Children's Care, Le
and Development

NVQ 2 · *Candidate Handbook*

Marian Beaver

Mandy Booty

Jo Brewster

Sally Neaum

Heidi Sheppard

Jill Tallack

Contents

Optional units

Published in 2005 by:
Nelson Thornes Ltd
Delta Place
27 Bath Road
CHELTENHAM
GL53 7TH
United Kingdom

05 06 07 08 09 / 10 9 8 7 6 5 4 3 2 1

A catalogue record for this book is available from the British Library

ISBN 0 7487 9560 X

Cover photograph: Image 100 36042 (NT)

Illustrations by Jane Bottomley and Angela Lumley

Page make-up by Florence Production Ltd

Printed and bound in Great Britain by Scotprint

Author Acknowledgements

Jo: Thanks to Fay Beaver and Holly and Laurie Brewster for their photographs. Thanks to Lovers' Lane Primary School for the photographs of displays and equipment.

Mandy: I would like to thank all those who have inspired my own personal development within the children's care, learning and development sector, particularly Jo from St. Joseph's and Karen and Lorraine, now in the Early Years team at Bracknell Forest Borough Council. Thanks also to Charlie from Bracknell and Wokingham College for her support as I worked on this project. And, most importantly, love and thanks to the five people who mean the world to me – Martin, Nick, Tom, Sally and Joe.

Heidi: I would like to thank Robert for his unwavering support, encouragement and for making great tea, and my children Nicholas and Alexander for being my motivation and inspiration. I dedicate my work to the memory of my late father Eddie.

Many thanks to the staff and children at Leapfrog Nursery, Gloucester and Treetops Nursery, Cheltenham for their time and enthusiasm during the photoshoots. Thanks also to Karen and Steve Sweetman and their son, Ben.

The authors and publisher would like to thank the following for the use of copyright material:

Sally and Richard Greenhill, p. ix; Photodisc 69 (NT), p. xv; Photodisc 79 (NT), p. 4; Photodisc 18 (NT), p. 81; Corel 788 (NT), Photodisc 71 (NT), both p. 85; Digital Vision KS (NT), Photodisc 79 (NT), both p. 95; Photodisc 71 (NT), p. 98; Image 100 42 (NT), p. 108; Photodisc 24 (NT), p. 109; Digital Stock 12 (NT), p. 301.

Introduction

This book has been written for students and practitioners with the intention of providing a guide to children's care, learning and development from birth to 16 years. The book relates particularly to the **National Occupational Standards of the National Vocational Qualifications (NVQs)** and **Scottish Vocational Qualifications (SVQs)** at **level 2**. Students on any of the other courses that require a knowledge and understanding of children's care and education will also find this book useful. Childcare settings may find this book a valuable addition to their reference shelves and helpful in supporting in-service training.

How to use this book

Principles and values

The **principles and values** that are firmly embedded in the National Occupational Standards are explained on pages viii–xii. Your assessor must ensure that you have shown that you have applied these principles and values in each unit of the award in your everyday work with children and their families.

Assessment

The section on **assessment** (pages xii–xx) will tell you how the NVQ award is structured. For example, it explains what units, elements, and performance criteria are. This section also explains assessment and how this is done.

Units

The book is divided into **units**. Each unit relates directly to a unit in the National Occupational Standards in Children's Care, Learning and Development at level 2. At the beginning of each unit you will find an overview of the unit so that you will know what it is about.

Each unit contains information that links to the **knowledge criteria**. To help you make these links, you will find yellow stickers in the margin that tell you which criteria are covered, for example:

K2D48.15
K2D49.12

There is also valuable information to help you understand the **elements** and **performance criteria**. The role of practitioners and their responsibilities when caring for children is emphasised.

Practical examples are used throughout the book. They help the reader to relate theoretical points to real-life situations. For example:

Practical Example

K2C2
K2C1
K2D48.3
K2C1.2

Examples of interaction

Think about these different examples of interaction:

1. A nursery nurse holds a baby while bottle feeding him. She cradles the baby in her arms, maintaining eye contact with him while giving him her full attention.

2. A pre-school assistant leads a large group discussion about 'Myself' with a group of 4-year-olds. She passes around the Listening Pebble. The children know that they have to listen to the person holding the pebble, and that they will have their turn to talk when the pebble reaches them.

3. A playworker plays pool with a 10-year-old in the holiday club. He has a good understanding of her interests and experiences, and uses these as the basis of their conversation.

4. A teaching assistant is helping to settle a 4-year-old into the Reception class. The child is very shy in a large group situation, so the teaching assistant uses closed, yes/no, questions to encourage one word answers initially, until the child feels more comfortable in the setting.

➤ *Why is the topic 'Myself' a good basis for discussion? What other techniques could be used to ensure that all children get the opportunity to have their say? Why is this important?* **K2C2**

➤ *What else might the nursery nurse be doing as she feeds the baby, to interact with him? Why is this important?* **K2C1, K2D48.3**

➤ *What examples of good practice can you identify in the above situations? What do you do in your setting to develop positive relationships with individual children?* **K2C1.2**

At the end of each element in a unit, there is a section about assessment called **Are you ready for assessment?** This includes guidance and helpful tips about how to prepare to be observed by your assessor. For example:

Element 201.3

Are you ready for assessment?

Communicate with children

You need to show that you can competently communicate with children, using appropriate methods and language. To do this, you will need to be directly observed by your assessor and present other types of evidence.

The amount and type of evidence you will need to present will vary. You should plan this with your assessor.

Direct observation by your assessor

These materials have been developed by Nelson Thornes Ltd and the content and the accuracy are the sole responsibility of Nelson Thornes Ltd. The City and Guilds of London Institute accepts no liability howsoever in respect of any breach of the intellectual property rights of any third part howsoever occasioned or damage to the third party's property or person as a result of the use of this Work.

Preparing to be observed

You will need to plan your assessment carefully, so that you are observed at a time when there is the opportunity for you to communicate with children. Think about

times when you are giving information to and receiving information from them. You will also need to show that you are able to adapt the way you communicate with children according to their needs, and that you can encourage them to use a variety of communication techniques.

Read the performance criteria and range carefully before your assessment. Try to cover as much as you can.

> You will need to present different types of evidence in order to:
>
> - demonstrate the performance criteria
> - show that you have the required knowledge, understanding and skills.

Throughout this book 'parent' is used to refer to a child's primary carer and 'practitioner' is used to refer to any early years/childcare/playwork worker.

References are made to national legislation and/or local regulations. The home nations that make up the United Kingdom are England, Wales, Scotland and Northern Ireland. There are differences in the legislation and regulations for each of the four nations. You will find references to these differences in the book.

Principles and values of good practice

Throughout each unit of your NVQ/SVQ, you must show you are committed to the **principles and values** described in the introduction to the National Occupational Standards in Children's Care, Learning and Development. You are reminded at the beginning of each unit that you must work within these principles and values.

Principles and values are an important basis for everyone's practice. They are the professional rules and beliefs on which you should base all your actions. Your assessor must provide a statement that you are applying all the principles and values, stated below, as you work with children and their families.

Principles

1   The welfare of the child is paramount. This means that the well-being of the child is the first and most important aspect of your work.

2   Practitioners contribute to children's care, learning and development and this is reflected in every aspect of practice and service provision.

3   Practitioners work with parents and families who are partners in the care, learning and development of their children and are the child's first and most enduring educators.

Values

1 The needs, rights and views of the child are at the centre of all practice and provision

Children are individuals in their own right. They have differing needs, abilities and potential. Therefore, any care setting should be flexible and sensitive in responding to these individual needs. Adults should listen to what children say and respond to their views appropriately.

2 Individuality, difference and diversity are valued and celebrated

All children benefit from an environment in which practitioners understand value and celebrate differences. Children differ as individuals and in their family and cultural lives. Differences are more likely to be valued and understood in an environment where difference is seen as a positive quality. In all settings, including those where there is less diversity of background, the use of resources that reflect a multicultural and multi-ability society adds to the richness of provision. It prepares all children for their lives in a diverse society. Practitioners should accept family diversity and different childcare practices. This is essential if they are to have an anti-discriminatory approach to their work.

3 Equality of opportunity and anti-discriminatory practice are actively promoted

Equality of opportunity

Equality of opportunity is about recognising and providing for differences. Equality of opportunity enables people to have the opportunity to participate in every area of life to the best of their abilities. It can be promoted at government level by the passing of laws, at institutional level through working practices and codes of conduct, and at a personal level through increased awareness and skills in meeting needs.

Equality of opportunity:

- *is not* about treating all people the same and ignoring differences
- *is* about recognising differences and providing for all people according to their needs. Ignoring differences can be the very reason that people are not given equality of opportunity – because their needs are not recognised.

People are not the same. They have many differences and their individual and particular needs should be recognised and accommodated. There is now a commitment at many levels of society to promote equality of opportunity. People now try to combat oppression and discrimination by recognising differences.

Equality of opportunity is about recognising differences and enabling children to have the opportunity to participate in every area of life to the best of their abilities

Anti-discriminatory practice

Anti-discriminatory practice means recognising, opposing and changing any way that discrimination occurs or might occur in the way people work. Discrimination occurs when a person or an organisation behaves in an oppressive manner towards an individual or group of people.

The best way to oppose discrimination is to provide an environment that encourages a positive view of all the people of the world. A positive environment celebrates difference and actively opposes any discriminatory practice. To develop anti-discriminatory practice, you must understand the causes of discrimination. This includes being aware of vocabulary or jokes that are, or might be, abusive. You should also be sensitive and alert to unequal provision of resources and opportunities.

Any obvious abuse or discrimination should be challenged. Not to do so would be to accept and condone it. Challenging abuse can be a difficult thing to do, especially for a young worker. It is, however, a skill that needs to be learned. Practitioners may have to take advice about what to do. Supervisors should be able to give advice and support about the need for action or what to do if the situation arises again. It may be their duty to take the matter further. Many settings have an equal opportunities policy or code of practice setting out the steps that should be taken.

4 Children's health and well-being are actively promoted

You must actively promote children's physical and emotional health and well-being. You can do this well if you are aware of children's needs and how to meet them.

5 Children's personal and physical safety is safeguarded, whilst allowing for risk and challenge as appropriate to the capabilities of the child

It is essential that you protect children from serious harm and injury. However, children must also learn to be independent and allowed to explore their environment according to their age and capabilities. You must learn to judge how best to protect children while promoting their independence.

6 Self-esteem, resilience and a positive self-image are recognised as essential to every child's development

A child's self-image is their view of who they are and what they are like. Children who think well of themselves have a positive self-image. They are more likely to develop high self-esteem. This means they have a feeling about themselves that they are good and worthwhile. It is essential to every child's development that they have high self-esteem and a positive self-image. If they do, they are more likely to be able to cope well with difficulties and frustrations in life – that is they are more resilient. They are also more likely to be happy, successful, make better and more secure relationships with others and have better mental health. You can promote self-esteem, resilience and a positive self-image by always praising children's efforts and achievements. Show them that you value them and what they do, and give them appropriate assistance to overcome difficulties.

7 Confidentiality and agreements about confidential information are respected as appropriate unless a child's protection and well-being are at stake

All practitioners have a responsibility to maintain confidentiality at all times. Breaking confidentiality by talking to other people inappropriately is a serious matter and can lead to you losing your job. Maintaining confidentiality means that any information given to you should only be given to others, or received from others, according to the policies of the setting and in the interests of meeting the needs of the child.

However, to protect children from harm, the sharing of information among practitioners working with children and families is essential. In many cases, it is only when information from a range of sources is put together that a child can be seen to be in need or at risk of harm.

8 Professional knowledge, skills and values are shared appropriately in order to enrich the experience of children more widely

Working as a member of a team will help you to share professional knowledge, skills and values. This will help you to provide a richer experience for children. You should be prepared to work hard, be helpful and co-operative, share things and offer ideas and information to other members of the team. If other members of your team make suggestions, you in turn should accept them positively and use them constructively to improve your practice with the children.

9 Best practice requires reflection and a continuous search for improvement

As a professional worker you must take responsibility for your own development and performance. Other practitioners can help and guide you towards best practice, but you will only make good professional progress if you become aware of your strengths and weaknesses. You must want to improve your skills and take responsibility for this. You should try to think about, or reflect on what you do.

However, we all find it difficult at times to know how good or bad we are at something and to know our strengths and weaknesses. Most people need the help and feedback of others to do this. The most useful feedback will usually come from a line manager or an experienced worker. You should try to listen to others. Think about what they say to you and be open to suggestions about how you can change and improve how you work.

There is more information about the assumptions and values that apply to playwork in the introduction to Unit CCLD 210.

Conclusion

This book is based on these principles and values throughout. You must show, throughout each unit of this award, that you are committed to all the principles and values expressed in the National Occupational Standards. You should refer to them as you work through each unit and demonstrate that you are putting them into practice.

Assessment of National Vocational Qualifications

This section describes who and what is involved in the assessment of National Vocational Qualifications or NVQs, as they are called in England, Wales and Northern Ireland, and SVQs, as they are called in Scotland. Together these are referred to as NVQ/SVQs.

What is assessment?

Assessment involves making a judgement about whether a person has achieved a particular standard or not. A person's learning is judged against the criteria provided by an awarding body. An awarding body is an organisation that is able to award (or give) a certificate or diploma when a person successfully completes an assessment.

One of the reasons for assessment is so that everyone concerned knows what standard and level has been reached. It means that a practitioner knows which jobs to apply for and an employer knows whether it is appropriate to consider them for a job.

Assessment of NVQ/SVQs

The NVQ/SVQ2 in **Children's Care, Learning and Development (CCLD)** covered in this book is a National Vocational Qualification at level 2. To gain a vocational qualification, a candidate is assessed on their practical skills. An assessor observes (looks at) what a candidate does and assesses whether they are doing it competently (well enough according to the standards). You will be assessed as you carry out your everyday work with the children. The assessor also judges a candidate's knowledge and understanding by finding out if they know *why* they are doing things in a certain way.

Competence

In order to successfully complete an NVQ/SVQ2 in Children's Care, Learning and Development, you must show that you can care for children competently. This means providing for children's developmental needs and keeping them safe and healthy. Competent performance means that your performance meets specific standards. The specific standards are those laid down in the National Occupational Standards in Children's Care, Learning and Development.

The structure of an NVQ/SVQ

Performance criteria

The Standards are made up of a large number of **performance criteria**. These are 'bite-size' descriptions of a small piece of an activity. These are printed in your assessment handbook. Each performance criteria is numbered.

Elements

Performance criteria are grouped together in elements. An element contains a number of performance criteria, linked by subject matter. Each element has a number and a title. For example:

Element CCLD 202.1 Prepare and maintain a safe environment

Units

Elements are grouped together in units. There are between two and five elements in every unit. Each unit has a number and a title. For example:

Unit CCLD 201 Contribute to positive relationships

Unit CCLD 202
The National Vocational Qualification (NVQ/SVQ) you are undertaking is called an NVQ/SVQ in Children's Care, Learning and Development (CCLD) at level 2. For this NVQ/SVQ, you must successfully complete **seven** units to gain the whole award.

Mandatory units

There are six **mandatory units**. Mandatory means you have to do them. They are:

CCLD 201, CCLD 202, CCLD 203, CCLD 204, CCLD 205, CCLD 206.

Optional units

There are four **optional units**. Optional means you can choose which unit you do. You only have to do **one** optional unit out of the four. You should discuss your choice with your assessor and choose an optional unit that suits the setting where you work. You can, for example, only choose optional unit CCLD 208 about the care of babies if you are working with babies.

The optional units are:

CCLD 207, CCLD 208, CCLD 209, CCLD 210.

NVQ/SVQ levels

There is an NVQ/SVQ in Children's Care, Learning and Development at level 2 and above it at levels 3 and 4. Nearly all level 2 roles are for those who are working under supervision in face-to-face roles with children and families.

The assessment process

Registering with an awarding body

Every NVQ/SVQ candidate must register with an awarding body. You register by joining an assessment centre. Each assessment centre is linked to an awarding body. The assessment centre will give you forms to complete so that you can register with an awarding body.

You will be linked to an assessment centre whether you become an Apprentice, a student at a further education college or enrol with a private training organisation.

The role of your assessor

Your assessor is a very important person to you. She or he (in this chapter an assessor will be referred to as she) will help you with the following things.

Building up a relationship

Every NVQ/SVQ candidate must have a personal assessor. You should know their name and where to contact them. You and your assessor should meet regularly and build up a positive professional relationship.

Your assessor may either be

- work-based and work in the same room as you most of the time
- work-based and work in the same setting, but only be in your room some of the time
- peripatetic – based somewhere else and travel to see you at particular times.

Planning

Your assessor should regularly help you to plan how to collect evidence of your competence. You should make a record of this plan for your portfolio.

Observation

Your assessor should observe you while you are working in your setting; she should arrange to do this even if she works with you all the time.

Different types of evidence

Your assessor will help you to collect different types of evidence in addition to what she observes. These are described later.

Expert witnesses

In addition to your assessor, an expert witness can also be an important source of performance evidence for you. Expert witnesses are experienced people who can confirm that your performance in the workplace is competent. They may include your line manager or other experienced people you work with. There may also be other professional people from outside your workplace who observe you working

Your assessor should regularly help you to plan how to collect evidence of your competence and make a record of this plan for your portfolio

and can give evidence of your competence. Your Awarding Body and your assessor will decide how to use the evidence of an expert witness.

Other assessors

You may have more than one assessor carrying out assessments, especially when doing the optional unit or working in a different setting. However, there should always be one co-ordinating assessor who brings together all the evidence of your competence and makes the final judgement about your work.

Portfolio of evidence

You should collect your evidence and put it in a portfolio of evidence. This portfolio may be on paper or it could be stored as files on a computer. You organise your evidence in a way that you agree with your assessor. It should contain:

- records of the direct observations made by your assessor
- the other, different types, of evidence you collect
- plans that you make with your assessor about assessment
- feedback from your assessor.

Labelling evidence

Each piece of evidence must be labelled to show:

- the unit and element it belongs to

- that it is your own work
- that it has been accepted by your assessor as relevant and valid evidence.

Assessment

Your assessor will look at the evidence collected in your portfolio. She will judge or assess whether you have sufficient evidence for her to decide that you are competent.

Sufficiency

Having sufficient evidence means having enough. You need only to present sufficient evidence to show you are competent. It is not necessary to produce large amounts of evidence, much of which may be similar. This is time-consuming and costly. On the other hand, it is important that there is enough evidence for your assessor to make a decision that you are competent.

Making a decision

Your assessor will make one of two possible decisions. These are that you are either:

- competent, or
- not yet competent.

If she decides that you are not yet competent, your assessor should help you to plan how to gain sufficient experience and evidence to show that you are competent.

Feedback

Your assessor should give you feedback on your performance and on your performance evidence. She will tell you if your evidence is valid and relevant and meets the National Standards. Feedback should always be constructive and the key points should be given to you in writing. Feedback should review your progress and give you positive suggestions about how to collect further evidence if you need to. Your assessor should make it clear when you have successfully completed a unit.

Internal verifiers

Internal verifiers are appointed by your assessment centre to make sure that the right standard of assessment is maintained. You should know who your internal verifier is. Your internal verifier will want to see your work and your assessor's records to make sure they are at the right standard. Your internal verifier may also want to talk with you and observe your assessor assessing you.

External verifiers

The external verifier is appointed by the awarding body to check that the standard of your assessment centre is correct. This is called quality assurance.

At some stage, you may be asked to bring individual units or your complete portfolio to the assessment centre. This is so that an external verifier can check them. You must keep your portfolio of evidence after you complete your NVQ/SVQ as it may be called for even though you have completed your award.

Types of evidence

The unit assessment record in your candidate handbook will give you guidance about the types of evidence needed.

Direct observation by your assessor

The best type of evidence of competence is direct observation of you by your assessor or an expert witness, while you are working.

An assessor or expert witness may observe you when you carry out:

- a particular activity you have planned to carry out at a pre-arranged time
- an activity that occurs from time to time during a session
- a frequently occurring activity during your normal working day.

Preparing to be observed

When you prepare to be observed you should:

- plan with your assessor what she will observe
- read the performance criteria carefully beforehand
- make sure that you have the necessary skills and knowledge to perform competently.

In this book, the section 'Preparing to be observed', in 'Are you ready for assessment?' at the end of each element, should help you to make the best of being observed. It describes all the things you should aim to do.

Other types of evidence

You may need to present different types of evidence in order to:

- cover criteria that are not observed by your assessor
- show that you have the required knowledge and understanding.

Here are some descriptions of other types of evidence that you could collect.

Reflective accounts

A reflective account is a description, in your own words (written, oral or recorded), of something you have done.

You should:

- describe the activity you have done step by step
- link your description to the performance criteria and knowledge statements
- think about, or reflect on, what you did and how the children responded
- show, in your description, that you know *why* you did things in the way you did
- be critical of your performance. Think about how you could improve.

Reflective accounts can provide very good evidence of your competent performance and that you have the appropriate knowledge and understanding.

Professional discussion

Candidates discuss with their assessor how their evidence meets the standards. The discussion is recorded as part of the evidence.

Recorded oral and written questioning

Your assessor may decide to ask you some questions. This will probably take place after she has observed you. Questions can be used to check your knowledge and understanding or to add to the observed evidence. The questions *and* your answers must be written down so that they can be used as evidence.

Log books and diaries of day-to-day practice

Log books and diaries are records of your practice in the work setting.

Diaries can be very useful additional evidence and a way of showing your assessor that you have covered performance criteria that she has not observed. You should write and use diaries carefully. It is not necessary to record daily activities over and over again. Remember, you only need sufficient evidence. It can be useful to write a log of a specific activity and describe it showing the different ways you have done it.

For example, if your assessor has directly observed you preparing and maintaining a safe environment indoors (CCLD 202.1), you might record in your diary/log occasions when you have done this outdoors.

Work plans for activities and routines

Work plans are plans for activities and routines that you carry out at work. They can include:

- plans that you have written yourself
- activities you have planned as part of a team
- records of preparations you have made
- timetables or schedules of activities and routines.

You might use a format from your work setting to record plans. You should describe what happened when you carried the activity out. As with other evidence, you should always record what performance criteria, knowledge and understanding they give evidence for.

Work-based products

Work products are items that are produced for the workplace, for example minutes of meetings, reports, curriculum plans, child observations and assessments.

Child observations and assessments of development

Child observations and assessments are records, made by you, of aspects of a child's development. There are many different ways of recording your observations and assessments. They may provide some evidence of your competent performance. They will usually provide good evidence of your knowledge and understanding.

However, when using these records in your portfolio, it is essential that strict **confidentiality** is maintained. It must not be possible to identify a child from anything that you write in an observation or assessment. There is more information about child observations in Unit CCLD 203.

Simulations, role-play or skills rehearsal
Simulations in Children's Care, Learning and Development are permitted only in certain circumstances. These are specified in the Assessment Strategy and Unit Evidence Requirements.

Case studies, assignments and projects
When using case studies, assignments and projects, both candidate and assessor need to be clear about the aims and objectives of the work to be done and the performance criteria and knowledge and understanding that will be covered.

Evidence from the past
Evidence that is accepted of your previous experience and learning is sometimes called accreditation of prior experience and learning (APEL). Your evidence needs to be signed by an appropriate person who can say it is yours. This evidence can only be used in a limited way for your award.

Providing evidence of knowledge and understanding
It is good practice to provide evidence of your knowledge and understanding *at the same time* as you provide evidence of your performance. This encourages you to link practice to theory, rather than separating them. It will also help you to keep your portfolio to a manageable size!

For example, when you reflect on your practice in a reflective account, you can link it to evidence of your knowledge and understanding. Your assessor may also ask you questions after she has observed you. She will record your responses and these can be used as evidence of your knowledge and understanding.

You should get into the habit of putting the correct references to knowledge and understanding statements on your work as you write or record it.

Principles of good practice
Throughout each unit you must show you are committed to the principles and values for the National Occupational Standards described on pages vii–xi.

Relationship between units
Many units are related to each other. They cover similar aspects of work. These links are referred to throughout this book.

Units also interlink. When your assessor is observing you carry out what you think is a single task, she may be able to record evidence of your competence across more than one unit.

For example, while you are supporting physical play (CCLD 206.4), you may also be:

- preparing and maintaining a safe environment CCLD 202.1
- encouraging children's positive behaviour CCLD 202.4

When you are planning your assessment, it is useful if you can make these links and cover as many performance criteria as you can. The more familiar you are with the performance criteria, the easier it will be for you to demonstrate your competence across a number of units and elements while your assessor is observing you.

Conclusion

Providing evidence for NVQ/SVQ assessment becomes easier as you become more familiar with the process of assessment and with the performance criteria, elements and units.

You may find it difficult and confusing to begin with. Don't give up. If you are a competent practitioner, with the help of your assessor and through the use of this book you can and will succeed.

You may find it confusing to begin with. Don't give up. Providing evidence for NVQ/SVQ assessment becomes easier as you become more familiar with the process

Contribute to positive relationships

This unit is about interacting with and responding positively to children and adults. It covers the verbal and non-verbal skills needed when communicating with children and adults. It looks at how to demonstrate respect for people through your language and behaviour. This knowledge underpins everything else you will do in your work with children and their families.

While you are working through this unit, you may find it helpful to refer to Unit CCLD 203 on children's development.

This unit contains four elements:

⌣ *CCLD 201.1 Interact with and respond to children*

⌣ *CCLD 201.2 Interact with and respond to adults*

⌣ *CCLD 201.3 Communicate with children*

⌣ *CCLD 201.4 Communicate with adults.*

The national standards for this unit include a list of key words and explanations that you need to understand. You should read this carefully as you plan the activities for your assessment. Your assessor can help you to make sure that you are interpreting the standards correctly.

⌣ Introduction

Before starting this unit, you need to understand what we mean by communicating with others and what we mean by interacting with others. When we communicate with others, we exchange information, thoughts and ideas. We need to make sure that our communication is clear and understood. We also need to understand what others are trying to tell us. Interaction involves more than just sharing information; it is the way we develop relationships with others. It is the way we create an atmosphere where children and adults feel at ease in our presence and are happy to share their thoughts and feelings.

The care, development and learning of a child does not just happen in the setting where you work. Parents will have an enormous amount of information about their children to share with you. This information will enable you to do your very best for the children in your care. There may also be other adults involved with a child outside your setting. They too will be able to contribute to your knowledge and understanding of the individual child. You must find ways to communicate and interact with children's parents and other adults in order to develop a partnership with them. A relationship of mutual respect and understanding between parents and practitioners will result in consistency between home and setting for the child.

When you work with adults, children and their families, the success of your work will mainly depend on the relationship you develop with them. You will meet many people, all of whom will have different experiences, different expectations, different backgrounds and different lives. This is what makes us all individuals. It is vital that you develop positive relationships with them, respecting and valuing the differences and celebrating the diversity in your own community. How you communicate and interact with the children and adults will be key to this.

Make it positive!

K2C13
K2D48.1
K2D49.1
K2D49.3
K2D49.4
K2D50.1

The need to connect with others is part of human nature – it is instinctive and necessary for survival. From the moment we are born, we begin to reach out to others. We communicate our needs through gestures and sounds. The responses we get from those with whom we interact will define the people we become. If the responses are warm and encouraging, and our needs are met, we will develop confidence in ourselves as valuable people. We will believe that what we have to say is important, and we will build productive and strong relationships. If, however, our attempts to communicate are ignored or undermined, we will learn that our needs and views are worthless. Our self-confidence will be damaged and our self-esteem and self-image will suffer.

You will see from Unit CCLD 203 that we categorise children's development in order to make it easier to observe their learning, and to plan activities that are appropriate for them. However, children do not develop in categories like this. They do not do a bit of physical development one day, followed by some social development the next. All the different categories of development relate to each other and children develop in a holistic way – in other words, the whole child develops.

So, the way you interact with the children and adults with whom you work is extremely important because it will affect the child's whole development. If you get it right, you will be creating a positive, accepting environment, where everyone feels comfortable expressing their thoughts, needs and feelings.

How we communicate

K2D3
K2C6
K2D48.14

The ability to communicate through the spoken and written word is what makes human beings different from other animals. We have many ways of communicating through papers, books and magazines, telephones, mobile phones, text messaging, emails and video connections.

However, the most important form of communication between people is direct, face-to-face communication. This type of communication is particularly important for those who work with people rather than machines. Sometimes, however, people find direct communication the most difficult. A large part of your role, if you work with children, is to communicate directly and effectively with children as well as with other adults. The adults may be parents, other professionals and your staff team. Childminders work with children and also in partnership with parents and sometimes as part of a childminding network. In order to provide the best environment for children, you need to develop good direct, face-to-face communication skills.

Face-to-face communication involves conveying a message using verbal and non-verbal methods, as shown in the table below.

How we communicate

Method of communication	What it includes
Verbal communication:	Using spoken words appropriately
	Listening
	Writing effectively
Non-verbal communication:	Tone of voice
	Body language including:
	<ul><li>facial expression</li><li>eye contact</li><li>posture, gestures, body movement and actions</li></ul>

To communicate effectively and to convey your message clearly and positively you must use all these methods skilfully.

Good practice when communicating and interacting with others

K2C6

Verbal communication

Verbal communication involves using words in some form. For this it is important that you speak clearly, listen carefully, and write clearly. You should:

- *speak clearly* using words that you can reasonably expect the listener to understand. You should change the words you use and the way you say them to take into account:

  - the chronological and developmental age of the listener

  - whether the listener speaks English as their home language

  - any hearing or learning impairment the listener has.

You should use an interpreter if needed.

- *listen carefully* to what the other person is saying to you. It is important to give time to listen to the person and to show them that you understand what they are saying to you. This can be done by what is called 'reflective listening'. This includes repeating what the other person has said but in a slightly different way and also summarising what they have said. This shows them that you have understood what they have said to you. It also helps you to show warmth and concern. It is good not to interrupt a person when they are speaking.

- *write clearly* in plain English. Use short sentences, simple words and illustrations and drawings.

Non-verbal communication

Only a small part of what we understand comes from the actual words a person says. A much bigger part comes from the way a person says it; this includes their tone of voice and their body language.

When communicating with others it important to check your tone of voice, facial expression, eye contact, posture, gestures, body movement and actions. You should check your:

- *tone of voice*. You need to be aware of the tone, speed and pitch of your voice. Through these you can express a range of emotions from excitement and enthusiasm, to boredom and irritation.

- *facial expression*. This is very important as it shows what you are feeling and what really interests you. If you look bright and interested, your communication will be much better than if you look bored and disinterested.

- *eye contact*. Making eye contact with the child or adult you are talking with is very important. However, eye contact is interpreted differently in different cultures. For example, in British culture it is considered rude not to make eye contact but it is rude to stare. For some people from an Asian family background, making eye contact during a conversation with a stranger can be rude.

Making eye contact is very important in British culture

- *posture, gestures, body movement and actions*. Movements of different parts of the body can be very revealing. Young children quickly learn that they gain attention by moving their bodies. Movements can show how a person feels and what they are about to do, such as bring a conversation to an end. You should try to sit or stand at the same level as the person you are speaking to. Keep an appropriate distance. If you get too close you may 'invade' the space around a person (sometimes called their personal space). If you keep too far away you may be considered rude and distant. People also differ personally, socially and culturally in their use of physical contact with others. You need to be aware of these differences so that you do not offend other people.

Barriers to effective communication

K2C9

The environment

You may have developed effective communication skills, but there are other things that can make communication difficult. The environment can help or hinder communication. Some settings are based in church or community halls with high ceilings. This can cause echoes and therefore increase noise levels.

You should avoid trying to communicate with people if there is:

- a great deal of other noise in the environment. The noise of machines, vehicles, loud music or lots of other people talking can make it difficult. You cannot give your full attention to the other person and they will not be able to hear you
- a lot of physical activity going on around you. People moving around or moving objects is very distracting.

Putting boisterous activities next to quieter ones can also have an impact on effective communication. For example, children might find it difficult to listen carefully to discussion around the interest table if a lively construction activity is taking place next to it. Try to find an appropriately quiet, calm place in which to communicate with others.

The way you speak

The way you speak includes

- the type of language you use
- the way you use it.

When communicating with children or with adults it is important that you use language that they understand. You should aim to:

- make your vocabulary (the words you use) simple. Avoid using a complicated word if there is simpler one
- avoid the use of jargon. This includes technical words and abbreviations that the other person may not understand

- avoid the use of slang. Slang should be reserved for communicating with friends and not be part of your professional vocabulary. It also provides a poor language role model for children who may copy you
- be aware of local **dialects**. Dialects are patterns of speech of a particular area. If part of your speech pattern includes use of local dialect words and phrases, you should be aware that not everyone you speak to is local and that it can seem to them that you are speaking another language. They may also feel left out
- understand your mood and attitude. We all have days when we feel low, unhappy or cross about something. As professionals we should control the way we express our personal emotions. We should always be positive and pleasant in our communication with children and adults at work. We must not let our personal feelings affect our professional contact with others.

Element 201.1 *Interact with and respond to children*

K2D48.15
K2D49.12

The most important factor in children's language development is interaction with other people. It is important that people who work with children adopt practices that contribute positively to children's language development. There is a recognised link between the quality of adult input and the quality of children's language. Listed below are some important points to remember when interacting with children. However, these are only practical points. A sensitivity towards children's needs and knowledge of them as individuals are the basis of positive interaction.

The same guidelines apply when talking with children for whom English is an additional language to the language spoken at home. It is important to remember that many children who are learning English as an additional language are very proficient in their first language. This means that they are likely to have an understanding of the use and purposes of language, and have developed the skills involved in interaction with others.

When talking to children, remember the following:

- *The tone of your voice* Does it convey warmth and interest in the child?
- *How quickly you speak* Do you speak at a pace that is appropriate for the child or children you are talking with?
- *Listening* How do you show the child that you are listening? Eye contact and getting down to the child's level, together with becoming involved in the conversation, indicate that you are listening and interested.
- *Waiting* Do you leave enough time for the child to respond? Young children may need time to formulate their response. Remember that pauses and silences are part of conversation too.
- *Questions* Do you ask too many questions? This may make the conversation feel like a question-and-answer session, especially if your response is 'That's

right'. What type of questions do you ask? Closed questions require a one-word answer and do not give the child the opportunity to practise and develop their language skills. Open questions have a range of possible answers, and give the child the opportunity to practise and develop their language skills and to develop their thinking. Asking questions will also enable you to check that you fully understand what the child has meant.

- *Your personal contribution* Do you contribute your own experience and/or opinions to the conversation? Conversation is a two-way process. It involves both people sharing information. This should be the same with children. It is important that the choice of what to talk about is shared.

- *Your methods of communication* Are you using the most appropriate method of communication? There are a variety of language systems and supports that children may use alongside or instead of verbal communication. These are called Alternative and Augmentative Communication (AAC). They include photographs, pictures, symbols and signing. You should liaise with parents, your Special Educational Needs Co-ordinator (SENCO) and any other professionals involved in the care of the children to make sure that you are giving the children the most appropriate tools to help them express themselves.

- *What do you talk about?* How much of what you say is management talk? How much is conversation and chatting? How much is explaining? How much is playful talk? Children need to be involved in a wide range of language experiences to enable them to practise and develop their own language

- *Developing thought* Do you ask for and give reasons and explanations when talking with children? Do you encourage the child to make predictions in real and imaginary situations? Do you encourage the children to give accounts of what they are doing or have done? Children's language and cognitive skills can be developed in this way.

- *Expressing feelings* As children's language skills develop, they will move from behavioural indicators of their feelings to using language to express themselves. You can help by accepting children's expressions of feelings, and giving them the vocabulary with which to explain how they feel. For example 'I can see that you are getting a bit frustrated with that – can I help you?'

- *To whom do you talk?* You must talk to all children within the group. All children need the opportunity to practise their language. There will be a range of developmental levels within every group of children and it is important that each child's needs are met.

The methods you use to interact with children will vary, depending on the child's stage of development and personal preferences. You will find that some children respond well to physical contact, and others shy away from it. Some will initiate conversation and others will only give one-word answers to direct questions. Some will prefer the company of their peers, whereas others will seek out the adults in the setting. By carefully observing children's responses in different situations, you will come to understand how best to interact with them individually.

Activities and experiences that encourage young children to talk

K2D49.11
K2D50.9
K2D51.8

Talking and listening carefully are both learned skills. People who work with young children need to know how to encourage these skills.

Talking

To develop language successfully, young children need an environment with plenty of opportunities to practise talking. They need lots of time when they are using language in different ways and for different purposes. Children also need people who will provide good role models, and who will listen carefully and help them to adjust and refine their language. When children make mistakes the best practice is to reflect back the correction. For example:

Child: 'I wented to the park.'

Adult: 'You went to the park did you?'

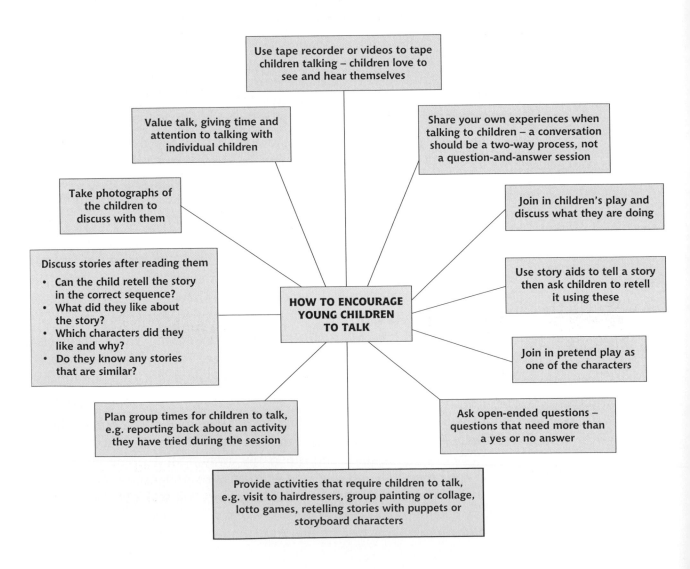

Use tape recorder or videos to tape children talking – children love to see and hear themselves

Value talk, giving time and attention to talking with individual children

Share your own experiences when talking to children – a conversation should be a two-way process, not a question-and-answer session

Take photographs of the children to discuss with them

Join in children's play and discuss what they are doing

Discuss stories after reading them
- Can the child retell the story in the correct sequence?
- What did they like about the story?
- Which characters did they like and why?
- Do they know any stories that are similar?

Use story aids to tell a story then ask children to retell it using these

HOW TO ENCOURAGE YOUNG CHILDREN TO TALK

Join in pretend play as one of the characters

Plan group times for children to talk, e.g. reporting back about an activity they have tried during the session

Ask open-ended questions – questions that need more than a yes or no answer

Provide activities that require children to talk, e.g. visit to hairdressers, group painting or collage, lotto games, retelling stories with puppets or storyboard characters

Practical Example

Examples of interaction

Think about these different examples of interaction:

1. A nursery nurse holds a baby while bottle feeding him. She cradles the baby in her arms, maintaining eye contact with him while giving him her full attention.

2. A pre-school assistant leads a large group discussion about 'Myself' with a group of 4-year-olds. She passes around the Listening Pebble. The children know that they have to listen to the person holding the pebble, and that they will have their turn to talk when the pebble reaches them.

3. A playworker plays pool with a 10-year-old in the holiday club. He has a good understanding of her interests and experiences, and uses these as the basis of their conversation.

4. A teaching assistant is helping to settle a 4-year-old into the Reception class. The child is very shy in a large group situation, so the teaching assistant uses closed, yes/no, questions to encourage one word answers initially, until the child feels more comfortable in the setting.

➤ *Why is the topic 'Myself' a good basis for discussion? What other techniques could be used to ensure that all children get the opportunity to have their say? Why is this important?* **K2C2**

➤ *What else might the nursery nurse be doing as she feeds the baby, to interact with him? Why is this important?* **K2C1, K2D48.3**

➤ *What examples of good practice can you identify in the above situations? What do you do in your setting to develop positive relationships with individual children?* **K2C1.2**

Element 201.1

Are you ready for assessment?

Interact with and respond to children

You need to show that you can competently interact with and respond to children in a warm and positive manner. To do this you will need to be directly observed by your assessor and present other types of evidence.

The amount and type of evidence you will need to present will vary. You should plan this with your assessor.

▶

Direct observation by your assessor

Observation is the required assessment method to be used to evidence some part of each element in this unit. Expert witnesses could supply additional evidence. Your assessor will observe you in real work activities and this should provide most of the evidence for the performance criteria for the elements in this unit.

Preparing to be observed

You will need to plan your assessment carefully, so that you are observed at a time when there is the opportunity for you to interact with and respond to children. This might be during a small group activity, during routine activities such as snack or meal times or during circle time. If you plan carefully with your assessor, you should be able to gather performance evidence as you are assessed for other units.

You will need to ensure that you use open questioning (questions that require more than a yes or no answer) so that the children have the opportunity to express their thoughts, feelings and ideas. Think about how you could adapt the ways that you interact with the children to ensure that they all are able to participate in the discussions. For example, how will you extend the fluent, confident child's language and understanding? How will you create opportunities for children with communication difficulties to be heard and listened to?

Read the performance criteria carefully before assessment. Try to cover as much as you can.

Other types of evidence

You may need to present different types of evidence in order to:

- cover criteria not observed by your assessor
- show that you have the required knowledge, understanding and skills
- cover other parts of the range.

Element 201.2 *Interact with and respond to adults*

During your work with children and their families, you are likely to come into contact with different kinds of adults:

- parents/carers
- colleagues
- managers/management committee members
- other professionals involved in the children's care, for example speech and language therapists, teachers, health visitors
- inspectors.

The relationship you build up with them is very important because you are working as part of an extended team of people. You will find more information about effective team working in Unit CCLD 207 and you should read this unit before planning your assessment for CCLD 201.

In a similar way to children, adults need to feel that they are being listened to. They need to feel that their views and opinions are respected and that you value what they have to say. It is only by working together with them, in a cohesive and consistent way, that you will recognise and meet the needs of all the children with whom you work.

Building relationships with adults

K2C8

There are many reasons why you should build positive relationships with the adults who come into your setting:

- Parents have the most knowledge and understanding of their children. If they are encouraged to share this with staff, all will benefit.

- Children need consistent handling to feel secure. This is most likely to occur if there are good relationships between parents, staff and other professionals working with the children and their families.

- Legislation contained within the Education Reform Act 1988, the Children Act 1989 and the Special Educational Needs Code of Practice 2001 places a legal responsibility on professionals to work in partnership with parents. Services provided for children in the public, private and voluntary sector must take this into account.

- It is a condition of receiving public funding for educational provision for 3- and 4-year-olds (known as nursery grant) that settings work in partnership with parents. Any future funding arrangements are also likely to insist on this.

- Research has demonstrated conclusively the positive effect that parental involvement in the care and education process has on the progress of children. If parents become involved early on in the child's care and education, they are likely to maintain this involvement throughout the child's educational career.

- Children's learning and development is not confined to either the childcare setting or the home. An exchange of information between your setting and home and from home to your setting will reinforce learning, wherever it takes place.

- Where parents are experiencing difficulties with their children, they may be able to share these problems and work towards resolving them alongside sympathetic and supportive professionals.

- As children get older, their needs and lives change. Through regular, positive interaction with families, you will be more able to support them both.

Relating to all

It is the responsibility of those who work with children to do everything that they can to make parents feel welcome and valued. The needs and feelings of all parents should be considered. This may include some parents who have had previous negative experiences of childcare or education settings and who may need encouragement to feel comfortable. Parents who are unfamiliar with the methods and approaches used in the setting may require explanation and reassurance.

To ensure good relationships with parents, practitioners should:

Avoid using jargon

Maintain confidentiality

Make time for parents to talk to you

Make the environment friendly and welcoming

Acknowledge and address carers by their preferred name

Listen to parents and respond, giving them your full attention

Organise help if you need someone to interpret

Be friendly and approachable

Resolve conflict

Share information

Show understanding

Provide information

Parents may be concerned that their child's cultural and religious background is understood. Provision should be made to ensure that parents who do not use the language of the setting are provided with the full range of opportunities to be involved in their children's care and education.

Colleagues and other members of your team will also have much to contribute to your work with children. A setting where everyone works together, sharing ideas and information will have a positive and accepting atmosphere.

K2C8

The best way to demonstrate that you value the views and opinions of the adults with whom you work is to take them seriously. You should:

- use the techniques you have read about previously in this unit to show that you are listening
- be prepared to discuss and negotiate
- accept that your own practice might need to be altered to accommodate the needs and wishes of other adults

- if you are not sure, consult with your managers or colleagues to ask for their advice

- be positive and confident in your responses. If you do not know how to respond, explain that you will need to discuss things with other people and will get back with a response

- be a reflective practitioner. Examine your own ways of working to see if you can take on board other people's views in order to become a better worker.

Dealing with disagreements

K2C10

There will be times when you have followed all the advice already given in this unit, and despite this, you feel unable to agree with another person's point of view. You might sometimes feel that the views being expressed are a criticism of your own practice and this can make you feel defensive and unwilling to change. You might completely disagree with the opinion being expressed. In these circumstances, you need to work even harder to listen. The way you cope with this situation will have a big impact on the future relationship you have with the adult in question.

Some dos and don'ts

- Don't lose your temper.
  Do keep calm.

- Don't stop listening.
  Do accept that others are entitled to their points of view.

- Don't react without thinking.
  Do step back from the situation and take time to consider your response.

- Don't try to cope alone.
  Do ask your colleagues, managers or other support workers for help and advice.

Remember, your policies are the rules of your setting. If the views and opinions can be accommodated within the policies, you should be considering them.

Element 201.2 Are you ready for assessment?

Interact with and respond to adults

You need to show that you can competently interact with and respond to adults in a warm and positive manner. To do this you will need to be directly observed by your assessor and present other types of evidence.

The amount and type of evidence you will need to present will vary. You should plan this with your assessor.

▶

Direct observation by your assessor

Observation is the required assessment method to be used to evidence some part of each element in this unit. Expert witnesses could supply additional evidence. Your assessor will observe you in real work activities and this should provide most of the evidence for the performance criteria for the elements in this unit.

Preparing to be observed

You will need to plan your assessment carefully, so that you are observed at a time when there is the opportunity for you to interact with and respond to adults. This might be at the beginning or end of a session, or when you are talking to a parent about his/her child. If you plan carefully, you should be able to gather performance evidence for CCLD201.4 at the same time. Make sure that you make parents feel comfortable in the setting and that you provide an opportunity for them to talk about their children as well as for yourself to talk about what has been going on in the setting.

Read the performance criteria carefully before your assessment. Try to cover as much as you can.

Other types of evidence

You will need to present different types of evidence in order to:

- demonstrate the performance criteria
- show that you have the required knowledge, understanding and skills.

Element 201.3 *Communicate with children*

K2C14
K2D49.11

One of the most important experiences adults can provide for children is to talk with and listen to them. It is widely believed that when adults stay in touch with children through attention and conversation, children may be less likely to behave in ways that create conflict. This is because when they learn to express themselves verbally or by using alternative communication systems, they are able to communicate their needs, feelings and choices.

To effectively communicate with children you will need to adjust your style according to the child's age and development. You will need a good understanding of the interests of the children in order for them to be able to relate to you, and you to them.

K2D3
K2D48.14

Children under 12 months will communicate through coos and gurgles, body movements and cries. You should:

- respond quickly to a baby's communication, by smiling or comforting
- give words to the baby's actions, for example 'Oh dear, you're crying. Are you hungry?' or 'You're smiling – do you like it when I play peek-a-boo?'
- make sure that the baby can see your face and use a sing-song tone of voice, with exaggerated facial expressions to keep a baby's attention.

Children aged between 12 and 36 months will gradually develop more verbal forms of communication. You should:

- respond quickly to his attempts to communicate, giving words to his actions – 'You're pointing at the book. Shall we look at it?'

- expand on her one word sentences – 'Juice, yes that's your juice. Would you like some?'

- label his emotions – 'Playing with the bubbles makes you happy!'

- talk through the daily routines of the setting, so that she begins to understand sequences – 'First we put on our coats, then we hold hands, then we go out to play.'

- explain why – 'Let's pick up the cars now – we don't want to fall over them, do we?'

- be a good language role model. Listen without distraction and model good use of language and grammar.

Children aged between 3 and 5 years old are beginning to talk in full sentences with the grammar improving as they get older. You should:

- talk about her past experiences, even if they are imaginary! Prompt and ask for more details to extend the conversation

- continue to label feelings, extending to discuss the possible causes of such feelings

- point out the written words around the children so that they begin to recognise the connection between the spoken and written word

- provide lots of creative and imaginative opportunities so that children can recreate their own experiences.

Older children will usually have well-refined communication skills, and will be able to use language to reason. You should:

- use conversation to keep up to date with children's likes, dislikes and needs

- use conversation to help the children to solve their own problems and talk through their plans

- help children to learn how to negotiate and consider other points of view by using these techniques with them.

Practical Example

K2D5
K2C6
K2C7

Surveys

The staff of the primary school have recently undertaken a parent survey to find out how the parents would like the school to develop. The survey covered issues such as choosing how to develop the outdoor play space, opinions on school dinners and whether they felt their children were happy in school.

They then decided to ask the children what they thought and asked the teaching assistants to produce some questions suitable for the different age groups in the school. Lisa, a teaching assistant from Year 1, realised that some of the younger children would have difficulty putting their thoughts down on paper, or expressing their opinions verbally. She therefore devised a lollipop voting system for them to use. She made happy and sad faces and stuck them onto lollipop sticks. She then translated the questions from the children's survey into questions that could be answered using the lollipop faces. In this way, she was able to record the views and opinions of the younger children, ensuring that their voices were heard.

➤ *Why do you think Lisa felt it was important for the younger children to be included in the survey?* **K2C2**

➤ *What would have been the main differences in those questions for the adults, those for the older children and those for the younger ones?* **K2C6, K2C7**

➤ *How do you find out the views and opinions of the children in your setting?* **K2D5**

Common communication difficulties in children

K2C9

Language is a learned skill. Some children have difficulties picking up and/or using speech and language. In a setting, it is good practice to be aware of particular children's difficulties and to adapt the activities that are planned so that all the children can participate together. Solving language and communication difficulties may need outside support, as there are many ways to help children who have difficulties. People who work with young children need to be aware of the early signs of speech and language difficulties so that advice and help can be sought if needed. Help and advice can be accessed in all pre-school settings through the co-ordinator of special educational needs (SENCO), a general practitioner, a health visitor or a social worker.

There may be a problem if you notice any of the following:

● By age 1 an infant doesn't cry, babble or pay attention to other voices.

● By age 2 a child can't put some words together in speech.

- By age 3 a child's speech is difficult for those outside the family to understand.
- By age 4 a child doesn't have a growing vocabulary, speaks in very short sentences and cannot make most sounds – or a child points to things instead of talking.
- By age 5 a child can't carry on a simple conversation, stutters or sounds very different from playmates.

Assessment may be needed if a school-aged child:

- is difficult to understand
- uses and pronounces words incorrectly
- consistently uses incorrect grammar
- can't seem to hear or understand others well
- speaks too loudly most of the time.

Helping children with communication difficulties

K2C4.6
K2D48.14

There are practical ways that you can help children to communicate, as shown in the table below. These techniques can be useful for all children, not just those who are experiencing difficulty.

Helping children with communication difficulties

Things to think about	Why this is important
Do you allow time for children to understand what you have said, think about a reply and then say the words?	Don't be tempted to finish children's sentences for them or they will feel that they need to speak more quickly. If children feel rushed to talk, they will feel less confident about what they have to say. They may have difficulty getting the words out.
Does your question have a right and wrong answer?	Children know that when you ask questions such as 'What colour is this?', 'How many are there?', 'What day is it today?', you know what the answer is. This immediately puts them under pressure. There are other ways to assess learning – direct questions and answers are often not appropriate.
Does the child know that he or she has to listen?	Many of the social rules about communication and interaction are learnt, and the child may not yet be aware of them. Using the child's name and touching his/her arm will send a message that it is time to listen.
How visual is your language?	Children understand best when we engage more than one of their senses. Pictures and objects are a great way to help children understand the routines of your setting and how they should respond in different situations. They can also be used by children who have limited verbal communication skills to interact with others and ask questions.
Do you model clear and correct pronunciation?	You are a powerful role model for the children in your care. When children make mistakes with grammar or sounds, you should model the correct way without undermining the child's attempt to

	communicate. You should not stop a child and make him/her repeat back to you.
Who else can help?	Working with other adults to support children who have difficulties will result in a shared and consistent approach. Your special educational needs co-ordinator (SENCO) may be in contact with other professionals, including speech and language therapists, who can share their strategies with you.

Take a look at Unit CCLD 209 for more information.

Element 201.3 Are you ready for assessment?

Communicate with children

You need to show that you can competently communicate with children, using appropriate methods and language. To do this, you will need to be directly observed by your assessor and present other types of evidence.

The amount and type of evidence you will need to present will vary. You should plan this with your assessor.

Direct observation by your assessor

Observation is the required assessment method to be used to evidence some part of each element in this unit. Expert witnesses could supply additional evidence. Your assessor will observe you in real work activities and this should provide most of the evidence for the performance criteria for the elements in this unit.

Preparing to be observed

You will need to plan your assessment carefully, so that you are observed at a time when there is the opportunity for you to communicate with children. Think about times when you are giving information to and receiving information from them. You will also need to show that you are able to adapt the way you communicate with children according to their needs, and that you can encourage them to use a variety of communication techniques.

Read the performance criteria and range carefully before your assessment. Try to cover as much as you can.

> You will need to present different types of evidence in order to:
>
> - demonstrate the performance criteria
> - show that you have the required knowledge, understanding and skills.

Communicate with adults

K2C6
K2C7

Settings communicate with adults in a variety of ways, both formally and informally. In this section, you will need to consider your telephone manner, writing style and notice boards, as well as the way you communicate face-to-face. You will also need to consider how to react if you are experiencing difficulties communicating with other adults.

You will communicate with parents in your setting in a number of ways. When parents are thinking about which setting to choose for their child, they will talk with staff about the day-to-day routine and about the facilities that are offered. Often they will visit a number of settings before deciding which is most suited to their child. Brochures, prospectuses and other written information is usually provided too so that a full picture can be given. All of these will provide starting points for questions from parents. Parents also gain information about the way that the group operates from the physical environment and how the setting is arranged. Once children start attending, you need to keep parents informed and up to date with what is happening.

Skills for talking and listening

Thinking about your own communication skills and how these might have an effect on your relationships with parents and other adults can be helpful. When talking with or listening to adults, consider the following points.

- Make eye contact but be careful – a fixed stare can be very off-putting.
- Don't interrupt and make comparisons from your own experiences. Encourage further conversation with phrases such as 'I see . . .', 'Tell me . . .'.

A notice board will keep parents informed and encourage involvement

- Make sure that you are at the same level. Try not to sit down if the parent is standing, and vice versa. Doing this will make communication seem less equal.

- If the adult seems upset or wants to discuss something in private, find somewhere suitable to talk.

- Summarise the points that have been made during and at the end of a discussion. This recap will be particularly helpful if the adult has come to discuss ways of dealing with a problem.

- Keep your distance. Everyone needs a space around them. If you get too close, the person you are speaking to may feel uncomfortable. (On the other hand, people from some cultural backgrounds may have a different view of personal space and could interpret your distance as unfriendly.)

- You may feel that an adult is worrying over something quite unimportant. Try not to dismiss these concerns as insignificant as the adult may be reluctant to confide in you in future. Try to be reassuring.

- Avoid using **jargon** (terms that only someone with your professional background would understand). This is off-putting and limits the effectiveness of your communication.

- Recognise that all parents, not just those who speak the language of the setting, will want to share information and be consulted about their children's progress and think about any arrangements you may need to make. (See 'Communicating with everyone' below.)

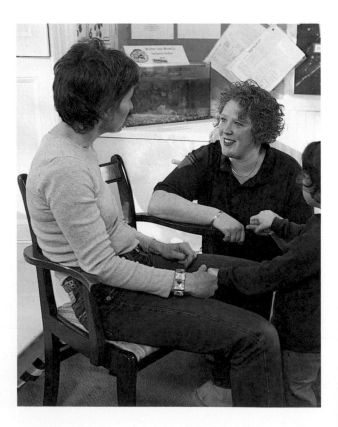

**Staff should be
welcoming to parents**

- Make the limits of confidentiality clear. Assure the adult that you will deal with any information shared professionally but be clear that you may have to pass some things on.

- Remember (particularly if you are a student) that you will usually need to discuss with colleagues and your line manager any requests that a parent might make. Don't make agreements or promises that you might not be able to keep!

Written communications

Most settings provide a variety of written information for parents. This is helpful for general information that parents might want to keep and consider and for keeping parents informed about current events and developments.

Brochures

All settings will have a brochure that they provide for parents giving them information about the services offered. Of course, these will vary, though there will be common factors. All will probably include:

- location, including address, telephone number, person to contact
- the times that the setting is open and the length of sessions
- the age range of children catered for
- criteria for admission (for example, a workplace nursery may require the parent to work in the establishment; social services establishments may require children to be referred through a social worker or health visitor)
- information about meals and snacks provided
- information about the facilities and accommodation available
- schedule of fees (if any) to be charged
- reference to any policies, especially those relating to special educational needs, equal opportunities and behaviour
- the qualifications of the staff and staff roles, and responsibilities
- an indication of the daily or sessional programme for the children
- what parents are expected to provide (for example, nappies, spare clothing, sun cream)
- details of any commitments the parent must make (for example, rota days, notice of leaving, regular attendance)
- details of any approach to learning followed (for example, learning through play, and the curriculum followed)
- information about the complaints procedure.

A brochure can provide the parent with a great deal of information which will also be useful to refer to once the child has started at the centre.

**A brochure provides
a great deal of
information**

Welcome to
TreeTops
"Home from home day care"

Caring passionately about children

Other types of written communications

Parents can expect to receive a whole range of written communications once their child has started at a setting. Some settings produce their own booklets, for example, about their approach to reading or other areas of the curriculum, indicating to parents the part they can play in their children's learning. Parents might also receive regular newsletters, invitations to concerts, parents' meetings, requests for assistance and support, information about the activities provided for children, advance notice of holidays and setting closures, and so on. These will often be reinforced with notices and verbal reminders. It is important that these notices and letters communicate the information in a clear and friendly manner.

Sometimes there will be a need for a more individual exchange of information, for example if a child has an accident during the session. This might be written in a note to the parent or it might be explained at pick-up time. Parents need to know what has happened and someone needs to have responsibility for passing on this information. Many settings provide regular written reports to parents on their children's progress

Communicating with everyone

K2C9

It is the responsibility of the childcare setting and its practitioners to ensure that they provide opportunities to communicate with all parents, remembering that for some, they may need to make special provision.

Some parents may not share the language of the setting. All parents, not just those who speak English, will want to share information and be consulted about their children's progress. Try to organise for someone to interpret for them – some local authorities will provide this service or have a list of interpreters. Remember that it is inappropriate to rely on an older child or another parent to interpret, particularly if the conversation is concerned with sensitive issues. Deaf parents who use sign language will require communication support too. (Sign language interpreters are usually very busy but your local deaf club or society should be able to help you to find one.)

Don't assume that all parents are able to read and write. If you are aware of this, you can talk to parents rather than rely on written information. Parents may speak a home or community language fluently but often may not read and write in it. You should be aware of this if you are having materials translated.

Some parents may be very pressed for time and cannot enjoy a relaxed chat with staff when they bring and pick up their children. You should not assume that they don't wish to talk about how their children are doing. Try to make alternative arrangements, perhaps for an out-of-hours appointment or a telephone conversation.

Confidentiality

**K2M11
K2M12**

The nature of your work with children means that you will learn a great deal about individual children and their families. All practitioners have a responsibility to maintain confidentiality at all times. Sensitive information concerning children and their families will only be available to you if you need it to meet the needs of the child and family concerned. Maintaining confidentiality means that any information given to you should not be given to others, or received from others, for any other reason than to meet a child's needs.

Although the idea of confidentiality may be easy to understand, the practice can be complex and will require self-control and commitment to the welfare of the child and their family. However, information about children and families will need to be exchanged within the work setting and you should ask your line manager about how and with whom it can be shared. You should not discuss identifiable children and families with anyone outside the work setting. Breaking confidentiality is a serious matter and can lead to you losing your job.

Respecting confidentiality means:

- You should not gossip about details of children or their families with others either in your workplace or outside. Imagine how you would feel if you were sitting on a bus and heard someone a couple of seats in front discussing your private life!
- You should discuss relevant information in a professional way with your supervisor and others who work with the child.
- Understanding that sometimes you will have to pass on information, even when a parent has asked you not to. You cannot guarantee to keep something to yourself if there could be a risk, however small, to the child.

You should refer to and become familiar with any workplace policy on confidentiality. Ask your supervisor to go through this with you.

Element 201.4 — Are you ready for assessment?

Communicate with adults

You need to show that you competently put adults at ease when you communicate with them, demonstrating respect for their individual needs and preferences. You will also need to show regard for confidentiality in your communications. To do this you need to be directly observed by your assessor and present other types of evidence.

The amount and type of evidence you will need to present will vary. You should plan this with your assessor.

Direct observation by your assessor

Observation is the required assessment method to be used to evidence some part of each element in this unit. Expert witnesses could supply additional evidence. Your assessor will observe you in real work activities and this should provide most of the evidence for the performance criteria for the elements in this unit.

Preparing to be observed

You will need to plan your assessment carefully with your assessor, so that you are observed at a time when there is the opportunity for you to communicate with adults. This might be talking with parents or meeting with your manager or colleagues. If you plan carefully, you should be able to gather performance evidence for CCLD201.2 at the same time. Make sure that you exchange information – receiving information as well as giving it. Read the performance criteria carefully before your assessment. Try to cover as much as you can.

> You will need to present different types of evidence in order to:
>
> • demonstrate the performance criteria
> • show that you have the required knowledge, understanding and skills.

Reflecting on your practice

Give some examples of the choices children make in your setting. How does this relate to their social and emotional development? What do you do to help them make choices?   **K2D5**

Why is it important for the development of positive relationships that you value adults' views and opinions?   **K2C8**

Explain how your setting's confidentiality policy affects the way you do your job. **K2M12**

What is the link between children's ability to communicate and their behaviour? **K2C14**

UNIT 202

Help to keep children safe

This unit is about keeping children safe during daily work activities. The unit covers responding to accidents, emergencies and illness. This unit requires you to know about the policies and procedures of your setting.

This unit contain four elements:

⌒ *CCLD 202.1 Prepare and maintain a safe and healthy environment*

⌒ *CCLD 202.2 Follow procedures for accidents, emergencies and illness*

⌒ *CCLD 202.3 Support the safeguarding of children from abuse*

⌒ *CCLD 202.4 Encourage children's positive behaviour.*

The national standards for this unit include a list of key words and explanations that you need to understand. You should read this carefully as you plan the activities for your assessment. Your assessor can help you to make sure that you are interpreting the standards correctly.

Introduction

Practitioners should plan and create an environment that is caring, stimulating and safe. The resources and equipment provided should be suitable. You should be aware of possible dangers and always ensure the safety of the children. It is essential to have knowledge of first aid. You must know about and follow the procedures of your setting when dealing with accidents, emergencies and illness. A valid first aid qualification is a very useful addition to your NVQ. Practitioners must be aware of the child protection procedures of their setting and be able to recognise and report any issues that give cause for concern to their line manager/supervisor. This will enable the proper procedures to be followed. Practitioners should encourage children's positive behaviour. To do this you will need to know what the expected behaviour of children should be at particular stages of development. There is more information about this in Unit CCLD 203.

Element
202.1

Prepare and maintain a safe and healthy environment

❮ Health and safety requirements

K2S15
K2S16
K2D48
K2D49
K2D50
K2D51

The Health and Safety at Work Act 1974 is the main Act of Parliament that regulates health and safety in the workplace. There have been additions to this legislation. Similar legislation is in force in Wales, Scotland and Northern Ireland.

❮ National standards for under 8s (SureStart)

There are national standards, legislation and regulations about health and safety that apply to your workplace. In England these standards come from the regulations under the Children Act (1989) and are inspected by Ofsted. Legislation and regulations in the four countries of the United Kingdom have differences. It is important that you know what applies to your own setting in your area.

Health and safety policies

Your setting will have a health and safety policy. It is most important that you know about this. You will need to follow this policy in your day-to-day work.

All child-care settings should have a health and safety policy that includes:

- clear safety rules for children's behaviour
- policies for the supervision of children
- safety equipment, for example safety catches on doors and windows, non-slip surfaces, safety glass, safe gym equipment
- procedures for using equipment
- policies for dealing with spills of bodily fluids
- procedures for staff to report potential hazards
- clear rules to ensure that staff work safely, for example closing and fastening safety gates, reporting any damaged or defective equipment, keeping hot drinks away from children
- policies for collecting children
- policies when taking children out of the setting.

Safeguarding the children

K2S17

The health and safety policies are there for the protection of the children and the staff. It is very important that these policies are made available to all staff. Policies and procedures must always be followed. There may be a temptation by some workers to cut corners or to ignore safety policies. This is a serious matter. It is important that you do not allow your own standards to be compromised. If you are worried by unsafe practices, you may be able to speak directly to the person concerned and tell them why you are worried. If this does not work then you should consult a more senior member of your team. There may be a member of your team who is responsible for health and safety and you should speak to them.

Potential hazards

K2S19
K2S20
KS21
KS223
K2D48
K2D49
K2D50

Potential hazards are possible dangers and threats to the children's safety. Many potential hazards are a normal part of everyday environments. It is up to the practitioner to be aware of things that might be a danger to children and know how to deal with them. Examples of potential hazards are electric sockets and cleaning fluids. You should use socket covers and keep cleaning fluids well out of the children's reach, in a high or locked cupboard. Practitioners need to create a safe environment. They should identify potential hazards and take action to prevent accidents.

Checking the environment

Reporting hazards

K2S17
K2S20

There may be times when hazards should be reported to a supervisor or the health and safety officer. Unsafe or broken equipment should be immediately removed. Children should also be removed from a dangerous situation. It is important to check areas that are going to be used by the children for any hazards, especially the outdoor play space. This is an area that may be used by other people who may create hazards for the children. For example, a playgroup or out of school club may use premises that are used by other people.

What to check before using the outdoor play space

- Are the gates securely locked, and the boundary fences secure?
- Can strangers come into contact with the children?
- Are there any litterbins and are they properly covered?
- Is the area clear of rubbish, poisonous plants, broken glass, and dog or cat faeces?
- Is there any risk from water?
- Are there any items or equipment left about that could cause accidents?
- Is the play equipment properly assembled according to the manufacturer's instructions and checked for defects?
- Are the surfaces suitable for the play equipment?
- Are any mats required in place?
- Is the number of staff supervising the children adequate?

Safety equipment

K2S17
K2S19

Using safety equipment can avoid some common hazards. Accidents often happen because simple safety precautions were ignored or the safety equipment was not used properly. Any safety equipment used should be fit for its purpose. It is possible to find this out by checking that safety equipment has a safety mark on the label. The labels will show that toys and other equipment, such as prams and cots, are safe and that they are suitable for the age group shown. It is very important to check for the safety mark before buying equipment or toys.

Safety marks

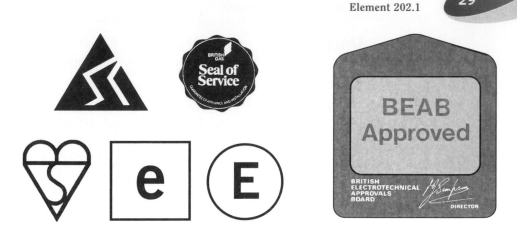

Safety equipment and how it is used

Safety equipment	Use
Harnesses, reins	To prevent falls from prams, pushchairs, and high chairs. To stop children running into the road. Harnesses and reins should be purchased with the pram, etc.
Safety gates	To prevent access to kitchens, stairways, outside. Always guard the top and bottom of stairways
Locks for cupboards and windows	To prevent children getting hold of dangerous substances or falling from windows
Safety glass/safety film	Prevents glass from breaking into pieces that would cause injuries
Socket covers	Prevent children poking their fingers or other objects into electric sockets
Play pens	Create a safe area for babies
Smoke alarm	Detects smoke and sounds the alarm
Cooker guard	Prevents children pulling pans from the cooker
Corner covers	Protects children from sharp edges on furniture
Fire fighting equipment, such as a fire extinguisher, fire blanket	May be used to tackle *minor* fires

---

Safety equipment can be a useful and practical aid to ensuring children's safety. However, this is no substitute for close supervision. It is always important to know where children are and what they are doing.

Adapting the environment

Ensuring accessibility

All activities and areas of the setting must be accessible to all children, although there will always be some areas where the children are not allowed, such as the kitchen.

- Children with a physical disability may need wider doorways, ramps, and larger toilet area. Space to allow them to move around classroom furniture.

- Children with a sensory impairment may need additional equipment. For example, a deaf child may need a hearing aid or a practitioner who can use British Sign Language.

- Children with a visual impairment will need the reading area to be well lit. Natural light is best but if the area does not get enough daylight then extra lights will be needed. Books with large print and clear pictures will be helpful. There should be extra space to help movement around classroom furniture. The floor must be kept clear of obstacles. Any changes to the physical environment should be planned and explained to the child in advance.

Lifting and carrying

K2P18

You should be aware of the policies and practices of your setting when lifting children and equipment. It is easy to injure yourself if you attempt to lift anything that is too heavy. Lifting incorrectly will also result in injury. If you are lifting children or equipment you should always:

- get a firm grip on whatever it is that you are lifting
- bend your knees as you lift, not your back
- plan your lifting, for example can the child stand up before you lift, so that you do not have to bend down so far?
- get help if the equipment is too heavy or too awkward for one person to lift.

You should never attempt to lift anything that is too heavy for you.

Always check the apparatus and supervise the children

Preventing infection

Encouraging children to develop good personal hygiene practices

K2S24
K2D48
K2D49
K2D50
K2D51

Infections like coughs, colds and tummy upsets can be passed from one person to another. This is very likely to happen in places where children are cared for in groups where they have close contact with each other. Teach children the basic rules of hygiene like washing their hands after using the toilet and before eating. This will help to prevent germs being spread.

Providing a hygienic environment

K2S24
K2D48
K2D49
K2D50
K2D51

Children are very vulnerable to infection, and diseases can spread very quickly in a childcare setting. Infection can be transmitted between adults and children and also between the children themselves. Basic workplace routines can prevent diseases being spread if they are carried out efficiently, thoroughly and regularly. Three important areas of routine hygiene in childcare settings are:

- personal hygiene
- environmental hygiene
- disposing of waste materials.

Hand washing is especially important because it is the single most effective means of preventing the spread of infection. Practitioners should ensure that they:

- wash their hands often throughout the day. Always wash their hands after going to the toilet, cleaning up after accidents and *before* handling food
- use warm water and a mild liquid soap, rub hands on both sides and rinse thoroughly
- dry hands thoroughly using a paper towel or hand drier
- keep nails short and free of nail varnish. Bacteria grow where the varnish is chipped
- disinfect nail-brushes
- use disposable paper towels or hot air hand dryers. If this is not possible, towels should be washed at least daily and kept as dry as possible
- cover any cuts or abrasions with a waterproof plaster
- wear latex gloves when changing nappies or dealing with blood or any other body fluids
- keep hair clean, brushed often and tied back. Check regularly for head lice.

Good hygiene practices

K2S24

A clean childcare setting is not only more welcoming but also less likely to contain harmful germs. Spread of infection can be prevented by:

- ensuring good ventilation
- supervising children when they use the lavatory and making sure that they wash and dry their hands properly afterwards
- avoiding overcrowding. The national standards stipulate how much space is required
- providing separate rooms for babies and toddlers
- using protective clothing, such as plastic aprons and gloves, when handling bodily fluids such as urine, blood, vomit or faeces
- keeping laundry facilities separate from food preparation areas
- cleaning toys and play equipment regularly. Toys should be cleaned daily, more often if used by babies
- using separate cloths and mops for different areas, for example one floor mop for the toilet area and a different mop for the playroom. Floor mops and cloths should be washed in hot water and detergent, rinsed and allowed to dry
- regular checking of the toilet/bathroom area. Hand washbasins should not be used as a source of drinking water
- using paper towels and tissues
- using covered bins with a foot pedal for disposal
- washing and sieving the sand regularly
- ensuring that any pets are kept clean and well cared for
- encouraging parents and carers to keep children at home if they are unwell. Including this in the written policies may prevent misunderstandings
- observing strict hygiene procedures in the food preparation areas
- checking the outside area for animal excrement or other hazards, like broken glass or refuse.

Disposing of waste materials

K2S24

All childcare settings should have a health and safety policy that covers the disposal of hazardous waste. Care must be taken with all bodily waste (blood, faeces, urine, saliva) to prevent the transmission of diseases. Infections can be present without showing signs so the policy must be strictly maintained.

The following guidelines should be implemented when handling and disposing of waste materials:

- Cover any cuts or grazes with a waterproof dressing.
- Wear disposable latex gloves and plastic aprons when dealing with bodily waste.
- Cover bodily waste with a 1% hypochlorite solution (such as bleach) before wiping up.

- Wash hands with an antiseptic soap.
- Dispose of nappies, dressings and used gloves and aprons in a sealed bag and place in a covered bin for disposal. Take off used gloves by peeling them back from the wrist to turn them inside out.
- Provide areas with covered bins with foot pedals for different types of waste.

Cleaning

Cleaning toys and equipment is important to ensure good standards of hygiene and to prevent infections spreading. Feeding equipment and toys used by babies should be cleaned each time they are used. Any toys that are regularly handled should be cleaned using soapy water or a disinfectant solution. This will also provide an opportunity to check toys and equipment for wear or damage. Surfaces also need to be cleaned, at least daily, using hot soapy water or a suitable anti-bacterial cleaner.

Most settings will have a routine for cleaning. This will include washing floors, bathrooms and toilets, kitchens, vacuuming and cleaning carpets.

Safe storage

K2S15
K2S20

All the cleaning materials and other items such as medicines, food items and waste must be kept safely. Locked storage for these items will make sure that they kept away from the children. Practitioners also need to be very careful when they are using these items. Make sure the children cannot get hold of them while they are in use. Check carefully that they have been replaced in the locked storage after use. Be very aware that common household items like washing-up liquid and washing powder are also potentially dangerous and need to be kept well out of the reach of children. Keep children out of the kitchen and laundry areas.

Supervising children

K2P25
K2S26
K2D48
K2D49

The number of adults required to care for children in day care is regulated by national standards. For example, the National Standards for Under 8s Day Care and Child Minding regulates the number of adults required to care for the children in England. This is also related to the age of the child. These figures are described as ratios; the number of children that can be cared for by one adult in these age groups in full day care is:

- children under 2 years – 1 adult to 3 children (1:3)
- children aged 2 years – 1 adult to 4 children (1:4)
- children aged 3–7 years – 1 adult to 8 children (1:8).

These numbers are the minimum requirements. You would expect to have fewer children per adult if some of the children had special needs. Children also need to get out and about to enjoy local outings to the shops or park. You would need more adults in these circumstances. Different ratios apply to childminders and these are also described in the national standards.

The adult:child ratios relate to staff available to work directly with the children. Suitable arrangements must be made to cover unexpected emergencies and staff absences. There should be enough staff to cover breaks, holidays and time spent with parents. All this will need careful planning by the management to make sure that the ratios are kept up and the children's safety ensured.

Encouraging children to be aware of personal safety

Providing a good role model

K2S26

Children are great imitators but they will learn and copy both good and poor behaviour. It is very important that adults always follow the safety rules and never compromise their own safety. This is especially important where road safety is involved. Always set a good example. Talk to children about road safety and use the Green Cross Code yourself. If there is a controlled crossing, use it and don't be tempted to cross at a red light even if the road is clear.

The adult role and risk assessment

K2S26

Having the adults there is only the beginning of good supervision. Adults must be alert and aware of what the children are doing. Supervising the children well makes sure that they remain safe but also lets them try out new and more challenging activities. Practitioners must always be aware of potential hazards. Then they can see any possible dangers for the children, before there is an accident, and take action to stop this happening. However, children do need to learn to do new things and to become more independent, so it is important not to limit the children to activities that are too easy. They will need to do more challenging things so, think about what simple measures will reduce the risk. For example, you may need to supervise a child more closely if they are trying out their climbing skills on more difficult climbing apparatus or using the woodwork tools.

Children and safety rules

All settings will have safety rules and the adults must make sure that children follow the rules. However it is also very important to explain to the children why there are rules and how the rules will help to keep them safe as they play and learn. Help the children to understand about risk and staying safe. For example, practitioners can explain the safety rules to the children before they use the apparatus. They must also explain the rules again during the activities if the children are not playing safely. Always explain why the child is in danger or putting others in danger.

Children will be able to play safely as they begin to understand about the dangers that are around them. However this awareness takes time to develop and all children will always need to be supervised as they play. Younger children and babies, because of their stage of development, will be less aware of dangers and will require greater supervision.

Children and adults together can make a list of the safety rules together. This can give the children a chance to talk about what is safe behaviour and what is not.

Playground rules

Make sure the list is not too long and that it includes the most important points. Examples that the children might suggest could be:

- No running indoors.
- No pushing, shouting or fighting.
- No walking around with scissors.

Include some positive rules, such as:

- Let everyone take a turn.
- Always fetch an adult if someone is hurt or crying.
- Sit down when having a drink.

Safety and security procedures

K2S33

Childcare settings should have strict security measures:

- Doors and gates that lead to the outside or to areas where children are not allowed must have a suitable lock. The lock must be well out of the reach of the children. All the adults in the setting must make sure that the locks are used at all times.

- Fire exits must be checked to see that they are not locked or blocked with equipment.
- Window locks must be fitted and used.
- Name badges for all staff and students.
- Door entry phones and bells will give the staff the opportunity to enquire about the nature of the business of any visitors before letting them enter the building.
- Supervised outdoor play times.

At the start of the day/session

All settings will have a procedure for receiving children at the beginning of a session. Babies, young children and their parents will be welcomed directly by their key person. Older children may be brought into the pre-school, nursery or classroom by their parent. There will be a method of registering each child's arrival. It is very important that a register of all the children present is taken at the very beginning of the day/session. This register must be updated if a child leaves early. It is a legal requirement that a register is kept. The register is most important. For example, if there is a fire it can be used to ensure that all the children have left the building safely. The start of the day is a very busy time. Practitioners will need to be watchful. You must make sure that children are properly supervised to ensure that children do not go back outside when parents leave.

Home times

Practitioners must ensure children's safety at home times. Most settings have a policy that only allows children to be collected by a named adult. Parents should inform staff about who will be collecting the child if they cannot do so themselves. Every setting should have a procedure for collecting children.

Practical Example

K2S33

Collecting Laurie

Laurie's mum, Wendy, came to the nursery today to collect him. She asked to speak to Janice who is in charge. She explained that she would not be able to collect Laurie herself the next week, as she would be delayed at work. She said that Laurie's Granny would come and fetch him. Janice explained that there would be several things that Wendy needed to do to make sure that the staff at the nursery could be certain that it was his Granny collecting Laurie.

➤ *What arrangements do you think Janice could make with Wendy to ensure that Laurie was safely collected?*

Taking children out of the setting

Outings with children

K2S38

Children enjoy going on outings. These can be short trips to the shops or to post a letter, or longer outings to farms or parks. All will provide valuable learning opportunities. The amount of preparation needed depends on the scale of the outing. Whenever you are taking children outside the setting, there will be local regulations that must be followed. Always make sure that you know about the regulations and follow them carefully.

Consider these things when planning to take children on an outing:

- safety
- permissions
- the place
- supervision
- transport
- food
- clothing
- cost.

The age and stage of development of the children

There are differences in the physical capabilities of children. Very young children, for example, will be restricted to areas where you can push a buggy. Children will vary in their ability to concentrate and sit still. Choosing a destination that meets the needs of all the age groups you are taking is important. It may be necessary to group children. Each group can then do different things. For example, during a visit

Outings with young children should be educational and fun

to a park, the younger children will enjoy feeding the ducks. The older ones will also wish to play ball games, or follow the nature trails.

The distance of the destination will decide whether the trip will last for a morning, afternoon or whole day. Younger children do not like spending a long time travelling. This should be thought about when choosing where to go.

Permissions

Permission to take children outside the setting will always have to be obtained from the person in charge of the setting. This person will be responsible for carrying out a risk assessment. The risk assessment will reflect the kind of outing planned. A short local visit will need less planning than a longer visit to a place that is further away. It is important to inform parents about the outing and get their written permission for children to take part

Adult help/supervision

It is essential to arrange to have a higher adult:child ratio on any outing away from the setting. This will depend on the risk assessment. A general guide for ratios on trips away from the setting is:

- children 0–2 years – 1 adult to 1 child (1:1)
- children 2–5 years – 1 adult to 2 children (1:2)
- children 5–8 years – 1 adult to 6 children (1:6)
- children 8–12 years – 1 adult to 8 children (1:8)
- children 12–16 years – 1 adult to 10 children (1:10).

There will be local regulations that apply to your setting. Find out about these.

It is always good to have extra adults to help cover any emergencies. For example, if a child is separated from the group and is lost, extra adults will be free to search. The remaining children will still be adequately supervised.

Cost

If there is an entry fee or travelling costs, some families may not be able to afford to pay. Check whether there is enough funding to cater for all the children.

Transport

Is the place within walking distance or will transport be required? If arranging transport with an outside organisation, make sure that:

- they are insured
- the vehicle is large enough to seat everyone – adults and children
- there are sufficient child restraints, booster seats and seat belts
- the vehicles are safe.

Records must be kept about vehicles in which children are to be transported. This includes:

- insurance details
- a list of named drivers.

Drivers using their own vehicle to carry any children must have insurance cover. Avoid travelling during rush hours. When on foot, plan to use the safest route.

Stages in the planning process

1   **Check** the national and local authority regulations that apply to your setting that cover outings. Any arrangements must comply with these regulations.

2   **Find out** about the destination, for example, travel routes, opening times and accessibility for children, toilet facilities, picnic areas, refreshments, first aid provision. It may be possible to visit to find this out before you go.

3   **Prepare** a timetable for the day. Everyone will need to know times of departure and arrival. Ensure that your programme is practical and there is enough time to do everything that you have planned for.

4   **Plan** to take all the necessary equipment with you, for example:
    - first aid kit
    - emergency contact phone numbers and a mobile phone (check the battery)
    - registers
    - any medicines and inhalers
    - camera
    - money
    - audio tapes for the journey
    - worksheets and bags for collecting items of interest
    - packed lunches
    - wet weather wear
    - sun cream, sun hats
    - spare clothes
    - pushchairs, nappies and harnesses for younger children.

5   **Consult** parents. It is necessary to get written consent from parents for any trip away from the setting. They will need to know about the cost, the day's programme, transport, special requirements – lunch, clothing, etc. A letter home with a consent slip is the best way to achieve this, perhaps combined with posters or notices displayed in the setting.

6   **Prepare** the children for the outing. Discuss the outing and explain what will be happening. Talk about safety issues, such as staying with adults, not speaking to strangers. Discuss any activities related to the outing. Make sure the children know what to do if they become separated from the group (for example, not to wander about but to stay in the same place). Older children may be shown a central meeting point or the ticket office. Show children the staff uniform or name badges so they know who to ask for help. Name badges for children are not used nowadays, as they enable strangers to find out the child's name. You could use a system of number badges that link to the register.

7   **Brief** all the adults who are helping on the outing. They will need to have all the information about the outing, who is in charge and has the registers and the contact numbers. They must also have a list of all the children and know which children they are responsible for. Make sure adults know what to do in an emergency.

8   **Plan** to meet up and have regular head counts and register checks.

9   **Consider** the 'what ifs'. Planning includes taking proper safety precautions, supervising the children carefully and preparing for the unexpected. However, unexpected events may still happen during an outing. It is important to think about what might happen beforehand. You can then think about how you would cope.

Element 202.1

Are you ready for assessment?

Prepare and maintain a safe environment

You need to show that you can competently prepare and maintain a safe environment. To do this you will need to be directly observed by your assessor and present other evidence. The amount and type of evidence you need to present will vary. You should plan this with your assessor.

Direct observation by your assessor

Observation is the required assessment method to be used to evidence some part of each element in this unit. Expert witnesses could supply additional evidence. Your assessor will observe you in real work activities and this should provide most of the evidence for the performance criteria for the elements in this unit.

Preparing to be observed

You will need to show your assessor that you can maintain and clean equipment. This is often done as the equipment is put out and put away. Make sure that, as you use any equipment, you follow any instructions and guidance provided.

Your assessor will need to see that you can safely dispose of waste materials so make sure that you know how to wrap waste and which bins are used for different types of waste. Be sure that you wear gloves and any protective clothing provided.

Your assessor will need to see that you work in a safe way so make sure that you pay attention to the locks on doors and windows. Be ready to act if you can see a hazard to the children's safety.

You should make sure that the children pay attention to personal hygiene. Encourage them to wash their hands after going to the toilet and before eating or drinking.

Your assessor will need to see you supervising the children during their usual activities. Make sure that you can tell your assessor how many adults there should be for the number and age of the children. ▶

As you supervise the children you will need to make sure that the children are safe. You should explain any safety rules. Help them as they attempt more difficult things, perhaps in their physical play, while still making sure that that are safe.

Check carefully when children come into the setting and when they go home. Make sure that you know about, and follow the procedures of your setting.

You will need to show that you know about any regulations, local and national, that are concerned with the safety of the children in your setting.

> You may need to present other types of evidence in order to:
>
> • cover criteria not observed by your assessor
>
> • show that you have the required knowledge and understanding.

Element 202.2 — *Follow procedures for accidents, emergencies and illness*

Emergency procedures

All establishments should have:

- written emergency procedures
- staff who have been trained in first aid
- first aid equipment
- an accident book for accurate recording of all incidents requiring first aid
- regular review of incidence accidents to highlight areas of concern.

Evacuation and fire procedures

Evacuation and fire procedures must be clearly displayed and pointed out to anyone who comes into the building. Law requires regular practices. All staff must be familiar with evacuation procedures. A fire officer will make regular checks.

Part of the introduction to your setting will include an explanation of the emergency procedures. Any visitors to the setting, such as parents staying with their children, will be shown the procedure for evacuating the setting if there is a fire or other emergency. These procedures should be displayed in every room where everyone can see and read them. They should be simple and easy to follow. A plan will show more clearly where the fire exits are positioned. Fire exits must never be locked or blocked by furniture or any other equipment

Other emergencies

Emergencies other than fire could involve a gas escape, electricity failure or leaking water. Security incidents such as a bomb threat or intruder alert may also need staff to use the emergency procedures.

Important things that must be included in emergency procedures:

- a reminder that the alarm should be sounded
- a clear statement or plan to show where the assembly points and fire exits are located
- the route to follow to get out of the building
- how to call for help, for example where the nearest telephone outside the building is located
- a reminder *not* to go back into the building
- the name of the person responsible for the procedure and collecting the registers and parents' contact numbers.

Children should leave the building by the quickest route. This will be shown on the evacuation procedure. It is important that someone is responsible for taking a register outside. An accurate count can then be done as soon as the children and staff get to the assembly point. The first thing the emergency services will want to know when they arrive is if anyone is still in the building. As well as the register it is important to have a record of the parents' contact numbers. These need to be kept close to the register or actually written in the register. Parents will need to be contacted and kept informed about what is happening.

Missing children or persons

If children or others are thought to be missing, it is important to check the register and the records of staff and visitors that are present. If you find that someone is missing, report to the person in charge immediately so that all the other registers and records can be checked. In the case of a fire evacuation, the fire officer in charge should be told immediately if someone is missing.

Fire-fighting equipment

Settings will have fire-fighting equipment; it is important to know where any fire-blankets, fire extinguishers and other equipment are kept and that you know how to use them safely. There are different kinds of fire extinguishers that are used for different kinds of fires. It is important that you have been fully informed about the fire-fighting equipment before you attempt to use it. Never put yourself at risk by attempting to put out a fire. It is much better to sound the fire alarm and evacuate the building safely.

There are different types of fire extinguishers. It is important that you know which kind of fire they can be used for. For example, fire extinguishers containing water must not be used on fires involving electrical equipment. There are special extinguishers that can be used for these fires. Suitable fire-fighting equipment should be placed near any potential fire hazard. For example, a fire blanket would be most useful in a kitchen.

**Fire-fighting
equipment**

Practising the evacuation procedure

Regular practices should take place to make sure that all staff and children know how to leave the building quickly and safely.

If you work in a home setting, you will be required to work out an evacuation procedure for each room in your home and practise leaving the building.

A record must be kept of each practice and the staff should discuss how well the practice went. Changes should be made to the procedure if there are any difficulties, or if staff can see how to make the procedure work better to ensure the children's safety. It is also very important to have practices that take place without any prior warning. Staff and children can then respond as they would in a real emergency.

Discussing the evacuation procedure and explaining what will happen will help to make the practice go more smoothly. The children will also need time to talk about the practice afterwards. Parents need to be aware of any fire practices. They can also talk this over with their children at home. Stories about fire-fighters and fire engines will help the children to talk about any worries they may have. Successful practices will mean that there is a good chance that all will be well in a real emergency.

Responding in a calm and reassuring way

A real emergency that leads to an evacuation of the setting will be a worrying and frightening experience for the adults and children. However, it is important to stay calm and to reassure the children by talking to them, while carrying out the evacuation procedure as quickly and safely as possible. Give clear and positive instructions in a clear calm voice. It will help if you and the children have practised what you need to do.

Coping with accidents and injuries to children

K2S27

What follows is an outline of basic first aid for children, it is not intended to replace a recognised training in first aid. It is important that all practitioners undertake recognised training in first aid so that they can act confidently and safely in the event of an accident. The British Red Cross and St John Ambulance run recognised first aid courses in most areas. A recognised first aid certificate will provide evidence for this element.

First aid box

All settings should have a first aid box. The first aid box should be clearly labelled and put in a dry place, where the children cannot reach it. All the staff should know where the first aid box is kept and it should be in a place where it can be easily and quickly reached in an emergency. The first aid box may contain all the items shown in the illustration below. There should be a list of the contents kept in the box.

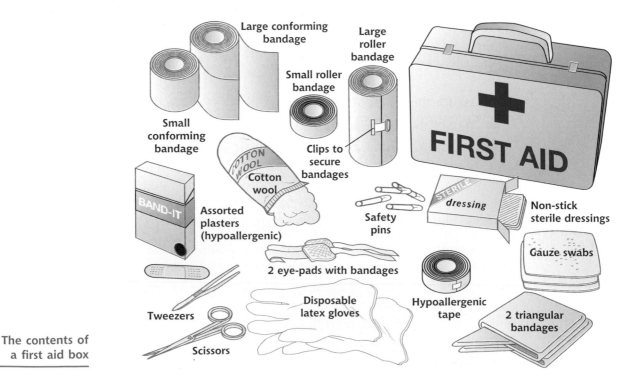

The contents of a first aid box

It is very important that the contents of the first aid box are checked. Things that have been used must be replaced at once, as people using the first aid box will be relying on everything being there. Most settings will have a designated member of staff responsible for first aid. There should be a foolproof system for checking and replacing first aid items as they are used.

The contents of first aid boxes may vary. Have a look to see what is in your setting's box.

First aid in emergencies

It is important to remain calm in any emergency situation. If you are the first person on the scene you should:

- *Assess the situation:* Find out how many children are injured and whether there is any continuing danger. Are there any other adults who can help? Is an ambulance required?
- *Put safety first:* Include the safety of all children and adults, including you. Remove any dangerous hazards. Move the injured child only if it is absolutely essential.
- *Prioritise:* Treat the most serious injuries first. Conditions that are immediately life threatening in children are:
  - *not* breathing.
  - severe bleeding.
- *Get help:* Shout for help or ask others to get help and call an ambulance. **If you are not trained to give emergency aid, you should concentrate on getting help as quickly as possible**. When the trained first aider arrives, she/he will take charge, so follow instructions carefully.

If you are told to telephone for an ambulance:

- Dial 999.
- Ask for the ambulance service.
- Answer the questions that you will be asked accurately and clearly.
- Know the telephone number from which you are calling.
- Know the exact place of the accident.
- Give the details of the accident and what you know about any injuries.
- Do not put the phone down until you have given all the information requested.

Examining a casualty

Find out if the child is conscious or unconscious.

- Check for response – call the child's name, pinch the skin.
- Open the airway and check for breathing.
- Check the pulse.

How to manage an unconscious child who is breathing

An unconscious child who is breathing and has a pulse should be put into the recovery position. This will keep the airway clear. Keep checking the airway and pulse until medical help arrives.

The recovery position

1 Lay the child on their back, tilt the head back, lift the chin forward, ensure airway is clear.
2 Straighten the child's legs, bend the arm nearest to you at a right angle.
3 Take the arm furthest away and move it across the chest, bend it and place it on the cheek.
4 Keep the inside leg straight, place foot flat on ground. Clasp thigh of the outside leg and bend it at knee.
5 Pull the bent leg towards you to roll the child on to their side. Keep hand against cheek.
6 Bend top leg into a right angle to prevent child rolling forward, tilt head back to keep airway open. Adjust hand under child's cheek.

How to manage an unconscious child who is *not* breathing

If a child is **unconscious** and **not breathing**, you will need to breathe for them. **You will need to have done a recognised first aid course to be able to do this. If you are not trained to do this, you must get help as quickly as possible.**

First aid for minor injuries

It is essential to remain calm when dealing with an injured child. They need to be reassured that everything will be all right.

Minor burns and scalds

Immerse the burnt area in cold water for at least 10 minutes. Avoid touching the burn or any blisters. Cover with a clean smooth cloth, such as a clean tea towel, and seek medical aid. For all but the most minor burns, you should get medical aid as quickly as possible.

Bleeding

Minor bleeding wounds should be cleaned and covered with a dressing. For major bleeds:

- Send for help immediately.
- Apply direct pressure to the wound and raise the injured part.

Dealing with bleeding

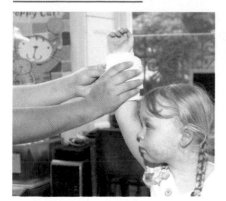 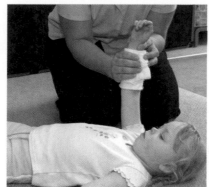 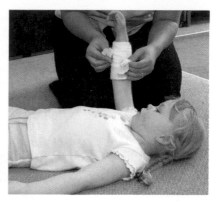

1 Apply pressure to the wound and raise the injured part

2 Lay the child down, while continuing to apply pressure and keep the injured part raised.

3 Keeping the injured part raised cover the wound with a firm, sterile dressing and bandage.

Nose bleeds

Sit the child leaning forwards and pinch the soft part of the nose above the nostrils for 10 minutes. If the bleeding continues, seek medical aid.

Managing a nosebleed

Remember that you should always wear gloves when dealing with blood or any other body fluids. This will protect you from infection.

Splinters

Children may get splinters of wood from rough wooden objects so check equipment carefully.

If the splinter is sticking out from the skin it may be possible to remove it using a pair of tweezers. The wound should be cleaned carefully. If the splinter is deeply embedded, medical aid will be needed.

Check to make sure the child's tetanus immunisation is up to date.

Sprains

Raise and support the injured limb to minimise swelling. Remove shoe and sock if it is a sprained ankle. Apply a cold compress – a polythene bag of ice or a pack of frozen peas would do. Keep the limb raised until you can get medical aid. The ankle should be checked to ensure that nothing is broken.

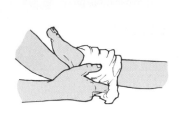

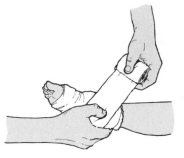

1 **Remove the shoe and sock, and raise the foot**

2 **Keeping the ankle raised, apply a cold compress.**

3 **Wrap the ankle with cotton wool padding and hold in place with a firm bandage, keeping the ankle raised and supported all the time.**

Objects in noses or ears

Children who have poked anything into their nose or ears should be taken to the nearest Accident and Emergency Department. The object will be safely removed.

Choking

This could be a very serious situation. Send for help immediately. If you are dealing with a young child, put the child over your knee, head down then:

- Slap sharply between the shoulder blades up to five times.
- Check to see if the object has become dislodged and is in the mouth.
- If the object has not been dislodged, call for urgent medical aid – take the child to the phone with you if you are alone.
- Try the back slaps again until help arrives or the object can be removed.

Poisoning

Eating poisonous plants or medicines, swallowing bleach or cleaning fluids are all serious situations.

- Send for help immediately.
- Check to see if the child is breathing and conscious.
- Put into the recovery position if unconscious.
- Take any samples of what has been eaten or drunk to the hospital with the child.

Asthma

Asthma attacks are very frightening for children. The airways go into spasm making breathing difficult. This could be a serious situation.

Management of an asthma attack

- Reassure the child.
- Give the child's inhaler if they are known asthmatics.
- Send for help.
- Sit the child upright and leaning forward in a comfortable position.
- Stay with the child.
- Continue to comfort and reassure the child.
- If this is the first attack or if the condition persists, call for an ambulance and contact parents.

When to call an ambulance

Call an ambulance immediately, or get someone else to do so if:

- this is the first asthma attack
- the above steps have been taken and there is no improvement in 3–5 minutes.

Cuts and grazes

Any cut or graze that breaks the skin will mean that there is a risk of infection.

- Sit the child down and comfort them.
- Explain what you are going to do.
- Wash your hands.
- Put on gloves.
- Gently clean the graze or cut using clean water and a gauze pad (do not use cotton wool or any fluffy material that could stick to the wound).
- Cover the cut or graze with a pad and a light bandage.
- Put all the soiled material and gloves into a sealed bag for disposal.
- Wash your hands thoroughly.

Some settings may use plasters, but this is risky as many children are allergic to them. It is best to use special plasters (hypo-allergenic) that are specially made to avoid allergic reactions.

Anaphylactic shock

This is a severe reaction to a substance, such as peanuts or a bee sting.

The child will be very anxious and distressed. There is severe difficulty in breathing; the pulse may be rapid and the face red with swelling. Call an ambulance immediately. Meanwhile move the child into a position that will help them to breathe more easily.

Note: Some children with a known allergy may have an Epi-pen that contains the drug adrenaline to be used in the event of an attack. They may be able to use this themselves, or a member of staff may be trained to use it. If so, it should be given without delay.

Maintaining standards of hygiene when dealing with accidents and emergencies

When dealing with accidents and injuries, it is important to make sure that you protect yourself and the injured child from infection. Always:

- wear protective clothing, such as gloves and aprons
- wash your hands before and after attending to an injury even if you wear gloves
- make sure that anyone helping you also wears protective clothing and washes their hands
- avoid touching the cut or graze or the dressing that will touch the cut. Don't let the child or anyone else touch either
- avoid coughing or sneezing over the injury by you or others
- clean up carefully and get rid of any dirty dressings or other material by sealing in a marked plastic bag for disposal preferably by burning
- clean up spills of blood, urine or other bodily waste carefully. Always wear gloves and use a solution of bleach (one teaspoon to a half a litre of water) to clean surfaces. Dispose of the waste as described above.

Recording accidents, injuries and other incidents

All settings will have a way of recording any accidents, injuries and other incidents. This is often a special book (the accident book). All accidents, injuries and incidents, however small or minor, must be recorded as soon as possible. This information should be shared with parents so that they are fully aware of what has happened. It may be that a child, who has had a minor accident at nursery and seems fine, will become ill later in the day or during the night.

The records should include:

- the full name of the child
- the date and time of the accident
- the exact details of the accident and any injury
- who was involved
- what treatment was given
- who was informed
- what action was taken
- the signature of the member of staff dealing with the accident.

Accident books should be kept for at least three years.

Settings will usually ask the parents to sign the book to show that they have read the details.

Informing parents

If an accident is serious, the parents should be contacted immediately. This is the responsibility of the senior member of staff or person in charge. If the child has to go to hospital, then the parent will need to go with them, or meet the ambulance there if this is a quicker option. Parents will need to be involved in any decision about their child's treatment so it very important to be able to contact parents as quickly as possible. Parents' contact telephone numbers must be kept up to date

More minor accidents are usually reported to parents when they collect their children at the end of the session. Again this is the responsibility of a senior member of staff. Parents may well be upset about accidents, however minor. It is very important to keep accurate records so that you can give parents clear information about what has happened and what was done. Parents will need time to talk about this, perhaps more than once. They may need to talk over their worries about what has happened with the person in charge.

Children's reactions to accidents and emergencies

After any accident children may be upset and crying. This is often because they have been frightened by what has happened. They may have injuries that need treatment and it is important to get help and to treat any injuries. However, it is also very important to comfort and reassure children after an accident. Take care not to blame children for accidents. They may have been acting in a dangerous way, but save the discussions about this for later. The important thing to do immediately is to sit with the child and talk to them while they recover. Children may want a particular comfort object, such as a toy. Try to fetch this or ask someone else to get it for the child as soon as you can. Children may also ask for their parent. The decision to send for a parent will depend on what has happened and how the child recovers.

Other children, who were not directly involved in the accident, may also be upset. They may be worried about a friend who has been hurt. Try to give simple explanations about what has happened and help the children to settle back into their normal activities. There should be a time later for the children and adults to talk about what has happened.

Allergies

K2S28

Children may be allergic to some foods, for example nuts or milk. It is very important that staff members are fully informed about any allergies that children may have. **Always check before giving food and drinks to babies and children.** If children are not allowed certain foods or drinks, this should be made clear to all staff. As well as recording this in the children's records, notices in the kitchen and the room where children are cared for should clearly display this information. Information about children's allergies to food and drink must be regularly updated.

This should be discussed with the parents when a child is admitted. The staff must be told about any changes. Practitioners must be aware that some foods could contain quite small quantities of substances that will cause a reaction. In some cases, if children are very allergic, this may only need the food to have been in contact with the ingredient that causes the allergic reaction. Many foods have a warning on the label about this.

Symptoms of food allergy may include:

- vomiting
- diarrhoea
- skin rashes
- wheezing and difficulty in breathing
- convulsions.

Recognising when children are ill

K2S29

It is very important to know about diseases that are common in childhood and to be able to recognise the signs that tell you that a child is ill. Most illnesses begin with the same general signs and need the same general care.

Causes of disease and how diseases spread

Diseases are caused by **pathogens**. The common name for pathogens is **germs**. The most important pathogens are:

- bacteria
- viruses
- fungi.

Once pathogens enter the body, they multiply very rapidly. This period of time is called the **incubation period** and can last for a few days or weeks depending on the type of disease. Although the child is infectious during the incubation period, they only begin to feel ill and show signs of the illness at the end of the incubation period.

How diseases are spread

Method of spread	Example of disease
Droplet infection. The pathogens are contained in the droplets of moisture in the breath and are breathed out.	Colds, coughs, measles, chickenpox
Touching infected people or material	Impetigo, athletes foot, thrush, coughs and colds
Drinking infected water	Food poisoning, gastro-enteritis, polio
Eating infected food	Food poisoning, gastro-enteritis, diarrhoea, typhoid
Pathogens entering through a cut or graze	Tetanus, hepatitis, HIV/AIDs

Common childhood illnesses

Colds

Viruses cause colds, so antibiotics will not help. There are things you can do to help the child breathe more easily: keep the nose clear; make sure the child has plenty to drink; and give light, easily swallowed food. Don't fuss if a child does not want to eat for a while, just give plenty to drink.

Coughs

A virus causes most coughs, like colds. If a cough persists or the chest sounds congested, a doctor should be consulted.

Diarrhoea

Young babies' **stools** are normally soft and yellow, and some babies will soil nearly every nappy. If you notice the stools becoming very watery and frequent, with other signs of illness, consult the doctor. In the meantime, give as much cooled, boiled water as you can.

Ear infections

Ear infections often follow a cold. The child may be generally unwell, pull or rub the ears or there may be a discharge from the ear. There may be a raised temperature. The child may complain of pain, but small babies will just cry and seem unwell or uncomfortable. If you suspect an ear infection, it is important that it is treated promptly.

Bronchitis

Infection and inflammation of the main airway cause **bronchitis** (chest infection). The child will have a persistent chesty cough and may cough up green or yellow phlegm. There may be noisy breathing, a raised temperature and the child feels very unwell. Consult the doctor as soon as possible. Meanwhile, allow the child to rest quietly. Sitting well propped up will help breathing.

Raised temperature

Children, especially babies, can develop high temperatures very quickly. If a baby has a raised temperature and/or other signs of illness, always consult the doctor as soon as possible. It is important to bring the temperature down to avoid any complications. Do not wrap a baby up; take off a layer of clothing and let older children wear light clothes. Keep the room cool and give plenty of cool drinks, little and often.

Febrile convulsions

Febrile convulsions are fits that occur as the direct result of a raised temperature. They usually occur in babies and younger children between the ages of 6 months and 5 years.

It is important to act effectively and quickly.

- Stay with the child and protect them from injury or falling.
- Get medical aid.

- Put the child in the recovery position when the convulsions have stopped.
- Take the measures described above to bring down the temperature.

Thrush

Thrush is a fungal infection that forms white patches in the mouth, usually on the tongue and the inside of the cheeks and lips. A baby may also have a sore bottom because the thrush has infected the skin in the nappy area. Consult the doctor, who will give the specific anti-fungal treatment to clear up the infection.

Vomiting

All babies will bring up some milk from time to time. If the baby is vomiting often or violently and/or there are other signs of illness, contact the doctor. Babies can lose a lot of fluid if they vomit frequently. Keep up the intake of fluids.

The table below lists the infectious childhood illnesses you need to know about. It outlines the signs to look for and the specific care needed.

Infectious childhood illnesses

Disease	Incubation	Symptoms	Care
Chickenpox	14–16 days	Spots on chest and back, red at first, becoming blisters, then forming a dry scab. Spots come in successive crops and are very itchy.	Discourage scratching and ease the itching by keeping the child cool and applying lotion such as calamine.
Coughs and colds	2–10 days	General signs of illness, nasal congestion, cough.	General care, but monitor coughs carefully in case the chest becomes infected. Watch carefully in case other symptoms develop, which would indicate a more serious illness. Consult doctor if unsure, especially with a baby.
Diarrhoea (caused by infected food or water)	2–7 days	Loose, frequent, watery stools, pains in the stomach.	Give plenty of fluid to avoid dehydration. Consult a doctor for a baby, or if the diarrhoea persists, or the child shows signs of dehydration or other illness.
Diphtheria	2–6 days	Difficulty in breathing. White membrane forms in the throat.	Medical aid and hospital treatment is needed. Immunisation available.
Ear infections (otitis media)	Variable	Pain, discharge from the ear, high temperature.	Medical aid, antibiotics and pain relief may be prescribed by a doctor.
Gastro-enteritis (caused by infected food or dirty water)	1–14 days	Severe and persistent vomiting and diarrhoea.	Medical aid and hospital care may be needed. Give plenty of fluids. Oral rehydration solutions may be given.

Disease	Incubation	Symptoms	Care
Measles	7–14 days	Raised temperature, sore eyes, Koplik's spots in the mouth, red blotchy rash that quickly spreads over the whole body.	Medical aid. Eyes and ears may need special attention as complications include sensitivity to light and ear infections. Immunisation is available.
Meningitis	2–10 days	Symptoms include high temperature, headache, irritability, vomiting, rash, pain and stiffness in the neck, and sensitivity to light,	**Get medical aid. Early hospital treatment will be needed.** It is very important to recognise meningitis early as the progress of this illness is very rapid and serious. Immunisation is available for some types of meningitis.
Mumps	14–21 days	Pain, tenderness and swelling around the jaw and ear, usually on one side of the face, then the other.	Doctor may advise pain relief. A rare complication in boys is inflammation of the testes. Immunisation is available.
Poliomyelitis (water-borne infection)	5–21 days	Headache, stiffness in neck and back, loss of movement and paralysis.	Hospital care. Immunisation is available.
Rubella	14–21 days	Mild general symptoms, rash lasting for about 24 hours.	General care. Keep the child away from any women who may be pregnant as the rubella virus can damage the foetus. Immunisation is available.
Scarlet fever	2–6 days	Red tongue, sore throat, rash on face and body.	Medical aid. Doctor may prescribe antibiotics.
Tetanus	4–21 days	Painful muscle spasms in neck and jaw.	Hospital treatment required. Keep immunisation up to date.
Thrush (fungus infection)	Variable	White patches in the mouth, usually on the tongue and inside the cheeks. A baby may have a sore bottom.	Consult the doctor who will prescribe a specific treatment. Check that all feeding equipment is sterilised.
Tuberculosis	28–42 days	Cough, weight loss, investigation shows lung damage.	Medical aid. Specific antibiotics are given. Immunisation is available.
Whooping cough	7–14 days	Long bouts of coughing and choking, difficulty in breathing during the coughing, whooping noise as the child draws in breath. Vomiting during coughing bouts.	Medical aid. Support during coughing bouts, and give reassurance. Give food after coughing if vomiting is a problem. Possible complications are permanent lung damage, brain damage, ear infections and bronchitis. Immunisation is available.

Asthma

Asthma is a condition in which the airways in the lungs become narrowed. Allergy to substances such as pollen, dust and pet hair causes the airways to swell. Spasms of the airways may cause further narrowing, making breathing difficult. The child wheezes and becomes breathless. Attacks vary in severity, but a bad attack can be very frightening. Severe asthma attacks are serious and require prompt medical aid.

Inhalers help to get medication into the lungs and relieve the affected airways. These medicines are called bronchodilators and help to reduce swelling and spasm in the airways at the time of an attack. Other medicines given by regular use of inhalers help to prevent attacks occurring. There are different types of inhaler, which children can learn to use. It is very important that a child's inhaler is immediately available.

In an emergency

If a child in your care has an asthma attack, follow the procedure described in the first aid section above.

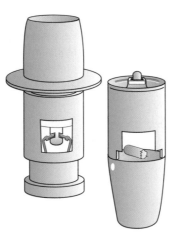
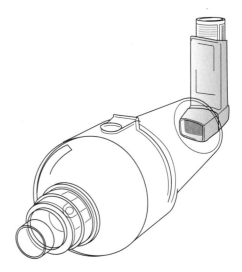

Different types
of inhaler

Infestations

Parasites obtain their food from humans and may affect children. Common parasites are:

- *fleas:* small insects that feed on human blood and live in clothing next to the skin. The bites can be seen as red spots
- *head lice:* insects that live in human hair close to the scalp, where they can easily bite the skin and feed on blood. You may see the lice or more likely nits. Nits are the empty white egg cases that are left stuck onto the hair after the louse has hatched

- *ringworm:* a fungal infection seen on the skin as a raised red circle with a white scaly middle
- *threadworms*: small thread-like worms that are found in the bowel. They cause a very itchy bottom. You may see the worms around the bottom
- *scabies:* tiny mites that burrow under the skin causing itching and raised red spots.

Each of these infestations has a specific treatment. Consult the child's doctor.

Caring for sick children in the work setting

When a child is ill outside the home environment, it is important to report any concerns. At school or nursery this will be to a senior member of staff, who will decide when to contact the child's parent. A childminder or nanny should contact the parents direct.

It is important to keep a record of the child's symptoms and how they change, as you may need to explain this to a parent or doctor. Information should be kept so that contact can be made in an emergency.

Giving medicines

These are the important points to remember when giving medicines to any child in a childcare setting:

- Follow the policy of your setting.
- Get the parents'/carers' written consent.
- Only give medicines advised or prescribed by the child's GP or hospital doctor.
- Follow the instructions for dosage and frequency carefully.
- Store medicine safely in a locked cupboard.
- Keep a record of all the medicines given, include the date, time and dose.

Practical Example

K2S29

Feeling ill at nursery

Leroy is 3 years old and comes to the nursery on three days each week while his parents are working. He has been coming for two months now and has settled in happily. He is very sociable and loves to play with the other children. Leroy came into nursery this morning his usual bright cheerful self. As the morning went on Sandra, the worker in charge of his group, noticed that he was sitting alone looking miserable. She tried to involve him in the activities, but he was reluctant to join in and became tearful. When Sandra went to comfort him, she noticed he was hot and decided to take his temperature. Leroy's temperature was raised and Sandra noticed that he had a flat, red rash on his face and body.

➤ *What should Sandra do now?*
➤ *What information should Sandra record?*

Element 202.2

Are you ready for assessment?

Deal with accidents, emergencies and illness

You need to show that you can competently deal with accidents, emergencies and illness. To do this you will need to be directly observed by your assessor and present other evidence. The amount and type of evidence you need to present will vary. You should plan this with your assessor.

Direct observation by your assessor

Observation is the required assessment method to be used to evidence some part of each element in this unit. Expert witnesses could supply additional evidence. Your assessor will observe you in real work activities and this should provide most of the evidence for the performance criteria for the elements in this unit.

Simulation is permitted for 202.2.

Preparing to be observed

You will need to make sure that you know all about the emergency procedures for your setting. Be ready to show your assessor where the information about how to evacuate the building is displayed. Be familiar with what you would be expected to do to help the children and others involved. Find out where all the fire-fighting equipment is located and be sure that you know how it can be used and for what kind of fire.

You will need to show your assessor where the registers and the information needed to contact the parents are kept. Make sure that you know how to call for the help needed in different situations. You should be able to contact the emergency services with the correct information if needed.

Show your assessor the records of previous practices at your setting, including the discussions and comments about the practices and any action taken.

You should show that you could recognise that a child is ill by knowing the signs of illness. You should be able to follow your settings procedures so that you can help the child.

You may need to present different types of evidence in order to:

- cover criteria not observed by your assessor
- show that you have the required knowledge and understanding.

Element 202.3

Support the safeguarding of children from abuse

Child protection

K2D48
K2D49
K2D50
K2D51

Children of all ages, male and female, from all cultures and all social and economic groups can be the victims of abuse. Abuse includes:

- the deliberate harming of children physically, sexually or emotionally
- the neglect of children's basic needs.

There are laws that aim to protect children from harm in any setting. England, Wales, Scotland and Northern Ireland have their own laws.

All those who work with children must put the interests and welfare of children first and protect them from harm. To be able to do this, a practitioner must know:

- the signs and symptoms of the different forms of abuse
- how these signs might show themselves in everyday situations
- what to do if they suspect abuse, including following the policies of their setting, the observation and recording of possible signs of abuse, and reporting these signs accurately and appropriately.

Types of abuse

K2S31

The four main types of abuse are:

- physical abuse and injury
- neglect
- emotional abuse
- sexual abuse.

Physical abuse and injury

Physical abuse involves someone deliberately harming or hurting a child physically. It includes hitting, shaking, throwing, biting, squeezing, burning, scalding, attempted suffocation, drowning, and giving children poisonous substances. This also includes giving a child inappropriate drugs or alcohol and the use of excessive force when punishing children or when carrying out tasks like feeding or nappy changing.

Signs of physical abuse

Bruises are a common sign of physical abuse. Where the bruises are on the body is important. Bruises on the cheeks, eyes, chest, back and shoulders are more likely to have been caused deliberately. Frequent bruising or bruises that are in a pattern may also be an indicator of abuse. Bruises resulting from deliberate injuries may be in the shape of fingertips, hands or other implements.

Bruising on the legs, below the knees, and arms below the elbows often occur accidentally as a result of physical play.

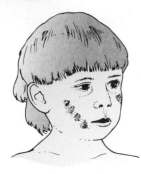

Bruises are a common sign of physical abuse

Other possible physical signs of abuse include:

- unexplained marks such as bites, outlines of weapons, nail marks, scratches and cuts, burns (particularly from cigarettes), scalds, certain fractures, internal damage, poisoning

- signs of head injury. These signs may include irritability, drowsiness, headache, vomiting or head enlargement. Medical attention is needed urgently. Head injury can result in brain damage, blindness, coma and death. Shaking a child or injuring the head can result in a subdural haematoma (bleeding into the brain)

- a torn frenulum in a young child (the frenulum is the web of skin joining the gum and the top lip). This usually results from something being forcibly pushed into the mouth, such as a spoon, bottle or dummy. It hardly ever occurs in ordinary accidents.

Blue spots (sometimes called Mongolian spots) are smooth, bluish grey to purple skin patches, often quite large. They are sometimes seen across the bottom of the spine or buttocks of infants or young children of Asian, Southern European and African descent. It is very important that Mongolian spots are not confused with bruises or seen as a sign of abuse. Children are born with them; they may disappear as the child gets older.

Behavioural indicators of physical abuse

Significant changes in a child's behaviour might show that a child is being abused. These may include:

- clinging, being withdrawn, aggressive behaviour, 'acting out' behaviour in role-play

- developing learning difficulties including a lack of concentration

- having an inability to enjoy life

- showing symptoms of stress, for example, regression including wetting, tantrums, strange behaviour, eating problems. Abused children often appear sad, preoccupied and listless.

Effects of physical abuse

Children's development is likely to be affected if they live in a family where violence, aggression and conflict take place. Children's reactions to abuse vary. Their reactions may often be observed in their behaviour. Physical abuse can affect all aspects of children's development. It may:

- lead to physical injuries, brain damage, disability and death

- be linked to aggressive behaviour, emotional and behavioural problems and educational difficulties

- cause long-term damage to a child's self-esteem and this may last into adult life.

Neglect

Neglect involves failing to meet the basic needs of a child over a period of time and not protecting their health, safety and well-being. It involves failing to meet children's need for adequate food, clothing, warmth, medical care, hygiene, sleep, rest, fresh air and exercise. It also includes failing to protect children, for example leaving young children alone and unsupervised.

Signs of neglect

- Constant hunger, a large appetite, large abdomen, too fat or too thin, failure to thrive, inadequate/dirty clothing which is inappropriate for the weather.
- Constant ill-health, untreated medical conditions, long-term nappy rash, repeated stomach upsets and diarrhoea.
- Uncared-for appearance, poor personal hygiene, dull matted hair, wrinkled skin, dirt in skin folds.
- Learning difficulties or poor social relationships, aggression or withdrawal.
- Constant tiredness or sleepiness.
- Frequent lateness or non-attendance at nursery or school.
- Repeated accidental injuries.

Effects of physical neglect

- Severe neglect affects health, physical growth and development. The term 'failure to thrive' is used to describe children who fail to grow normally. Growth charts (percentile charts) are used to record and assess such children. Neglect can result in death.
- Children may find social relationships difficult and their educational progress can be limited. Children who are neglected are more likely to be victims of other forms of abuse.

Emotional abuse

Emotional abuse can be extremely damaging. It can create an environment in which children's needs are not recognised or nurtured. Neglecting children's emotional needs damages their development. Some adults may be emotionally abusive to children. They harm children by using constant threats, verbal attacks, taunting or shouting at them and rejecting the child. Domestic violence, adult mental health problems and parental drug/substance misuse may exist in some families where children are exposed to this form of abuse.

Signs of emotional abuse

As with physical abuse, emotionally abused children will usually show signs in their behaviour. They may turn their reactions outwards and become aggressive, destructive and uncooperative with others. Or they may withdraw and become quiet and unhappy. They may show similar behavioural signs to the physically abused child.

The effects of emotional abuse

There is increasing evidence of long-term negative effects on children's development where they have been subjected to continual emotional abuse. Emotional abuse affects children's developing mental health, behaviour and self-esteem and can be especially damaging to very young children.

Sexual abuse

K2S31

Sexual abuse is the inappropriate involvement of dependent, developmentally immature children in sexual activities. Sexual abuse covers a range of abusive behaviour not necessarily involving direct physical contact. It can include allowing children to witness sexual activity or watch pornographic videos. It includes exposure and self-masturbation by the abuser, through to actual body contact such as touching or penetration.

Child sexual abuse is found in all cultures and socio-economic groups. It happens to children in all kinds of families and communities. Boys and girls, including babies, are victims of sexual abuse. Both men and women sexually abuse children. It is becoming clear that the majority of children who are sexually abused know the abuser. This may be a member of the child's family, a family friend or a person the child knows in a position of trust.

Signs of sexual abuse

Early recognition of the signs (indicators) of sexual abuse is essential. Otherwise it can continue undiscovered for many years and cause great harm. There may be no obvious physical indicators of sexual abuse, so particular attention should be paid to behavioural indicators:

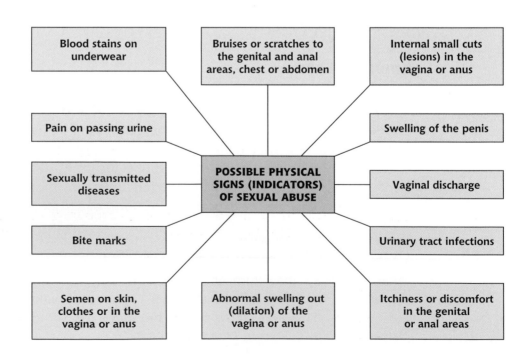

Blood stains on underwear

Bruises or scratches to the genital and anal areas, chest or abdomen

Internal small cuts (lesions) in the vagina or anus

Pain on passing urine

Swelling of the penis

Sexually transmitted diseases

POSSIBLE PHYSICAL SIGNS (INDICATORS) OF SEXUAL ABUSE

Vaginal discharge

Bite marks

Urinary tract infections

Semen on skin, clothes or in the vagina or anus

Abnormal swelling out (dilation) of the vagina or anus

Itchiness or discomfort in the genital or anal areas

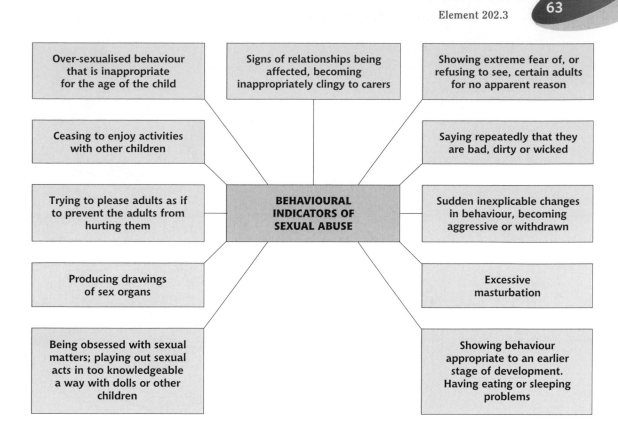

Over-sexualised behaviour that is inappropriate for the age of the child	Signs of relationships being affected, becoming inappropriately clingy to carers	Showing extreme fear of, or refusing to see, certain adults for no apparent reason
Ceasing to enjoy activities with other children		Saying repeatedly that they are bad, dirty or wicked
Trying to please adults as if to prevent the adults from hurting them	BEHAVIOURAL INDICATORS OF SEXUAL ABUSE	Sudden inexplicable changes in behaviour, becoming aggressive or withdrawn
Producing drawings of sex organs		Excessive masturbation
Being obsessed with sexual matters; playing out sexual acts in too knowledgeable a way with dolls or other children		Showing behaviour appropriate to an earlier stage of development. Having eating or sleeping problems

The effects of sexual abuse

Sexual abuse can lead to disturbed behaviour, inappropriate sexualised behaviour, sadness, depression and loss of self-esteem. The effects are likely to be more severe if the child is older and the experience of abuse is prolonged. The effects can last into adult life. However, only a minority of children who are sexually abused go on to become abusers themselves.

A child's ability to cope with this experience can be helped by the support of a worker who believes the child, helps the child to understand and offers help and protection.

Observing the signs of abuse in everyday situations

Practitioners are in a good position to observe the signs and symptoms of injuries to children. These may also include changes in their behaviour.

Babies and infants

Careful observation of babies can take place during routines such as nappy changing, when changing or removing clothing, during washing and hygiene routines, while feeding and playing with babies.

Toddlers and young children

Any hygiene, feeding or changing routines can be used to observe young children carefully. Play provides a good opportunity to observe and assess behaviour. Any

Practitioners are in a good position to observe the signs and symptoms of injuries to children, including significant changes in their behaviour

play that requires children to push up sleeves or remove clothing also enables carers to observe signs of injury unobtrusively. Good opportunities to observe the condition of older children occur when they are changing for physical exercise and swimming.

Protecting children from abuse

K2S33

The Children Acts (1989, 2004) are the laws that aim to protect children from harm in any setting. This legislation is based on the principle that all children have a right to protection. There are written procedures to protect children in all settings. Parents have a right to be consulted in most circumstances. Any disclosure by a child must be dealt with sensitively and professionally. There are ways to help children to protect themselves from abuse.

The policies and procedures of work settings

Every setting where children are cared for has policies and procedures that aim to protect children from abuse. In England these are based on the procedures written locally by each Area Child Protection Committee (ACPC). Procedures are also in place in Wales, Scotland and Northern Ireland. It is very important that all workers know about their local procedures and follow them. Policies and procedures ensure that all workers know what their duties are, provide clear instructions about what to do and make clear the steps that must be taken to protect children.

The policies practitioners should follow *may* include:

- routine and specific observation and assessment of children's behaviour and development. Settings will have ways of doing this and of recording observations. Policies may include keeping accurate, relevant records and signing and dating them

- using the *Framework for the Assessment of Children in Need and their Families* (published by the Department of Health in England in April 2000). It provides a way of collecting and analysing information

- discussing possible signs of abuse with a senior colleague, who may be the specifically named person in the organisation.

The procedures practitioners should follow *will* include:

- reporting concerns to a specific person in the setting. The specific person will decide whether there are grounds to refer suspicions to the statutory body, i.e. the Social Services Department (in England, the police and the NSPCC can also receive referrals)

- reporting the concerns themselves directly to the social services department if they work alone

- recording specific observations of what has been observed, signing and dating them.

After an investigation social workers will decide whether there are grounds to call a Case Conference with a view to placing the child on the Child Protection Register, or even going to court to remove a child from home. A practitioner may be asked to go to a Case Conference and present a report based on their observations.

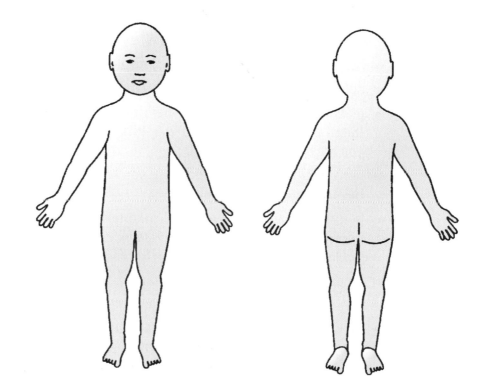

Physical indicators may be recorded on a chart like this

Involving parents

One of the principles of the Children Act is that people who work with children must also work in partnership with their parents. It is important to involve parents in the early stages of any enquiry into possible child abuse (with the exception of suspected sexual abuse). This is because:

- parents may be able to provide a clear and satisfactory explanation
- the way parents respond may give a clear sign that all is not well. This is particularly so if parents give an unsatisfactory explanation, are vague or inconsistent, delay seeking medical attention, or if they lack concern or blame others or the child for an injury
- positive partnership with parents is the best way to create good, constructive relationships with families
- if abuse is occurring, the best outcome is to work positively with a family to prevent further abuse and where possible to keep the child within the family
- enquiries that are not carried out sensitively and respectfully, involving parents, can bring unnecessary distress both to children and their parents.

Dealing with disclosure

The role of the practitioner in responding to disclosure

K2S33

In any day-care setting, it is possible that children will tell or demonstrate to a worker that they are being abused. In other words they will disclose. This could happen in an open way or through hinted words or behaviour. Adults need to respond sensitively and appropriately. They should:

- listen and be prepared to spend time and not hurry the child
- not ask leading questions, putting words into children's mouths
- reassure them truthfully. Tell them they are not odd or unique; you believe them; you are glad they told you; it is not their fault; they were brave to tell; you are sorry it happened
- find out what they are afraid of, so you know how best to help. They may have been threatened about telling
- be prepared to record what the child tells you as soon as possible (within 24 hours). Do this in detail, accurately and legibly. Include the date of the disclosure
- let the child know why you are going to tell someone else
- consult a senior person or an appropriate professional who will be able to help
- seek out support for your personal emotional reactions and needs from an appropriate colleague or professional
- not attempt to deal with the issue alone.

Helping children to protect themselves

K2S34

Practitioners can help children to protect themselves by ensuring that children:

- understand they have a right to be safe and learn how to do this
- develop an awareness of their own bodies, and understand that their bodies are their own and that no one should touch them inappropriately
- learn to recognise, trust and accept their own feelings
- gain self-confidence and assertive skills to help them, for example, to say 'no'
- recognise that they should talk and share their worries. That they have a right to be listened to and believed
- learn that kisses, hugs and touches should never be kept secret, even if they feel good.

These principles and the skills that children need to put them into practice can be taught through the existing curriculum in schools. They can also be incorporated into themes and topics in pre-school settings. If taught well, they will promote children's confidence, assertiveness and communication skills, as well as contributing to their protection. They are relevant to all children, including disabled children and children with learning difficulties who may be especially vulnerable.

Listen and be prepared to spend time and not hurry the child

Practical Example

Joseph

A 2-year-old child, Joseph, often comes to the day nursery with fresh bruises on his arms and upper body. His mother explains that these are the result of minor accidents while playing.

K2S31

➤ *What might lead you to suspect that the child was being injured non-accidentally?*

➤ *Describe the procedures you would follow in your setting. Describe what would you record.*

Element 202.3 — Are you ready for assessment?

Support the safeguarding of children from abuse

Direct observation may be difficult for some of this element. To show that you can support the safeguarding of children from abuse you will need to present other types of evidence. You should discuss this with your assessor.

Element 202.4 — *Encourage children's positive behaviour*

⟩ 'Normal' behaviour (age appropriate behaviour)

K2D48
K2D49
K2D50
K2D51

The theory of what is 'normal' behaviour at a certain age is useful when observing and assessing children's behaviour. Knowing what to expect also helps us to manage children's behaviour. Parents and carers sometimes show a lack of awareness of what is normal at a particular stage of the development (see Unit CCLD 203). As a result they may have unrealistic expectations of their children, respond negatively to their behaviour and then punish them. If we know that temper tantrums are normal in a 2-year-old child, that curiosity and the drive to explore are predictable in a very young child, this will help us to respond firmly yet positively to this behaviour.

Normal behaviour is the behaviour to be expected at a specific age (age appropriate behaviour). Different children achieve maturity in their behaviour at different ages. The age at which children develop specific behavioural patterns is only approximate and depends on:

- the characteristics of the individual child
- the child's family, social and cultural environment

- the expectations placed on the child within this environment
- whether the child has any individual special needs – for example, a physical or learning impairment.

Goals and boundaries

K2D35
K2D49
K2D50
K2D51

Most children will develop 'normal' and acceptable patterns of behaviour if adults:

- are consistent, loving and fair in their expectations
- are good role models
- set a clear framework for behaviour.

A framework is made up of a set of goals and boundaries:

- *Goals* are the behaviour that adults want to encourage. These goals should cover all aspects of behaviour within the setting, including social, physical and verbal. They cover how children and adults should behave towards one another, including sharing, taking turns, being courteous and helping others when they are distressed. Expectations of children's behaviour must be realistic. They must be achievable in relation to the children's age and stage of development. Everyone must be able to understand them.
- *Boundaries* are the limits of what is considered acceptable behaviour. Children need to know that if they cross the boundary of acceptable behaviour there will be sanctions. Boundaries are usually set to exclude physical aggression, verbal abuse, and throwing or destroying equipment.

Values and norms

A framework for children's behaviour should be based on a set of values and norms that can be understood by all.

The behaviour children learn at home is based on the values and norms of the social and cultural group to which they belong.

- *Values* are the things that are believed to be important and worthwhile, for example that everyone is worthy of care and attention.
- *Norms* are rules or customs of actual behaviour that are based on values and beliefs. A norm is that children should listen if their teacher is talking to them – the norm being based on a belief in the value of learning.

Many social and cultural groups share similar values and beliefs about what is acceptable or unacceptable behaviour, for example the belief that physical violence is wrong and that respect for other people is important.

Sometimes groups of people have differing values or beliefs, together with different rules and customs. For example, groups have different rules and customs about how to address and relate to other people; what is appropriate dress; how food should be eaten, etc. These differences may mean that parents and schools have different expectations of children's behaviour. However, such differences need not be negative and many can easily be accommodated positively within a childcare setting.

If they conflict with the values and norms of the setting, workers and parents must develop a clear understanding of what is acceptable within the childcare establishment. For example, there could be different beliefs about the value of punishment and how it should be carried out.

Practitioners also have their own personal set of values about acceptable or unacceptable behaviour. These are not necessarily the values that are appropriate to a childcare setting. It is essential that workers develop a professional approach when working with children and adopt the values of the setting.

Accepting the child

It is not useful to describe a child as 'naughty' or 'bad'. This can have a negative effect on a child's self-esteem and feelings of worth. It can lead to the child feeling rejected and unwanted. Criticism should focus on the behaviour, not the child. Behaviour is most usefully described as 'acceptable' or 'unacceptable'.

K2D35
K2D37
K2D49
K2D50
K2D51

Managing children's behaviour

Behaviour modification is a useful tool for practitioners to use when managing children's behaviour. It involves identifying positive aspects of behaviour and encouraging them through praise and recognition. Unwanted behaviour can be discouraged by ignoring it or through the use of sanctions. Management of persistent problem behaviour requires a team approach to adopting appropriate policies and responses.

What is behaviour modification?

Behaviour modification is the name given to techniques used to influence children's behaviour. It works by:

- promoting and rewarding positive aspects of children's behaviour
- managing and discouraging negative aspects of children's behaviour.

It is a useful tool for practitioners to use when managing children's behaviour.

Behaviour modification involves the following techniques.

Identifying behaviour

The first aim of behaviour modification is to identify different types of behaviour. These are both the behaviour that the adult wishes to encourage, for example:

- playing co-operatively and sharing toys
- being considerate and helpful
- working well and completing a task

and the behaviour that the adult wishes to discourage, for example:

- aggressive, abusive or challenging behaviour
- behaviour that is disruptive, destructive or damaging to people or property
- self-damaging or personally unconstructive behaviour.

Rewarding positive behaviour

The second aim is to reward positive behaviour by encouraging and promoting it. This may involve giving a child:

- positive attention through words of praise or encouragement or through non-verbal attention such as smiles or nods
- practical treats such as sweets, stickers and badges or, for older children, being allowed to go out or stay up later
- the opportunity to share rewards. This might be done by, for example, recording each child's positive behaviour on a chart, so that the 'points' gradually accumulate and the whole group gets a reward when the chart is full.

Discouraging negative behaviour

The third aim is to discourage negative behaviour. This may involve:

- ignoring the behaviour
- directing attention to another child who is behaving acceptably
- removing the child to a different, unrewarding situation
- showing disapproval verbally or non-verbally
- applying the sanctions agreed by the establishment, for example loss of privileges
- using physical restraint if it is in the interests of the safety of the child or others.

Note that physical punishment is illegal and should never be used in a childcare setting.

Behaviour modification techniques can be very effective, but they need to be used consistently by all the adults concerned with the child. This can be difficult to achieve and requires both a team approach and partnership between practitioners and parents. Adults need to have a clear idea of the behaviour they are trying to modify and then observe, record and assess changes in behaviour in order to monitor the effectiveness of their approach.

Managing problem behaviour

Management of persistent problem behaviour presents a challenge to practitioners. A clear policy and a team approach are needed.

K2D36
K2D37
K2D49
K2D50
K2D51

Behaviour that is directly challenging should be responded to calmly, using the techniques described above. Challenging behaviour is usually attention-seeking and may be self-destructive. It is often the result of a child only being given attention when they misbehave. An effective method of changing such behaviour is consistently to give the child lots of positive attention and to praise them when they behave acceptably. Attention-seeking behaviour should then be ignored, providing it is not too destructive or placing anyone in danger. The child then learns to associate attention with acceptable rather than unacceptable behaviour. It is important to share concerns with colleagues and discuss the management of children's behaviour with them. The benefit of a team approach is that it provides support for colleagues and consistency in dealing with a particular child or group.

Why does difficult and negative behaviour happen?

Most children want the approval of adults and others. They therefore wish to behave in an appropriate way. Most children develop acceptable patterns of behaviour if adults are loving, fair and consistent, set clear boundaries and are positive role models.

Behaviour is not 'naughty or bad' just because it does not conform to adult standards of behaviour. Children need to learn which behaviour is acceptable and which is unacceptable.

There is often a reason why behaviour occurs. This reason may be hidden, unconscious or in the past. The reasons are not always straightforward or obvious. Some behaviour is well established and it is difficult to understand why it occurs. The table below gives some of the possible reasons for a behaviour occurring.

Why does difficult and negative behaviour happen?

Cause	Explanation
Feelings	• Behaviour can often be caused by how a child is feeling. We must accept that feelings are real. It is the behaviour that results from the feeling that is either acceptable or not acceptable. You must never reject a child's feelings, only their behaviour. • Similar feelings in children can lead to very different behaviour. For example, feelings of anger may result in one child being physically or verbally aggressive but another child being withdrawn.
Curiosity	A child learns by being active and curious about their environment. There may be a clash between the child's curiosity and the adult's wish for the child to be safe.
Imitation	Children often imitate what they see others doing. Sometimes what they imitate may be acceptable behaviour for an adult or an older child, but not for a young child.
Developing independence	Children need ways of showing their growing independence. This may result in them trying to influence others in unacceptable ways.
Attention-seeking	Human beings need and want attention from other people. Children's behaviour can be a way of seeking attention. This means attracting the attention of other people. Some children learn that they only get attention if they misbehave.
Anger or frustration	A lack of experience of the world sometimes means that children have unrealistic expectations of what is and what is not possible. This may result in anger or frustration. Children may show frustration in their behaviour. For example, a child may have a tantrum when told that mummy cannot stop it raining so they can go to the park.
Anxiety or fear	Children have lack of experience and understanding of the world. They may become anxious and/or fearful when changes in familiar patterns and routines

occur. This can affect their behaviour. Examples might be a change in nursery, starting school, changes in friendships, lack of sleep. The feelings are often short term and their behaviour usually settles down.

Emotional needs	Children have many emotional and social needs, for example, the need for love and affection, belonging, consistency, independence, achievement, social approval and to develop self-esteem. When these needs are not met, a child may show unwanted behaviour as they struggle to get what they need.
Short-term stress	There are likely to be times in all children's lives where they experience short-term stress caused by, for example, moving house, a new baby in the family or a short period of hospitalisation. If these situations are handled sensitively any behavioural difficulties are not likely to be long term.
Long-term stress	When a child's emotional needs are not met over a long period of time, their behaviour can be badly affected. For example, during long-term separation or if the child is abused. Their distress is likely to be shown in their behaviour. This may be anything from extreme withdrawal to violent behaviour.

Managing behaviour effectively

Tom, aged 3, was normally a quiet and gentle child. However, he often became upset and difficult when activity time ended and the children came together for a story. He wouldn't put his toys away and shouted at the staff that he didn't want to have a story. This was clearly upsetting to Tom and disruptive to the group.

K2D36
K2D37

The staff decided to observe Tom over a period of a week to try to learn the pattern of events that led up to this behaviour. They noted many things:

➤ *Tom often became very involved in activities, especially construction activities.*

➤ *He produced quite complicated structures with the equipment.*

➤ *When the children were asked to clear up, he became worked up. He quickly tried to finish his construction. He became anxious that the other children were going to break it up.*

➤ *This behaviour only occurred when he was partway through an activity at story time.*

The staff agreed the following behaviour management plan:

➤ *Tom was told, 10 minutes before story time, that the session was ending soon. This was to give him time to complete what he was doing.*

➤ *Completed models were kept until the following day and not taken to pieces straightaway.*

➤ *If Tom didn't finish what he was doing, his partly finished model would be saved until the following day. Then he could choose either to finish it or to break it up himself.*

> *What were the events that led to Tom's behaviour?*
> *What unwanted behaviour did he show?*
> *How did this behaviour affect others?*
> *How did the staff find out what was causing his behaviour?*
> *How did they plan to manage Tom's behaviour?*

Reporting to parents

Persistent unwanted behaviour should be reported to parents promptly and accurately.

Physical punishment

Appropriate policies and responses should be discussed and agreed so that everyone is working to the same goals. The use of physical punishment is not allowed in childcare settings. Physical restraint to prevent injury or damage must be very carefully administered.

Significant incidents should be recorded accurately and objectively. This means only recording what actually took place, not the reactions or opinions of workers.

Element 202.4 Are you ready for assessment?

Encourage children's positive behaviour

You need to show that you can competently encourage children's positive behaviour. To do this you will need to be directly observed by your assessor and present other evidence. The amount and type of evidence you need to present will vary. You should plan this with your assessor.

Direct observation by your assessor

Observation is the required assessment method to be used to evidence some part of each element in this unit. Expert witnesses could supply additional evidence. Your assessor will observe you in real work activities and this should provide most of the evidence for the performance criteria for the elements in this unit.

Preparing to be observed

During your normal work with the children, you should show your assessor how you can encourage children's positive behaviour. You could do this by recognising and praising children's efforts and achievements. You can do this by looks, smiling or words. You may offer the child or young person some kind

▶

of reward for their positive behaviour. This will show that you are aware of the required goals and boundaries. Your own behaviour in dealing with any dispute or unacceptable behaviour should be sensitive and fair. It should follow the procedures of the setting.

You may need to present different types of evidence in order to:

- cover criteria not observed by your assessor
- show that you have the required knowledge and understanding.

Reflecting on your practice

- How is positive behaviour encouraged in your setting? Think of at least two successful examples of when you have done this. **K2D37**
- What is the policy in your setting for dealing with bodily fluids and waste? **K2S24**
- What general signs of illness in children have you observed in your setting? What action was taken? **K2S29**
- What are the procedures for identifying and reporting any safety hazards in your setting? **K2S19**
- How does your setting ensure that the environment is safe for the children? **K2S19, K2S20**

UNIT 203

Support children's development

This unit requires you to know and understand children's development from ages 0–16 and to demonstrate competence with the children you are working with. It covers observing children, sharing observational findings, and contributing to the planning and implementation of activities to support children's development.

This unit comprises four elements:

◟ *CCLD 203.1 Contribute to supporting children's physical development and skills*

◟ *CCLD 203.2 Contribute to supporting children's emotional and social development*

◟ *CCLD 203.3 Contribute to supporting children's communication and intellectual development*

◟ *CCLD 203.4 Contribute to planning for children's development needs.*

The national standards for this unit include a list of key words and explanations that you need to understand. You should read this carefully as you plan the activities for your assessment. Your assessor can help you to make sure that you are interpreting the standards correctly.

◟ Introduction

This is a key unit in your qualification. In order to work successfully with children you need to understand how they develop in all areas. Observing the children that you work with, and making careful assessments of their development, will enable you to understand a child's achievements and needs, and to plan for them.

This chapter on supporting children's development covers:

- understanding the principles of children's development with charts that show developmental sequences for physical, emotional, social and behavioural development; and for communication and intellectual development

- supporting children's development using observation as a starting point for planning and the principles and practice of observation. The role of planning and assessment in supporting children's transitions is also considered.

This unit is fundamental to your whole qualification because it underpins your work with children and their families. It is impossible to separate the performance criteria and knowledge for this unit from the other units in this book. It is most likely that your assessor will help you to gather evidence for this unit as you work on other units in this qualification – for example, when you are observed communicating with children for unit 201, you will probably be gathering evidence for this unit as well. For this reason, you will only find one 'Are you ready for assessment?' section, at the end of this unit. Your assessor will help you to identify how your knowledge and performance can be demonstrated as you work through all the other units.

Children's development

The term 'development' is used to refer to the ways in which children grow and change. Development occurs in an order or sequence, for example babies sit before they walk. Developmental patterns are seen in all areas of growth and change. The charts in this section cover children's:

- physical development and skills
- emotional and social development (including behaviour)
- communication development
- intellectual development.

Practitioners **need to know about children's development**. It is essential that people who work with children know about development sequences so that:

- expectations about what a child can do are realistic
- appropriate experiences and activities can be provided for the child
- experiences and activities can be offered that lead a child onto the next stage of development
- children's individual progress can be monitored against the developmental sequence.

Influences that affect children's development

Children's development is influenced in two ways:

K2D44

- Development happens because children are born genetically programmed to be able to do certain things. This is called nature.
- Development happens because of children's experiences after they are born. This is called nurture.

Children's development happens because of a combination of nature and nurture. For example, they are born with the potential to learn to talk, but need to hear and use language for this skill to develop.

When considering children's development it is important to remember that:

- children develop within family systems. All families are different and will influence each child differently
- families exist within a social and cultural system. These social and cultural systems interact with and affect children's developing skills.

This diagram shows how each aspect of development consists of what the child is born with and their experiences after birth. The balance between nature and nurture is different for different aspects of development.

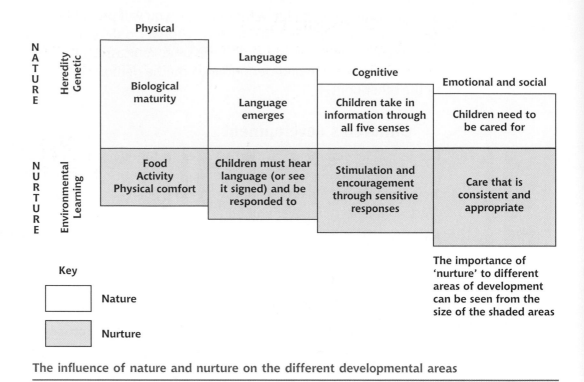

The influence of nature and nurture on the different developmental areas

The rate and sequence of development

KD2
KD45
KD46

The development of a child is an individual progression through the stages. All the areas of development are interconnected. Children are different and they have different life experiences. This means that they will develop at different rates. However, almost all children will progress in the same sequence. Ages at which children are likely to have reached a stage are often given in developmental charts. These are usually average ages and many children will reach the stage before that age and many children will reach the stage after that age. This is absolutely normal. In a group of children who are the same age there will always be a range of developmental stages. Whilst a child is within this range of development there is no cause for concern. The development of children who have special needs may be outside the general range of development depending upon what their needs are. You will find more information about the range of children's special educational needs in Unit CCLD 209.

Element 203.1
Contribute to supporting children's physical development and skills

K2D47

Physical development is described in two areas: gross motor skills and fine motor skills.

Gross motor skills

The ability of humans to use two legs and walk involves the whole body. These whole-body movements are described as gross motor skills.

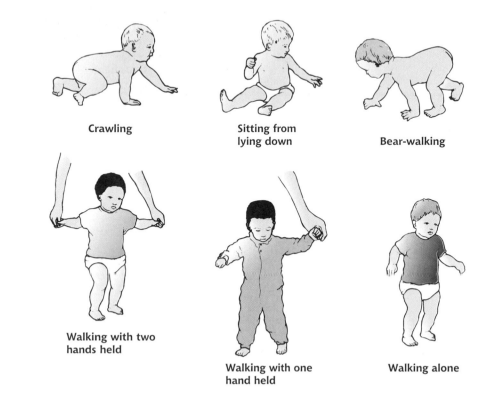

Crawling

Sitting from lying down

Bear-walking

Examples of gross motor skills involved in the development of walking

Walking with two hands held

Walking with one hand held

Walking alone

Fine motor skills

The use of the hands in co-ordination with the eyes allows human beings to perform very delicate procedures with their fingers. These manipulative aspects of physical development are called fine motor skills. They include aspects of vision and fine and delicate movements. The development of vision takes place alongside the development of fine motor skills.

The neonate

The newborn baby in the first month of life is often called the **neonate**, which means newly born.

The following tables show:

- the main stages of physical development from 1 month to 7 years (pages 81–84)
- age and physical developmental indicators from 8 to 16 years (pages 85–86).

Examples of fine motor skills in the development of manipulation

Holding and exploring objects

Palmar grasp using whole hand

More delicate palmar grasp involving the thumb

Inferior pincer grasp

Exploring with the index finger

Delicate/mature pincer grasp

Fine motor development – fists are clenched

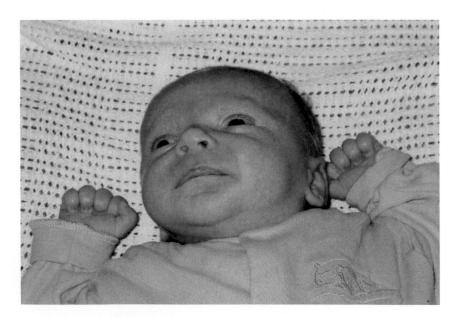

The main stages of physical development, 1 month to 7 years

Age range	Gross motor skills	Fine motor skills and vision
1 month	*Prone (lying face down)* The baby lies with its head to one side but can now lift its head to change position. The legs are bent, no longer tucked under the body. *Supine (lying on the back)* The head is on one side. The arm and leg on the side the head is facing will stretch out. *Sitting* The back is a complete curve when the baby is held in sitting position.	The baby gazes attentively at carer's face while being fed, spoken to or during any caring routines. The baby grasps a finger or other object placed in the hand. The hands are usually closed.
3 months	*Prone* The baby can now lift up the head and chest supported on the elbows, forearms and hands. *Supine* The baby usually lies with the head in a central position. There are smooth, continuous movements of the arms and legs. The baby waves the arms symmetrically and brings hands together over the body. *Sitting* There should be little or no head lag. When held in a sitting position the back should be straight, except for a curve in the base of the spine. *Standing* The baby will sag at the knees when held in a standing position. The placing and walking reflexes should have disappeared.	Finger-play – the baby has discovered its hands and moves them around in front of the face, watching the movements and the pattern they make in the light. The baby holds a rattle or similar object for a short time if placed in the hand. Frequently hits itself in the face before dropping it! The baby is now very alert and aware of what is going on around. The baby moves its head to look around and follows adult movements.

Age range	Gross motor skills	Fine motor skills and vision
6 months	*Prone* Lifts the head and chest well clear of the floor by supporting on outstretched arms. The hands are flat on the floor. The baby can roll over from front to back. *Supine* The baby will lift its head to look at its feet. The baby may lift its arms, requesting to be lifted and may roll over from back to front. *Sitting* If pulled to sit, the baby can now grab the adult's hands and pull itself into a sitting position; the head is now fully controlled with strong neck muscles. The baby can sit for long periods with support. The back is straight. *Standing* Held standing the baby will enjoy weight bearing and bouncing up and down.	Bright and alert, looking around constantly to absorb all the visual information on offer. Fascinated by small toys within reaching distance, grabbing them with the whole hand, using a **palmar grasp.** Transfers toys from hand to hand.
9 months	*Prone* The baby may be able to support its body on knees and outstretched arms. May rock backwards and forwards and try to crawl. *Supine* The baby rolls from back to front and may crawl away. *Sitting* The baby is now a secure and stable sitter – may sit unsupported for 15 minutes or more. *Standing* The baby can pull itself to a standing position. When supported by an adult it will step forward on alternate feet. The baby supports its body in the standing position by holding on to a firm object and may begin to side-step around furniture.	Uses the inferior **pincer grasp** with index finger and thumb. Looks for fallen objects out of sight – is now beginning to realise that they have not disappeared for ever. Grasps objects, usually with one hand, inspects with the eyes and transfers to the other hand. May hold one object in each hand and bang them together. Uses the index finger to poke and point.

Age range	Gross motor skills	Fine motor skills and vision
12 months	*Sitting* Can sit alone indefinitely. Can get into sitting position from lying down. *Standing* Pulls itself to stand and walks around the furniture. Returns to sitting without falling. May stand alone for a short period.	Looks for objects hidden and out of sight. Uses a mature pincer grasp and releases objects. Throws toys deliberately and watches them fall. Likes to look at picture books and points at familiar objects. **Pincer grasp** using the thumb and first finger.
15 months	Walks alone, feet wide apart. Sits from standing. Crawls upstairs.	Points at pictures and familiar objects. Builds with two bricks. Enjoys books; turns several pages at once.
18 months	Walks confidently. Tries to kick a ball. Walks upstairs with hand held.	Uses delicate pincer grasp. Scribbles on paper. Builds a tower with three bricks.
2 years	Runs safely. Walks up and downstairs holding on. Rides a trike, pushing it along with the feet.	Holds a pencil and attempts to draw circles, lines and dots. Uses fine pincer grasp with both hands to do complicated tasks. Builds a tower of six bricks.
3 years	Can stand, walk and run on tiptoe. Walks upstairs one foot on each step. Rides a tricycle and uses the pedals.	Can thread large wooden beads onto a lace. Controls a pencil in the preferred hand. Builds a tower of nine bricks.

Age range	Gross motor skills	Fine motor skills and vision
4 years	Climbs play equipment. Walks up and downstairs, one foot on each step. Can stand, walk and run on tiptoe.	Builds a tower of 10 or more bricks. Grasps a pencil maturely. Beginning to do up buttons and fasten zips.
5 years	Can hop. Plays ball games well. Can walk along on the balancing beam.	Can draw a person with head, trunk, legs and eyes, nose and mouth. Can sew large stitches. Good control of pencils and paintbrushes.
6 years	Rides a two-wheeled bicycle. Kicks a football well. Makes running jumps.	Can catch a ball with one hand. Writing hold is similar to the adult.
7 years	Can climb and balance well on the apparatus. Hops easily on either foot, keeping well balanced.	Writes well. Can sew neatly with a large needle.

Physical developmental indicators, 8–16 years

Age	Developmental indicators
8–12 years	Initially, physical growth and changes to the body slow right down in this age band, compared with the speed of physical development up to the age of 5. Children will become more agile and adept. They will become more co-ordinated. Their muscles and bones will strengthen and many will enjoy becoming involved in particular sports – football, rugby, tennis, dance and swimming, for example. With regular coaching, the skills needed for them will become more refined. As their emotional and social skills continue to develop, children in this age band usually enjoy being part of a team and will participate in team games and sports with enthusiasm. It is important that children continue to stay active and fit. There will be more distractions from an active lifestyle as they become interested in games consoles and TV and DVDs/videos. Practitioners should aim to balance these interests with physical activity for all children. This may involve working with them to help them discover which sports or activity interests them most. Fine motor skills become far more refined, with handwriting becoming joined and fluent. Towards the end of this age band, puberty may begin. This marks the beginning of their transition from childhood to adulthood, a process which will affect their bodies and minds. Some children will enter puberty before the age of 11. although most will between the ages of 11 and 13 years. 
13–16 years	The teenager's body continues to change rapidly as he or she goes through puberty. Many will experience growth spurts, and physical activity continues to be important to maintain bone and muscle strength and physical fitness. With growth spurts may come an increased need to rest and it is therefore not unreasonable for young people to lie in when they have the opportunity. 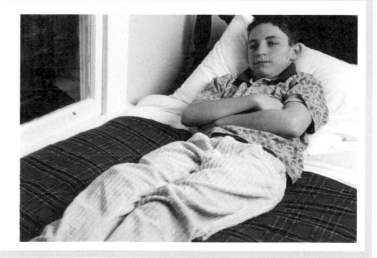

Age	Developmental indicators
	Curiosity about sexual matters will usually begin and accurate information and sources of advice and guidance should be readily available.
	Young people of this age may begin to rebel against authority, and this might show itself through refusal to take showers, clean teeth, etc. However, although they may not admit it, young people still feel more secure within structured routines.

Element 203.2

Contribute to supporting children's emotional and social development

Children's emotional and social development

Birth

K2D 47

- For the first month or so, a baby's behaviour is mainly controlled by inbuilt reflexes, such as rooting, sucking and swallowing. They startle to noise and turn to the light. They sleep most of the time and cry when hungry, in pain or unattended to.

- Infants begin to learn as soon as they are born, but at this stage they prefer to be left undisturbed. They cry to make their needs known and are peaceful when their needs are met.

- Newborn infants do not realise that people and things exist apart and separate from themselves. It is thought that carers are perceived only as 'relievers of their distress', whether this is hunger, pain or loneliness.

- At this stage babies are utterly dependent on others. They are usually content in close contact with carers, but are not aware of themselves as separate beings.

1 month

- Babies continue to sleep most of the time and cry for their needs to be met. They are observed to smile from birth; but when they are 4–8 weeks old they begin to smile and make noises in response to happenings outside themselves. They learn to smile at a voice and a face, especially if it moves, and will quieten in response to a human voice and smile.

- Babies begin to learn to tell the difference between themselves and other people and things. They do this through contact with their carers and by exploring using their five senses. They gradually come to understand who they are themselves (personal identity) and what they think and feel about themselves – self-image and self-concept.

- They are still totally dependent. They will grasp a finger if the hand is opened and the palm is touched.

2 months

- From 2 months, as babies begin to mature physically and to explore the environment, they gradually smile and become more responsive to others. The baby is capable of having 'conversations' with the carer. These are a mixture of movements and noises when one person is quiet while the other speaks. Infants start to recognise their carer's face, hands and voice. They may stop crying when they are picked up and sleep less during the day and more during the night.

- They are beginning to be aware of their separateness from their carer. Babies learn that touching a toy or a person's hand feels different to touching their own hand. These experiences help them to tell the difference between themselves and others.

- During this stage, early recognition of a child's sensory impairment, such as vision or hearing, enables carers to adapt their approach to meet the child's needs. They are still totally dependent.

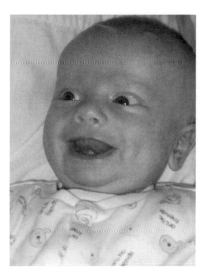

At 2 months, babies will gradually smile

3 months

- Babies take a lot of interest in their environment at this stage. They are maturing rapidly physically. Babies turn their heads when they hear sounds and to see what people are doing. Carers must take the time to talk, play and be with them. Babies need contact with other people. By 3 months, babies have learned to respond with pleasure to friendly handling. Infants react to the world as if they alone make things exist or disappear. If something or someone disappears from their view, babies will keep looking at the place where they were before they disappeared. If they do not return, the baby will probably forget about them. If it is a person who is important to them, they will probably cry.

- They are able to show an increasingly wide range of feelings, including pleasure, fear, excitement, contentment and unhappiness, and have some awareness of the feelings and emotions of others.

- Once children can tell they are separate, they will start to build a picture or image of themselves. Gradually they discover what kind of person they are and what they can do. This picture of themselves can be either:
  - a positive self-image – the child feels they are valuable and worthwhile, or
  - a negative self-image – the child feels worthless and useless.
- Children's ideas of their own value are based on the responses of those around them. They need to experience that people approve of and accept them in order to develop feelings of self-approval and self-acceptance.
- They are rapidly beginning to learn a range of social skills from the people around them. They have not yet developed the physical skills that lead to personal independence.

6 months

- Development during the first six months is very rapid. Infants are awake for much longer periods by 6 months of age. If they have been stimulated during this period, they will show great interest in their environment and respond happily to positive attention. Babies of 6 months laugh, show excitement and delight, and will also show likes and dislikes strongly. Around this age infants:
  - become more aware of themselves in relation to other people and things
  - show a marked preference for their main carer(s)
  - reach out for familiar people and show a desire to be picked up and held
  - begin to be more reserved with, or afraid of, strangers
  - smile at their own image in a mirror, or may like to play peek-a-boo
  - show eagerness, anger and pleasure by body movements, facial expression and vocally
  - play alone with contentment; stop crying when communicated with.
- This period may see the beginning of stranger anxiety and separation distress. This implies that babies recognise they are separate and feel unsafe without the support of their main carers. If carers meet babies' needs at this stage, they will help to reinforce the babies' view of themselves as separate, but worthwhile.

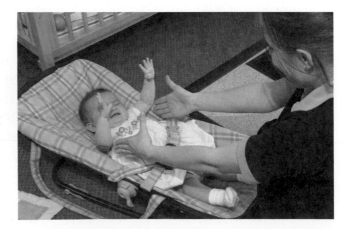

At 6 months, a baby will reach out to be picked up

- During this stage, children are learning that people and things have a permanent existence (object permanence). Even if they cannot see them, people and things still exist. This awareness is reinforced through games such as peek-a-boo: the infants are discovering that people and things that disappear temporarily are still there, but have to be looked for.
- They may have the following skills:
  - look at their hands and feet with interest
  - use their hands to hold things
  - drink from a cup that is held for them.

9 months

- Given the right opportunities, they will have formed strong attachments with their main carer(s). Infants take great pleasure in playing with their carers and learn a great deal from this. They can be a delight to be with.
- Around this age infants usually:
  - clearly identify familiar people and show a marked preference for them
  - show a fear of strangers and need to be reassured when in their company
  - often cling to the adult they know and hide their face in them
  - play peek-a-boo, copy hand clapping and pat a mirror image
  - still cry for attention to their needs, but also use their voice to attract people to them
  - show some signs of willingness to wait for attention
  - show pleasure and interest at familiar words
  - understand 'no'
  - try to copy sounds
  - offer objects to others but do not release them.
- By this age, infants have become aware of themselves as separate from others, and have formed a clear image of other people who are significant to them.
- They will also usually have begun moving around independently, and put their hands around a cup or bottle when feeding.

1–2 years

- Between 1 and 2 years children become aware of themselves as individuals and begin to assert their will, sometimes in defiant and negative ways. At this stage children are very egocentric. Their defiant and resistant behaviour can be seen as an attempt to protect their individuality.

15 months

- By this age toddlers use their main carer as a safe base from which to explore the world and are very curious about their environment. They are anxious about being physically separated from carers, have an interest in strangers but can be fearful of them.

- They tend to show off but do not react well to being told off, show interest but jealousy in other children, are emotionally changeable and unstable, throw toys when angry and resist changes in routine.

- Around this age children have a sense of 'me' and 'mine', begin to express themselves defiantly, and to distinguish between 'you' and 'me', and can point to members of the family in answer to questions.

- They may hold a cup and drink without assistance, hold a spoon and bring it to the mouth, help with dressing and undressing, and swing from dependence to wanting to be independent.

At 15 months, toddlers will hold a spoon and bring it to the mouth, spilling some food in the process

18 months

- At this age children tend to follow their carers around, be sociable and imitate them by helping with small household tasks, respond by stopping doing something when the word 'no' is used, imitate and mimic others during their play, and engage in solitary or parallel play but like to do this near a familiar adult or sibling.

- They show some social emotions, for example, sympathy for someone who is hurt, but cannot cope with frustration, show intense curiosity, have intense mood swings, move from dependence to independence, eagerness to irritation, and co-operation to resistance.

- They try to establish themselves as members of the social group, begin to copy their values, are conscious of their family group.

- They are still very dependent on familiar carers and often return to a fear of strangers.

- They can use a cup and spoon well, and successfully get food into their mouth, take off some clothing and help with dressing themselves, and can make their carers aware of their toileting needs.

2–3 years

- Children are still emotionally and socially very dependent on familiar adult carers, although they are capable of self-directed behaviour. During this period, extremes of mood are common. Children can change between aggressive and withdrawn behaviour, awkwardness and helpfulness very rapidly.

2 years

- By this age children can be sensitive to the feelings of others, display emotions such as sympathy and are capable of being loving and responsive.
- They demand their carer's attention and want their needs to be met immediately, and may have tantrums if crossed or frustrated or if they have to share attention.
- They will ask for food but can sometimes respond to being asked to wait; they are possessive of their own toys and objects, have little idea of sharing, tend to play parallel to other children, and engage in role play, but are beginning to play interactive games. They tend to be easily distracted by an adult if they are frustrated or angry, join in when an adult sings or tells a simple story, and can point to parts of the body and other things when asked.
- At this age children do not always fully accept that their parent is a separate individual. They are sometimes self-contained and independent, other times very dependent. They will feed themselves without spilling, lift a cup up and put it down, put some clothes on with supervision, say when they need the toilet, become dry in the daytime.

2 years, 6 months

- Around this age children develop their sense of self-identity; they know their name, their position in the family and their gender, play with other children, learn that different toys may be intended for girls and boys, and engage in 'pretend' play.
- They want to have anything they see and do anything that occurs to them, throw tantrums when stopped, are not so easy to distract, and are often in conflict with their carers.
- They have an awareness of some dangers and know they should avoid them (like stairs and hot stoves); they have the ability to use a spoon and some other tools to eat with well, to pour from one container to another and to get themselves a drink, dress with supervision, unzip zips, unbuckle and buckle, and unbutton and button clothing.
- They are toilet-trained during the day, and can be dry at night, especially if lifted.

3 years

- Around this age children can feel secure when in a strange place away from their main carers, can wait for their needs to be met, are less rebellious and use language rather than physical outbursts to express themselves, still respond to distraction as a method of controlling their behaviour, but are ready to respond to reasoning and bargaining, are beginning to learn the appropriate behaviour for a range of different social settings.

- They adopt the attitudes and moods of adults, want the approval of loved adults, can show affection for younger siblings, can share things and take turns, enjoy make-believe play, use dolls and toys to act out their experiences, and may have imaginary fears and anxieties.

- They call themselves 'I' and have a set of feelings about themselves. They are still affected by the attitudes and behaviour of those around them. They see themselves as they think others see them.

- They may have the ability to use implements to eat with, toilet themselves during the day, may be dry at night, will wash their hands but may have difficulty drying them, and are learning to dress without supervision.

Having a step by the wash basin or child-height sinks will enable children to achieve independence

4 years

- By this age children can be very sociable and talkative to adults and children, enjoy 'silly' talk, and may have one particular friend. They can be confident and self-assured, but may be afraid of the dark and have other fears. They have taken the standards of behaviour of the adults to whom they are closest, and turn to adults for comfort when overtired, and ill or hurt.

- They play with groups of children, can take turns but not consistently, and are often very dramatic in their imaginative play. They are developing a strong sense of past and future, are able to cope with delay in having their needs met, and show some control over their emotions. They can be dogmatic and argumentative, and may blame others, swear and use bad language.

- Most children have now developed a stable self-concept (i.e. a view of themselves that remains constant and fixed). Children who see themselves as likeable at this stage will not change this view of themselves when, from time to time, other children say that they do not like them.

- They may be able to feed themselves well, dress and undress, but may have difficulty with back buttons, ties and laces. They can wash and dry hands and face and clean teeth.

Children will gradually become able to dress themselves

5 years

- Children usually enjoy brief separations from home and carers and show good overall control of emotions, but may argue with parents when they request something. They still respond to discipline based on bargaining, although they are not so easily distracted from their own anger as when they were younger.
- They often show the stress of conflict by being overactive, but may regain their balance by having 'time-out'.
- They prefer games of rivalry to team games but enjoy co-operative group play, although they often need an adult to sort out conflicts. They may boast, show off and threaten.
- They are able to see a task through to the end, show a desire to do well, and can be purposeful and persistent.
- They develop a stable picture of themselves, are increasingly aware of differences between themselves and other people, including gender and status, and want the approval of adults They show sensitivity to the needs of others and a desire for acceptance by other children, and are developing internal social rules and an inner conscience.
- They may use a knife and fork well, dress and undress, lace shoes and tie ties, wash and dry face and hands, but may need supervision to complete other washing.

6 years

- At 6 years they have greater independence and maturity, have a wide range of appropriate emotional responses, and are able to behave appropriately in a variety of social situations.

At 5 years, children can dress and undress themselves

- They have all the basic skills needed for independence in eating, hygiene and toileting.
- However, they can be irritable and possessive about their own things, and have spells of being rebellious and aggressive.

7 years

- At 7 years children become very self-critical about their work. They may be miserable and sulky, and give up trying for short periods, or so enthusiastic for life that carers have to guard against them becoming overtired.
- They are more aware of their gender group and more influenced by the peer group.
- Much of the child's personality is established by the end of this period. By 7, children's experiences in their families and in their social and cultural environments will have led to the establishment of their personal identity, social and cultural identity, gender role, attitudes to life, and skills for independence.

8–12 years

- Peers become more and more important to children within this age band. It can be quite devastating when their friends turn their back on them. Children tend to play in same sex peer groups. It is most important to these children that they are accepted by their peers. They long to be part of the group or team and will strive for acceptance by mimicking their friends' attitudes, language, clothes and style. However, they can still be comfortable being alone.

13–16 years

- Young people continue to need time with their friends.
- They will have a strong sense of what is fair and right, although will continue to need good role models to help them make the right decisions.
- Strong bonds are formed with their peers and often, emotional attachments are made with girlfriends and boyfriends.

Children, aged 8–12, tend to play in same sex peer groups

Young people can form emotional attachments

⟡ Children's behaviour

1 year

- At 1 year, children do not have a clear perception of themselves as individuals; they have a close attachment to, and are sociable with, adults they know; are anxious if separated from them and shy with strangers.
- They are capable of varied and dramatic emotional responses; seek attention vocally and obey simple verbal instructions.

15 months

- Children are more aware of themselves as individuals, but not of other people as separate from them.
- They explore their environment indiscriminately (they are 'into everything'); are possessive of people they are attached to, and of objects they want ('It's mine!').

Pre-school-aged children are capable of loving, responsive behaviour

- They respond better to distraction than verbal reasoning or sharp discipline; may show off, throw toys in anger and have mood swings.

18 months

- Children respond to the word 'No', but usually need the command to be reinforced or repeated.
- They have become more aware of themselves as separate individuals; are very self-centred (egocentric) in their awareness and behaviour, having only recently discovered themselves as separate individuals.
- They are very curious about everything around them; are easily frustrated; can be defiant and resistant to adults and may react by shouting and throwing things.

2 years

- Children have a clear understanding of self but are still not fully aware of carers as separate individuals.
- They are able to be self-contained for periods of time; are often possessive of toys and have little idea of sharing; want their demands to be met quickly but can wait if asked.
- They may have tantrums if crossed or frustrated but can be distracted.
- They have a wide range of feelings and are capable of loving, responsive behaviour; are aware of and able to respond to the feelings of others.

3 years

- Children have developed a strong self-identity and a growing level of independence; show less anxiety about separation and strangers.
- They often resist efforts by carers to limit their behaviour; have mood swings and extremes of behaviour; are impulsive, and less easily distracted.
- They can wait for their needs to be met; are less rebellious and use language rather than physical outbursts to express themselves; are ready to respond to reasoning and bargaining.
- They are beginning to learn the appropriate behaviour for a range of different social settings; can understand when it is necessary to be quiet or noisy; adopt the attitudes and moods of adults; want the approval of loved adults.

4 years

- Children have more physical and emotional self-control; have more settled feelings and are more balanced in their expression of them; are more independent of their main carers; are happier, more friendly and helpful; can respond to reason and bargaining as well as to distraction; are less rebellious and can learn the appropriate behaviour for a range of settings.

- They are capable of playing with groups of children, tending to centre around an activity then dissolve and reform; can take turns but are not consistent about this; are often very dramatic in their play; engage in elaborate and prolonged imaginative play; are developing a strong sense of past and future.

- They can be dogmatic and argumentative; may blame others when they misbehave; may even behave badly in order to get a reaction; may swear and use bad language.

Being argumentative is part of pre-school-aged children's behaviour

4–5 years

- Children are constantly trying to make sense of the world around them and their experiences in it.
- They can be very sociable, talkative, confident, purposeful, persistent and self-assured.
- They can take turns and wait for their needs to be met, but may also be stubborn and sometimes aggressive and argumentative.
- They still turn to adults for comfort, especially when tired, ill or hurt.

5 years

- Children have achieved a greater level of independence and self-containment, generally show a well-developed level of control over their emotions.
- They show a desire to do well and to gain the approval of adults and are developing a sense of shame if their behaviour is unacceptable to the adult. They can also be argumentative, show off, boast and be overactive at times of conflict; argue with parents when they request something but still respond to discipline based on bargaining. They are not so easily distracted from their own anger as when they were younger, and may regain their balance by having 'time-out'.
- They prefer games of rivalry to team games; enjoy co-operative group play, but often need an adult to arbitrate. They boast, show off and threaten; show a desire to excel and can be purposeful and persistent.

6–7 years

- Children become increasingly mature and independent.
- They develop a wide range of appropriate emotional and behavioural responses to different situations, and are able to behave appropriately in a variety of social situations.
- They can be self-confident, friendly and co-operative, but may have spells of being irritable, rebellious and sulky.

8–16 years

- Behaviour within this age band can swing from growing maturity to childish behaviour quickly and easily. Hormonal changes can bring about moodiness and outbursts. However, children of this age are generally more able to describe how they feel and will have developed strategies to deal with their feelings.
- They will have a strong sense of fairness and will feel that it is important to stick to the rules.
- They may experience conflict between their parents' moral values and those of their peers. This can lead to difficulty as the influences of their peer groups become more important to them than the influences of their families.
- As they strive for independence, young people may appear to be breaking the rules. Adults need to let them make their own decisions as far as possible so that they learn to be responsible for themselves.

By the age of 6, children can be self-confident, friendly and co-operative

Adults need to let young people make their own decisions as far as possible

Puberty

Puberty is a stage in a person's life when they grow from being a child to being an adult. Changes occur physically, psychologically and emotionally, sometimes in a very short space of time. For this reason, it can be a very confusing time in a young person's life. He or she may feel too embarrassed to talk to anyone about what is happening to them. Sometimes their parents feel too embarrassed to explain what is happening.

Because puberty is a stage in a person's development, there is no fixed time when it will occur. Usually, a child will begin puberty between the ages of 11 and 14, but it can happen earlier or later.

Mood swings, rebellion and non-communication are common in young people going through puberty. An understanding attitude is necessary when helping young people through this time in their lives.

Young people will need:

- someone who will listen without judging them
- somewhere to get advice, guidance and information anonymously
- good role models in the adults around them, demonstrating healthy lifestyles and attitudes
- structure and routine to help them to feel secure when they feel uncertainty in other areas of their lives.

Contribute to supporting children's communication and intellectual development

Element 203.3

Children's communication development

The table below summarises a baby's communication development in the first year of life.

Communication development from birth to 1 year

Age	Communication developmental indicators
Birth 2–3 weeks	Involuntary cry. Signs of intentional communication: eye contact.
4 weeks onwards	Cries are becoming voluntary, indicating, for example, unhappiness, tiredness, loneliness May respond by moving their eyes or head towards the speaker, kicking or stopping crying.

6 weeks onwards	May smile when spoken to. Cooing and gurgling begin in response to parent's or carer's presence and voice, also to show contentment.
1–2 months	May move their eyes or head towards the direction of the sound.
3 months	Will raise their head when sounds attract their attention.
4–5 months	Playful sounds appear: cooing, gurgling, laughing, chuckling, squealing; in response to the human voice and to show contentment. Responds to familiar sounds by turning their head, kicking or stopping crying. Shouts to attract attention.
6 months	The beginning of babbling: regular, repeated sounds, e.g. *gegegegeg, mamamam, dadada*; baby plays around with these sounds. This is important for practising sound producing mechanisms necessary for later speech. Cooing laughing and gurgling become stronger. Begins to understand emotion in the parent's or carer's voice. Begins to enjoy music and rhymes, particularly if accompanied by action.
9 months	Babbling continues and the repertoire increases. Begins to recognise their own name. May understand simple, single words, e.g. *No, Bye-bye*. Continues to enjoy music and rhymes and will now attempt to join in with the actions, e.g. playing pat-a-cake.
9–12 months	Babbling begins to reflect the intonation of speech. May imitate simple words. This is usually an extension of babbling, e.g. *dada*. Pointing begins. This is often accompanied by a sound or the beginnings of a word. This demonstrates an increasing awareness that words are associated with people and objects.

1 year
- Vocabulary starts to develop. First spoken words appear (expressive language). Can respond to simple instructions.
- Children understand more than they can say (receptive language).

15 months
- Receptive language increases rapidly: active more limited.
- Points with single words.

18 months
- Expressive language increases – names of familiar things and people.
- Single words used, plus intonation to indicate meaning.
- Words and sentences repeated.

21 months
- Both receptive and expressive language increase – receptive still larger.
- Begins to name objects that are not there.
- Sentences begin as two-word phrases.

- Gestures important. Begin asking questions such as 'What?', 'Who?' and 'Where?'.

2 years

- Both receptive and expressive language continues to increase.
- Can generalise words. Use personal pronouns instead of names but not always correctly.
- Sentences become longer but still abbreviated.
- Questions asked frequently, particularly 'What?' and 'Why?'.

Reading with children is an excellent way to develop language skills

2 years, 6 months

- Vocabulary increases rapidly. Words used more specifically with less generalisation. Longer, more precise sentences, but still some abbreviation and incorrect word order.
- Uses language to protect their rights. Shows interest in listening to stories.

3 years

- Expressive language develops rapidly. New words picked up quickly.
- Sentences become longer and more adult-like. Children talk during play. Language is used for thinking and reporting on what is happening, to direct actions, express ideas and maintain friendships. Pronouns usually used correctly. Frequent questions are 'Why?', 'Who?' and 'What for?'. Rhymes are attractive.

3 years, 6 months

- A wide vocabulary develops. Word usage is usually correct. Language can be used to report on past experiences. Incorrect word endings sometimes used.

Talking with others is necessary for children to pick up language and to adjust and refine their language skills

4 years

- Extensive vocabulary. New words added regularly. Longer, more complex sentences, some joined with 'because'. Able to narrate long stories, including sequences of events. Running commentaries during play. Fully intelligible speech with minor incorrect uses. Questioning at its peak, including 'When?'.

- Can usually use language to share, take turns, collaborate, argue, predict, justify behaviour, create situations in imaginative play, reflect on their and others' feelings.

5 years

- A wide vocabulary and can use it appropriately. Sentences usually correctly structured, may be some incorrect grammar. Pronouns may still be childish. Language continues to be used and developed.

- Questions and discussions are used for enquiry and information; questions become more precise as cognitive skills develop. Children offer opinions in discussion.

5–7 years

- Children practise, adapt and refine their language skills. Language is used for a wide range of purposes in relation to themselves and other people, including

Children need opportunities to practise, adapt and refine their language skills

protecting themselves, directing others, reporting things, reasoning, predicting, projecting themselves into situations and imagining.

8–12 years

- Children will be able to communicate in a clear and fluent manner.
- Written communication skills become more refined, although children of this age will still be more able to express themselves verbally and non-verbally than in a written form.
- Vocabulary continues to increase, with children questioning, reasoning, chatting and telling jokes.
- The rules of grammar are learnt and are being increasingly used.

13–16 years

- Parents of teenagers of this age can often be heard saying, 'He never talks to me' or 'She stays on her own in her room when she is at home'. Young people usually prefer to communicate their inner most thoughts only to their closest friends. It is important, therefore that information and advice is easily accessible in an anonymous way for those young people who need it.
- The language young people use within this age band is often littered with phrases and sayings current to their times.

Children's intellectual development

Birth

- At birth, babies are able to explore using the senses.
- They are beginning to develop basic concepts such as hunger, cold, wet.

1 month

- Infants begin to recognise main carer and respond with movement, cooing.
- They will repeat pleasurable movements, thumb-sucking, wriggling.

3 months

- At 3 months, babies have become more interested in their surroundings.
- They begin to show an interest in playthings.
- They begin to understand cause and effect – if you move a rattle, it will make a sound.

6 months

- Infants expect things to behave in certain ways, for example the jack-in-the box will pop up but is unlikely to play a tune.

9 months

- At 9 months, babies recognise pictures of familiar things.
- They watch a toy being hidden and then look for it (object permanence established).

12–15 months

- Infants explore objects using trial and error methods, and begin to treat objects in appropriate ways, for example talk into a telephone and cuddle a doll.
- They begin to point and follow when others point and to seek objects in the most likely places.

18 months to 2 years

- By this age infants can refer to themselves by name.
- They begin to understand the consequences of their actions, for example, spilling their juice makes a surface wet.
- They may show the beginnings of empathy, for example, by comforting a crying baby.

3 years

- Children can match primary colours. They can sort objects into categories, but usually only by one criterion at a time, for example, all the cars, but not all the red cars.

- They ask a lot of questions.
- They can recite the number words to ten but are not yet able to count beyond two or three.
- They are beginning to understand the concept of time, talk about what has happened and look forward to what is going to happen.

Children can follow a point

Children can concentrate on an activity for a short time

- They can concentrate on an activity for a short period of time, leave it and then go back to it.
- They are beginning to understand the concept of quantity such as one, more, lots.

4 years

- At this age children can sort using more categories.
- They may solve simple problems, usually by trial and error, but are beginning to understand 'why'.
- They add to their knowledge by asking questions continually.
- Memory skills are developing, particularly around significant events like birthdays and holidays, and also of familiar songs and stories.
- They will confuse fantasy and reality, for example 'I had a tiger come to my house to tea too'.
- They can include representative detail in drawings, based on observation.
- They understand that writing carries meaning and use writing in play.

Children can include representative detail in pictures

5 years

- By this age they have a good sense of past, present and future.
- They are becoming literate – most will recognise their own name and write it.
- They will respond to books and are interested in reading.
- They demonstrate good observational skills in their drawings.
- They understand the one-to-one principle and can count reliably to ten.

Most children will recognise and write their own name

- Concentration is developing. They can concentrate without being distracted for about ten minutes at an appropriate task.

6 years

- Children are beginning to understand the mathematical concept of measuring – time, weight, length, capacity, volume.
- They are interested in why things happen and can form and test a simple idea, for example, that seeds need water to grow.
- They begin to use symbols in their drawing and painting – a radial sun and strip sky appear now.
- Many children will begin to read independently, but there is a wide variation in this.

7 years

- Children are able to conserve number reliably and will recognise that a number of objects remains constant, however they are presented. They may be able to conserve mass and capacity.
- They begin to deal with number abstractly and can perform calculations involving simple addition and subtraction mentally.
- They may be able to tell the time from a watch or clock.
- They are developing the ability to reason and an understanding of cause and effect.

Children are beginning to understand the mathematical concept of measuring

Children are able to conserve number reliably

8–12 years

- As children progress in school, they will develop a better understanding of the world around them. They will be better able to reason and think logically and will be able to communicate in a clear and fluent manner. They will continue to question and solve problems and will be able to retain many facts, particularly about subjects that interest them. They will enjoy telling jokes and understand past, present and future.

- Children of this age also have a stronger sense of morality – they understand right from wrong. Their families and main carers will continue to be the main influences and role models for them, although they will begin to be influenced by the behaviour and style of those they admire – music, film and TV stars having a great influence on this age band.

- From about the age of 10, children develop the ability for abstract thought, enabling them to question what goes on in the world around them as well as ideas and moral issues.

- Growing independence will mean that children will strive to make more decisions for themselves. This will include the friends they make, the food they eat and whether or not they wish to talk.

13–16 years

- Musical, artistic or academic talents may start to emerge at this stage.

- The pressure of the school curriculum can become overwhelming for some young people and those around them need to be alert to signs of anxiety. A balance of activity is necessary so that young people feel able to switch off from exam and school pressure.

Young people start to show musical talent

What you need to know to support children's development

Knowledge criteria	Age range	Information can be found in these units
K2D48.1–17	0–3 years	CCLD 201, 206 and 208
K2D49.1–15	3–7 years	CCLD 201, 202, 205, 206 and 210
K2D50.1–11	7–12 years	CCLD 201, 202, 205, 206, 209, 210
K2D51.1–12	12–16 years	CCLD 201, 202, 205, 206, 209, 210

Element 203.4 *Contribute to planning for children's developmental needs*

What we know about the children we care for should be the starting point for what we plan and provide for them. We need to consider their capabilities, their interests and their likes and dislikes. We find out about these by talking with their parents and through our observations and then plan appropriate activities and experiences. As we work alongside children supporting their play, we observe their responses and assess their skills and understanding. This enables us to plan for the next stage.

Observing and planning for children's experiences and activities is a continuous process. The diagram of the planning cycle shows the ongoing pattern of observing, planning and providing.

Practitioners observe children and act on these observations as part of their everyday practice, for example seeing that a child has fallen over and offering

The planning cycle

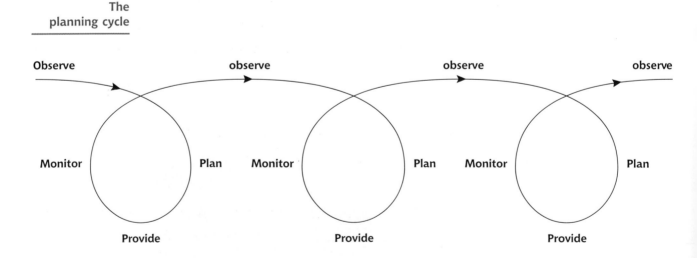

comfort, noticing that the glue pot is empty and refilling it. There is also a place for practitioners to observe a child or children, perhaps at a chosen activity and with a particular focus, and to record this. Considering this information will enable you to assess the children's achievements and plan for their needs. It is often helpful to discuss these observations and assessments with others who work with the child. With young children, this will be practitioners, parents and carers. Older children will benefit from being involved in the assessment of their own learning. This enables all involved to work towards the same goals.

The role of play in development

K2D 43

This unit requires you to understand the importance of play in children's development. Play is the most appropriate way to provide for all aspects of young children's learning and development. You will find a full explanation of how to promote children's development through play in Unit CCLD 206.

Observation

Why observe children?

K2D39

Observation of children is important in all childcare training as it enables us to examine and understand children's development. It is also a vital professional tool. As practitioners, we observe children so that we can:

- understand children as individuals and their likes and dislikes
- learn about the interests of a child or group of children
- meet the specific needs of individuals or groups of children
- assess what the child has achieved and then plan for the next stage
- evaluate the effectiveness of the provision made for children
- identify any particular difficulties a child may have
- note and record any concerns regarding child protection issues
- provide information about the child to parents and to others who have an involvement with the child
- collect information to assess a child's progress in relation to normal development
- measure the progress and achievements of children against national targets, for example the Foundation Stage profile.

What do you observe?

- *Individual children during their play and other activities* You will get the best results from observing children in familiar, naturally-occurring, everyday situations rather than those specially set up for the purpose of observation. All children will benefit from observation, not just those about whom you have a concern.

- *Children in groups,* to look at interaction and co-operation. Small groups will give you an opportunity to compare skills and responses.

- *A particular activity or a piece of equipment* to see how children respond to it.

- *Children's choice of activities during a session* Do they join in with all the activities? Are some avoided?

Recording observations

- Try not to let children know that you are observing a particular child or group of children as this might influence the way they behave.

- If you are not joining in the activity, place yourself where you can see the child but not within their personal space.

- Make notes while you are observing because you may not remember details later. A small notebook is better than a large folder.

- Write up your notes as soon as you can after your observation or you may forget what they mean.

- Always record the date you made your observation. This will be useful if you refer back to it later to assess a child's progress.

- Sometimes preparation is necessary. For example, if you are observing the spread of children around the classroom, then you should make a sketch of the layout beforehand. Checklists can be used for many purposes and are straightforward to complete particularly, if you are with a group at an activity.

- If you want to observe children using their language skills, you could use a small tape-recorder.

Position yourself unobtrusively when you observe

• You could use a video camera to record observations but filming will raise issues of confidentiality. Children will often play to the camera too.

Different techniques

Practitioners will use a variety of different techniques to record their observations of children. Some simple techniques are outlined below. Each method has advantages and disadvantages. With experience, you will be able to choose the method that is most suitable for the purpose of your observation.

Checklist

This is a useful way of gaining a lot of information and recording it in a straightforward way, usually by ticking against a chart. Published developmental scales and checklists can be used or you can devise your own, perhaps to assess a particular skill or stage of development. Checklists are also useful to compare different children. The main disadvantage of checklists is that they have a narrow focus and are not designed to enable you to record anything other than the skill or skills you have been looking for. The checklist below enables you to record and then compare the dressing skills of four 3-year-olds.

Narrative

This is a detailed account of everything that you see a child doing. It helps if you have a clear focus for your observation so that you can choose an appropriate activity to observe. For example, if you want to find out about how well a child gets

A checklist observation

Aim: To observe children putting on their coats
Purpose: To see if they can manage unaided

Task	Child A	Child B	Child C	Child D
Find own coat?	√	√	√	√
Put it on the right way?	√	√	√	√ (turned it right way round)
Put it on unaided?	√	√	√	√
Zip it up?	X (needed help)	n/a	n/a	√
Fasten buttons?	n/a	√	√	n/a
Put on hat?	√	√	n/a	√
Put on gloves?	X	√	n/a	√ (but struggled with fingers)
KEY: √ Can do it X Cannot do it n/a Not applicable				

on with others, you would need to observe him or her in an activity with a group of children. Observing the child, say, alone at the sticking table would not give you a picture of his or her social skills. With this method, you should observe for a short time, about 5 minutes or so. It can be hard to observe so closely and write down everything that you see for much longer.

Here is an example of a narrative observation of a 6-year-old at a computer activity, looking at her fine motor skills:

> *K. sat down using her arms to hold the chair. She then placed her right hand tightly on the mouse and put her finger on the left button. She gripped the mouse with her fingers and palm but as she moved it around she held her middle finger up. She clicked on the paintbrush and picked a colour but her hand was wobbling. She clicked on a file and dragged the arrow over using the mouse. It took her quite a bit of time to do this. She then started to draw some flowers using the paint brush. She filled in the sky by clicking on the paint tin at the side of the screen. She drew a sun and some grass, using different colours for each, by very slowly moving the mouse and keeping her finger pressed down all the time.*

Time sampling

This method involves observing at regular intervals, say, every 15 minutes and noting down what the child is doing. It can be used for a number of purposes. Noting the range of activities chosen by a child would show whether a child was taking part in everything on offer. Recording a child's interactions with others would give a picture of his or her social skills and friendship groups. A disadvantage of this method is that you have to be disciplined, recording only what happens during your watching slot and ignoring anything else.

The example below of a time sample observation provides a picture of E's ability to concentrate throughout a session.

Snapshot

This is a useful method for looking at the provision that you make for children. You can use it to show which activities are popular, where staff are located and demonstrate how space is used. The example below shows how the children were spread around the room during a session and shows where the adults were based to support activities.

Jottings, notes

In many settings, practitioners make quick observations of children, perhaps on post-it notes, on sticky labels or in notebooks. Often this is linked to key person groups but other practitioners will make and contribute their observations too. These notes can be very helpful in making assessments of children's learning and development and useful in helping the team to discuss and respond to children's interests and needs when planning for the group. Making these concise, evaluative observations whilst working alongside the children is a skill that requires practice, confidence and a secure knowledge of child development.

AIM – to observe E throughout the session, for three minutes every 15 minutes.

PURPOSE – to identify any factors affecting his performance and to assess any need for support.

TIME/SETTING	OTHERS PRESENT	ACTIONS & REACTIONS	LANGUAGE
9.00 Classroom.	Whole class for register and assembly.	Sitting attentively. Hands up to face, starts to look around.	Answers "yes" to name. Body language, leaning across desk.
9.15 Classroom.	Whole class spelling test.	Gets ready with spelling book and pencil.	Waits quietly as teacher reads out spellings group by group.
9.30 Classroom.	Whole class.	E wanders round tables with spelling sheet. Should be in line to take new spellings to cloakroom.	Teacher asks E if he knows what he is supposed to be doing. He smiles at her, and says "yes". Teacher asks E to join the line of children.
9.45 Library, giving me instructions to work Roamer.	J and C.	E very interested, gave me precise instructions of how to use the Roamer.	E said, "To work the Roamer you switch on the button on the side, press CM, press one of the arrows, forward press a number and GO."
10.00 Craft table in area between library and classroom.	J and T.	Cutting paper and card for owl nest.	E said, "You give the paper a twist, on the floor of the nest is where the babies play", pointing, "that's their rattle".
10.15 Craft Area	J, P and T.	Standing to table making owls habitat. Stopped working to look at J and P making their nest. E was supposed to be working with T.	Staring at J and P working. Teacher walks through and asks E if he is helping T with their model. E nods his head.
10.30 Classroom milk time	Whole class and a teacher from another class.	Sits drinking juice from flask.	Does not enter any conversation with peers; concentrates on drinking.
10.45 Playtime	In line with whole class, standing between S and T.	Standing between S and T. Rocking backwards and forwards, knocking into them.	E smiles, nods head.

A time sampling observation

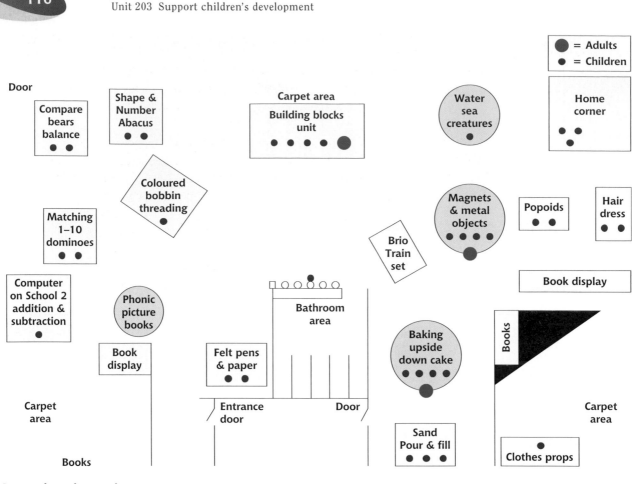

A snapshot observation

Quickly made observations can be useful

Using observation

Alex had been attending nursery for about six months. At this nursery, staff make focused observations of individual children on a regular basis and discuss their findings at team meetings. The general feeling was that Alex had settled well and enjoyed most activities. The nursery nurse observed Alex for the whole of a morning session, focusing on his social interactions with other children and on the activities he chose. She found that although he appeared to be part of a group, for much of the time he was watching others play and was not able to take a real part in the activity. He chose a range of activities but during that session avoided painting and craft. This observation was discussed at the team meeting with other staff. They had seen him enjoying painting and craft on other occasions and did not feel his missing those activities this time was significant. However, they were concerned about his social skills and felt that he needed some support in this area.

➤ *Why was observation useful in this situation?*

➤ *From this observation, what did staff identify as their main concern about Alex?*

➤ *In your own placement or work setting, what use is made of observation?*

Policies and procedures relating to observation

K2D40
K2D41
K2D42

Observing children will help you to understand their development and is a very important professional skill. As a candidate, you must make sure that you follow any policies or procedures your setting has about observation.

Generally, the following will apply:

- Ask your supervisor's permission *before* you carry out an observation. (In most settings where candidates are trained, parents will have been told that their children will be observed and will have given their permission for this.)

- Show your observations to your supervisor *before* you take them away from your workplace. Sometimes parents might like to have a copy too.

- Ask permission from both supervisor and parents before you take and use any photographs/videotapes of children in your observations.

- Make sure that you are aware of how your setting complies with the Data Protection Act regarding information about children and their families

- Maintain confidentiality and protect the child's identity by using initials and recording age as years and months, rather than date of birth. Do not identify the setting by name.

- Talk about what you have observed only with your colleagues and, where this is appropriate, the child's parents.

- If you have any concerns about what you have observed, discuss these with your supervisor straightaway. There will be procedures in your setting for responding to concerns.

Being objective

You must make sure that your observations of children are **objective**, that is, free of any personal feelings or thoughts. The way you see a child may be linked to:

- your previous experience of the child or other children
- your own attitudes and values
- any comments made by other people about that child.

If you approach a child or a situation with an idea of what you expect to find, then this will influence what you see. One way of making sure your observations are objective is to record exactly what you see without making any assumptions. For example:

- 'Jamie threw himself onto the floor screaming, kicking his feet and hammering the air with clenched fists.' *not* 'Jamie was in a rage.'
- 'Sarah snatched the doll from Nicola, kicked her and then bit her arm' *not* 'Sarah is an aggressive child.'

It will also help you to be objective if you avoid:

- jumping to conclusions, for example 'He is a naughty boy'
- making generalisations, for example 'All children cry when their mothers leave them'
- expressing personal opinions, for example 'She is a lovable child'
- labelling children, for example 'She is a bully.'
- ascribing feelings to children, for example 'They were frightened'.

These examples give a subjective view. Describing exactly what you see will make your observations objective.

Transitions

K2T1112

Knowledge about children's development and information gained from observation will enable you to plan for children's transitions. A **transition**, in childcare, is the movement of a child from one care situation to another. This usually involves a change of physical environment and a change of carer for part or all of the day. Transitions could include a child going to a childminder, day nursery, family centre, crèche, nursery school, primary school or secondary school.

Transitions involve change and loss of familiar people. This is threatening to children's feelings of security and trust. Children of all ages may find coping with this difficult. Even adults will find transitions, such as changing jobs or leaving home, stressful.

Multiple transitions

Some children may experience frequent moves. This may be because of constant and unpredictable family breakdowns. A move to foster care, for example, will probably also include a change of school.

Children who experience multiple transitions become increasingly distrustful of adults. They become accustomed to change, but become increasingly unable to relate closely to any carer. Their emotional and social development is disturbed and this makes them difficult to care for. It is for this reason that frequent changes of environment for young children are avoided if at all possible. Social workers try to make long-term permanent plans for children. These may involve placing children with adopters or long-term foster parents.

There is more information about separation and transitions and how this affects children aged 0–3years in Unit CCLD 208.

Ways of helping children and families to cope with transitions

Young children need stability and security in their environment so they need help to cope with any transitions they make.

Preparation

Children's reactions to separation can be affected by the way they are prepared for change. In the past, there was little or no awareness of the value of preparation. Children were taken to school and left to cope with the experience. Good preparation is now accepted as beneficial to all children when moving to any setting. Preparation has become part of the policy of most institutions, including nurseries, schools, hospitals, childminders and long-term foster care.

Preparation should be part of the procedures of a day-care setting or school. Practitioners dealing with children at times of change need to understand and be sensitive to children's needs.

The following guidelines for preparation can be applied to a variety of settings including schools and hospitals.

Before a transition, prepare children by:
- talking to them and explaining honestly what is about to happen
- listening to and reassuring them
- reading books and watching relevant videos with them
- providing experiences for imaginative and expressive play, which will help children to express their feelings
- arranging introductory visits for them and their parents
- making sure that any relevant personal details about a child, including their likes and dislikes and cultural background, are available.

Caring for children during separation and transition

When caring for children the following points are important:
- Children under 3 need a one-to-one relationship with a key person.
- The particular needs and background of children need to be known.
- Prepare the other children and adults in the setting. Tell them when a new child is coming and what their name is. Explain that they should make the new child welcome.

- Welcome new children warmly when they arrive and call them by the name they prefer.
- Show children around so that they can begin to know where things are. Give them their own coat peg with a picture or label.
- Provide a place (a tray, drawer or locker) to keep personal things.
- Introduce them to other children and to other workers.
- Make sure that children's comfort objects are readily available to them.
- Reassure and comfort them if they appear anxious or upset.
- Help them deal with routines and timetables.
- Children should be provided with activities appropriate to their developmental age and stage, especially play that encourages the expression of feelings.
- Honest reassurance should be given.
- Children's parents should have access to them, if appropriate, whenever possible.
- Children should have reminders of their parents, such as photographs, when they are apart. This is particularly important if children are in hospital.
- Positive images of parents and reminders of home culture should be promoted.
- Allow young children time to adjust to the new setting and routines. Children will vary in the time it will take them to settle. This will depend upon their previous experience of change, and on their age and personality.

Reuniting children with their parents

Children who have been prepared for separation and cared for appropriately will find it easier to be reunited with their parents and to readjust to their home environment. This can apply as much to children starting school as to children who are returning home from full-time care. Children can be helped with being reunited if practitioners remember to:

- be honest about when they will be reunited
- allow them to talk and express their feelings through play
- advise the parent(s) to expect and accept some disturbance in their child's feelings and possibly some regressive (going back to an earlier developmental stage) behaviour.

Transitions to a pre-school setting or school

Most children go to school. Some may start by attending a pre-school setting, others start when they are the statutory school age of 5. Whatever their age, children may experience anxiety and stress when they start school.

Possible sources of anxiety when starting a pre-school setting or school are:

- separation from their parent
- being among a large unfamiliar group of children who may already be established in friendship groups
- the day may seem very long

- they may be unfamiliar with the predominant culture and language of the school
- the routines will be unfamiliar and they may have a fear of doing something wrong
- different activities such as PE, playtime, milk and dinner time can feel strange to them
- the scale and unfamiliarity of the buildings may be frightening
- being directed and having to concentrate for longer than they are used to.

Starting school

Practical Example

K2T1112

Ben started in the reception class at his local infant school the week after his fifth birthday. This was the school policy for all admissions. Previously, he went to a day nursery full-time for four years while his mother and father worked. His parents were given a helpful information brochure about the school and attended a meeting held for parents of all new children. Ben attended pre-school sessions with other new children during the term before he started. These were held in one of the school classrooms on one afternoon a week, with the reception teacher.

➤ How was Ben prepared for the reception class?

➤ How could Ben's parents use the information they were given about school?

➤ How well do you think Ben settled into school and why do you think this?

➤ Why might Ben not have settled without this preparation?

Changing schools

As children get older, they will be faced with changing from their familiar school to another. This transition can be made less stressful if it is approached in a positive way. Parents, teachers and practitioners should be well informed and positive about the move. Good preparation is very important. This should include visiting the new school and meeting the new teachers. Time should be set aside to talk about moving on and to allow the children to ask questions. For older children, written information, that can be read and referred to, will help them to be clear about what to expect. It is also helpful if children are moving on in groups and that the new class will include some familiar faces.

Strategies to help children when starting and moving school

Policies

School policies can include:

- an appropriate admission programme with pre-visits to the school

- an admission policy that staggers the intake of children
- a helpful and informative brochure, provided in the home languages of parents and children
- appropriate classrooms and staff
- good liaison with parents
- a welcoming environment.

Staff

Practitioners can provide:

- a relaxed classroom routine
- appropriate activities and expectations, individual attention
- observation and monitoring of new children
- an awareness of cultural and language differences
- a welcome to parents to participate.
- information about the school timetable and the school day.

Parents

Parents can help by:

- talking with their children about the new school
- encouraging independence skills, for example dressing, washing, eating
- giving children some experience of separation before they start school
- being there for the child when they need reassurance
- having a positive attitude towards school
- reading books about starting school and encouraging realistic expectations establishing routines (such as bedtime) that will fit in with school
- providing the appropriate equipment (for example, lunch box, PE kit).

Children whose admission to school is handled sensitively with attention to the points above usually learn to cope with attending school each day.

Reflecting on your practice

- How is observation used in your setting? Think about when you observe children and how you record the information. **K2D39**
- List the ways in which this information is used to plan appropriate activities and experiences for the children. **K2D39**
- Find out about your setting's policies and procedure relating to observation, for example issues of confidentiality, data protection and how to share information. **K2D41, K2D42**
- What kinds of influences affect children's development? **K2D44**
- What do you understand by the term holistic development? **K2D45**

Unit 203

Are you ready for assessment?

Support children's development

Throughout this qualification, you will need to show how you competently support the physical, emotional and social, communication and intellectual development of the children with whom you work. To do this, in this unit you will be observing their current skills and abilities and helping to paln for their future development. You will need to demonstrate a basic understanding of child and young person development across the whole age range of 0–16 years.

The amount and type of evidence you will need to present will vary. You should plan this with your assessor.

Direct observation by your assessor

Observation is the required assessment method to be used to evidence some part of each element in this unit. Expert witnesses could supply additional evidence. Your assessor will observe you in real work activities and this should provide most of the evidence for the performance criteria for the elements in this unit.

Preparing to be observed

Read through the key words section at the front of your unit to make sure that you fully understand what is needed. You should then plan carefully with your assessor to make sure that you are able to demonstrate the national standard required. Think about

how you observe and record children's development. Plan for our assessor to observe you encouraging the children's skills and development described in each element. By planning carefully, you will be able to gather evidence for units 201, 202, 205 and 206 at the same time.

Read the performance criteria carefully before assessment. Try to cover as much as you can.

Other types of evidence

You will need to present different types of evidence in order to:

- Cover criteria not observed by your assessor
- Show that you have the required knowledge understanding and skills.

UNIT 204

Use support to develop own practice in children's care, learning and development

This unit concentrates on ways that you as a practitioner can develop your own practice. It provides information to help you to identify your strengths and weaknesses. It helps you to get support from other staff in your setting and from organisations and networks outside your setting. It provides information about asking for and responding to feedback and also about professional development and training opportunities. The aim of the unit is to encourage you to improve and develop your practice in relation to the work that you do.

This unit contains two elements:

⌣ *CCLD 204.1 Make use of support to develop your practice*

⌣ *CCLD 204.2 Use new knowledge and skills to improve your practice.*

The national standards for this unit include a list of key words and explanations that you need to understand. You should read this carefully as you plan the activities for your assessment. Your assessor can help you to make sure that you are interpreting the standards correctly.

⌣ Introduction

As a practitioner, it is important that you are aware of the support that is available to you. We all like to be told when we are doing something well. It is not quite so easy to be told that we are not doing well. But, if you do not know how you are getting on and you never receive any feedback about your practice, you will not be in a position to develop and progress.

It might help you to know that staff at all levels within your organisation will

- receive feedback on their performance
- be encouraged to ask for and use support that is available
- be expected to take part in professional development activities.

Element
204.1

Make use of support to develop your practice

The systems available for supervision and support

K2P55

Within your setting, members of your work team will be able to support you in many different ways.

If you are a new member of staff, you might be allocated a workplace mentor. This person will be available to support you and help you to get to know the setting and how it works. Your mentor should be able to answer questions and offer support on an informal basis.

If you have been employed recently, you might be offered a probationary review as a condition of your contract. At this review, you will have the opportunity to discuss your progress with your manager. Your manager might ask your supervisor or colleagues for a progress report. Part of this process might be to set specific targets for development or improvement. These targets will be reviewed within a period of time agreed with the manager.

Whether you are new to the role or an established member of staff, support will be available to help you to develop your practice. Some settings will carry out regular staff supervision.

As part of the staff development procedure at your setting, all staff should expect to have an annual appraisal. The appraisal system and format vary from setting to setting. You might not be familiar with this term as this system might be called something different at your setting.

Appraisal structure

The structure of a basic appraisal is as follows:

1 An appointment for your appraisal will be made.
2 There will be an opportunity to evaluate your own practice prior to the meeting (see advice about how to do this in the next section).
3 Your progress will be reviewed.
4 There will be an opportunity to discuss development or training.
5 Action points and time-scale will be agreed.
6 A record of your appraisal will be kept on file and reviewed (you should also receive a copy).

It is also important that those working alone find ways of getting feedback and support on their practice. If you are a nanny, your employer might carry out supervision or some form of appraisal. Childminders should seek feedback about their practice and provision from the parents.

All registered settings are inspected by Ofsted and feedback about the provision is given. However, a childminder will experience direct supervision of their practice

A supervision meeting with your manager will provide a good opportunity to ask for support and feedback

when they are inspected. The inspector provides feedback and support about them as a lone worker.

Discussion with others in a similar role can be supportive. There are a number of nannying networks and childminder networks developing in various parts of the United Kingdom. Information about these networks can be found at your local Children's Information Centre or you could use the internet to find out what local or national support is available.

Remember that you should also expect to receive regular support and feedback from your assessor.

Are you a reflective practitioner?

To progress in your career you will need to find ways to develop your skills, knowledge and understanding. You will also need to identify what you enjoy doing and what you prefer not to do; you will need to know your own strengths and weaknesses. You will need to **reflect**. Reflection is not always something that we find easy. It may help you to develop as a practitioner if you:

- think about what you have done
- review and consider your actions
- plan ahead.

Identifying strengths and weaknesses

K2P52

Help and feedback from others is very important to get a clear and balanced picture of your practice. Before asking for feedback, it will help if you have already taken the time to reflect on what you do well and on things that you feel you do not do well. We all find it difficult to **evaluate** our own performance. To evaluate our performance means that we try to understand how good or bad we are at something and to identify our strengths and weaknesses. Most people need the help of others to do this.

To work out your strengths and weaknesses, to evaluate your professional performance and to improve your skills, you must:

- want to do this
- take responsibility for it
- identify what your needs are
- be realistic about what you can achieve
- take responsibility for your own development and learning
- take feedback from others positively in order to improve.

It can be very difficult to do this on you own. You could try to write down what you think are six of your strengths and six weaknesses. We often find it easier to see our weaknesses rather than our strengths. You can also identify your strengths and weaknesses by talking to your assessor and/or your colleagues.

You should try to:

- listen to others
- understand what they say to you
- be open to suggestions about how you can change and improve how you work.

By identifying the strengths and weaknesses of your own practice, you will be able to share your thoughts with your supervisor. You will also be in a position to ask for help and support in areas that you are already aware you need to develop. This will help to improve your future work performance.

It is important that those working on their own also find ways of getting feedback on their practice. They also need support and professional development. Discussion with parents and with others in a similar role can be very supportive.

Asking for feedback

K2P53

Try to make a suitable time to gather feedback. If your setting is particularly busy, it might be better to wait until the end of the session. Making a time for feedback will be more constructive. Your supervisor will be able to suggest ways that you can improve in a less hurried way. You will be in a better position to listen and to respond to the feedback that you are given.

The experiences that you have had in the past might affect your current and future practice.

Practical Example

Roberto's review

Roberto has recently joined the crèche as an assistant. His supervisor has noticed that he does not praise and recognise the efforts of the children as often as he could. His supervisor raises this issue with him at his probationary review. Roberto is surprised, as this has never been pointed out to him before.

The supervisor thinks that there may be many reasons why Roberto does not naturally praise the children. She feels that some of these reasons may be linked to his experiences in other settings and the practice that he observed there. She also feels that he may not understand the purpose and benefits of praise and recognition. Roberto's supervisor gives him advice about what he can do to improve this area of his practice. She asks him to observe and listen to the way that other members of staff praise the children. She also asks him to read about praising children and recommends some books and articles.

Her advice includes encouraging Roberto to accept the feedback because it is intended to help him to learn and to develop his skills and childcare practice.

➤ *Why do you think Roberto's supervisor was unhappy with his practice?*

➤ *What effect do you think Roberto's previous experiences were having on his practice?* **K2P53**

➤ *Why was it important for Roberto to be given feedback and support? How will this help him to develop his practice?*

You will need to be open to suggestions for changing your methods of working. This could be achieved in a number of ways:

- supervision by experienced practitioners
- observation of experienced practitioners both at your setting and if possible in other settings
- in-service staff development
- attending courses.

Good training will give you ideas on how to improve your practice.

Learning styles

K2P54

Before undertaking professional development, it will be useful for you to consider the way that you learn – your learning style. Being aware of the way that you learn can help you to understand why you find some tasks easier than others. Your preferred learning style will also help you to make choices about the types of development training that you do.

People learn in different ways and at different speeds. It will help you if you know that there are particular ways that help you to learn:

- *Visual learners* learn best through the use of visual aids – these include the teacher, textbooks, diagrams and video.
- *Auditory learners* learn best through listening to lectures and discussions, listening to audio tapes.
- *Tactile/kinaesthetic learners* learn best by doing things, using a hands-on approach to learning.

Many people learn through a combination of styles. If you are not sure about your own learning style, there are lots of resources available to help you to decide, including textbooks and online questionnaires. Whatever your learning style, you need to make sure that the type of learning or training that you commit to will complement this.

Professional development activities will help you to develop your role

Personal and professional development

K2P56
K2P58

Continued professional development is a common factor in most contracts of employment. As a practitioner you should aim to identify your own needs for development. You can do this and review your progress when you have supervision time with your line manager.

- You may set professional goals and targets and decide to take further training in order to do your job better.
- You will have to decide what further training you are able to do and the time that is available to you.

- You should think about your personal career aims and whether your current work is helping you to move towards them.

- There may be personal and professional obstacles to your development. You should think clearly about what these are and go through each of them with your manager. These could be:

  - your educational achievement so far

  - your domestic situation

  - skills that you have not yet achieved

  - changes in practice that you are not aware of (for example, health and safety procedures).

There may be ways you can deal with some or every one of these obstacles and make them less of a barrier.

Types of professional development

K2P57
K2P58

In this unit, you have been encouraged to reflect upon your own practice and to think about how you can progress within the children's care, learning and development sector. There are many ways that you can progress, including professional development opportunities within the sector. These opportunities include:

- training for appropriate children's care, learning and development qualifications on the Qualifications and Curriculum Authority (QCA) framework. This framework is available online.

- short courses to gain specific skills to meet the National Standards for Under Eights Day Care and Childminding, for example First Aid, Basic Food Hygiene, Child Protection.

- short courses to increase your professional skills in meeting the care, learning and developmental needs of children

- training and development opportunities to understand new developments, for example the Foundation Stage, Assessment, Inspection and Regulation, Quality Assurance

- general education opportunities, for example Key Skills.

Advice may be available locally. Opportunities for updating and further training and advice will be available through your local Early Years Development and Childcare Partnership (EYDCP) and National Childminders Association (NCMA).

Examples of professional development opportunities

Opportunity	What's involved	How do I find out about it?	How do I get onto this training?
Training courses	Long- or short-term programmes such as a range of childcare courses, NVQs, first aid, child protection. A local college, training organisation or EYDCP may run these	Flyers and information may be sent to your setting. College prospectus – available from the college, your local library or online. Many settings are given an EYDCP training programme each year. Link workers and advisers should be able to tell you about the training that is available to you	Check with the setting and then enrol with the college or training provider
Seminars	Day or half-day meetings where a particular aspect of children's care, learning and development is discussed and training is carried out	Normally local information may be found in the EYDCP training programme. Link workers and advisers should also be able to tell you about seminars that would be of use to you	Check with the provider to see if there are spaces – you may need to complete a booking form or go onto a waiting list if the seminar is very popular
Information days	May be about a specific aspect of your role for example an information day run by a local college about the childcare courses available	Information sent to your setting – make sure that you check the staff notice board if you have one. Prospectus. Link worker or adviser	Enrolment or booking form as above.
Conferences	Might be local or national. A variety of workshops are usually available. People attending book into these in advance. Conferences that are specifically for childcare workers generally offer a broad range of workshops to include a variety of settings	May be advertised locally. Nationally, you can find out about conferences in publications such as childcare magazines. Information is also available online	When you contact the organiser of the conference, they will send you a booking form. At this point, you will need to choose the workshops that you wish to attend. In most cases, you should expect to receive confirmation of your booking
Exhibitions	Companies and organisations often attend conferences to exhibit goods, resources and equipment. Sometimes exhibitions are held at support and resource centres	National and local advertising – newspapers, leaflets. If you are working in a school, companies and organisations often come to parents' events to exhibit; they may also attend in-service training days	Often free and reasonably informal – you just turn up when you can
In-service training	There are different ways that settings carry out in-service training. A day nursery may offer training for all staff in first aid or customer service; a school will offer a broad in-service training programme for support staff	Information about in-service training will be given out at staff meetings or will be displayed on staff notice boards	May be compulsory. Within a day nursery setting such training might be held after the nursery has closed or at weekends. Schools have set Inset days that you will be made aware of

Element 204.1

Are you ready for assessment?

Make use of support to develop your practice

You need to show that you can make use of support to develop your practice. To do this you will need to be directly observed by your assessor and present other types of evidence. The amount and type of evidence you need to present will vary. You should plan this with your assessor.

Direct observation by your assessor

Observation is the required assessment method to be used to evidence some part of each element in this unit. Expert witnesses could supply additional evidence. Your assessor will observe you in real work activities and this should provide most of the evidence for the performance criteria for the elements in this unit.

Preparing to be observed

You need to show your assessor that you have identified and used the support that is available to you. Observation for this element could be carried out during a supervision session (with the prior agreement of your workplace supervisor).You should plan with your supervisor to discuss:

- your recent performance while carrying out an activity with children, including the strengths and weaknesses of your performance and areas that need developing
- your personal development objectives – what you are aiming to achieve in the short and long term

- which of these aims are achievable and realistic
- how they might be achieved
- information about training and development activities that you could do to help you to develop your performance

During this discussion with your supervisor, your assessor will be able to see you using the support available to you and that you are taking responsibility for your own development, learning and performance. Your assessor will also be able to see you getting feedback from your supervisor, discussing your performance constructively and positively, and showing that you understand how you will use this in the future to improve your work performance.

Your assessor may also observe you receiving feedback from others at other times. This might happen during observation of activities and routines.

Read the performance criteria carefully before your assessment. Try to cover as much as you can.

▶

Other types of evidence

You will need to provide different types of evidence in order to:

- cover criteria that are not observed by your assessor
- show that you have the required knowledge and understanding.

Such evidence could include:

- copies of your appraisals
- certificates from development training (these would make good evidence if supported by a reflective account about the training and how the training has helped you to develop your practice)
- an individual learning plan that you may have developed as part of your course programme induction. This plan might include the identification of your own learning needs and gaps in your knowledge. Talk to your assessor, as you should be able to use this plan as evidence for this unit
- diary/log entries of any times when you receive support and feedback from others and make comments about how you responded to this.

Element 204.2

Use new knowledge and skills to improve your practice

If you have read the performance criteria for this element, you will notice that there is an overlap with Element 204.1. This is because development of your practice is continuous. This can be illustrated as a cycle as shown on page 134.

As discussed in the previous element; there are a variety of ways that you can gain new knowledge and skills. This element considers the ways that you can use new knowledge and skills to improve what you do. You might find that you gain skills that will help you in other aspects of your life, which will be an additional benefit. For example, through attending training you may have developed your organisational skills. Improving such skills will obviously be of use both professionally and personally.

It is important that you continue to take advantage of opportunities to gain new knowledge and skills. If you think back to the practical example in the previous element, you will remember that the worker, Roberto, was encouraged to observe the way that his colleagues praised the children. You will also be aware that there are lots of opportunities to observe adults praising children in your setting. You can probably think of aspects of your own knowledge that are developing on a daily basis too.

The cycle of
practice
development

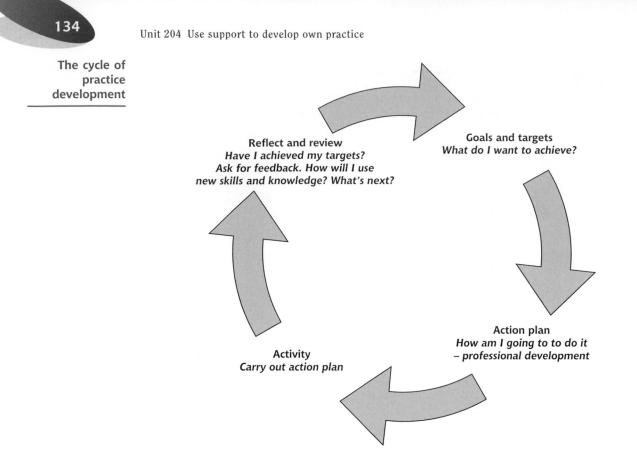

Reflect and review
Have I achieved my targets?
Ask for feedback. How will I use
new skills and knowledge? What's next?

Goals and targets
What do I want to achieve?

Action plan
How am I going to to do it
– professional development

Activity
Carry out action plan

Using new knowledge and skills

You may have worked on developing the delivery of a particular activity. You can ask for further support to ensure that you are doing things according to the procedure. You may observe colleagues and then request that colleagues observe you and give you feedback on the way that you do things now. Hopefully your practice will have improved and your feedback will be positive.

It is important to ensure that any new skills and ideas that you bring back to the setting are shared with senior staff. You might learn from fellow students on your college course and therefore you should ensure that anything new that you want to try is consistent with the policies, procedures and the practice of your setting.

Make sure that you use the correct methods of communication to inform colleagues of your new skill or things that you have learned. One way of doing this could be to put copies of training course materials on the staff notice board. If you have staff meetings, you might notice that colleagues give feedback to staff about training they have attended.

Ali improves her practice

Earlier this term, Ali had a supervision meeting with her manager. At the meeting, Ali was told that her supervisor felt that she was not enjoying her work. Ali admitted that she felt bored. She also felt that life in the baby room was very routine, as were the toys and activities that were provided.

Her manager was concerned about Ali's comments. She explained that the aim of the setting was for all staff to experience all of the age groups. They decided that Ali would benefit from some training. They found out that there was going to be local training about the *Birth to Three Matters* framework (see CCLD 208).

Ali attended the training with some colleagues. When she returned to the setting, she was full of ideas and was keen to share these with her manager. A room meeting was organised where the staff discussed ways that the framework could be implemented within the room. Once the framework was up and running, the manager came to observe Ali's practice. She gave Ali feedback about her practice and the difference that she had noticed in Ali's behaviour and enthusiasm. She was impressed with the way that Ali was using her new skills and gave Ali positive feedback about the improvements in her practice.

➤ *How were weaknesses and concerns about Ali's practice identified?* **K2P52**

➤ *How did her manager support Ali?* **K2P55**

➤ *Why do you think Ali's practice improved?* **K2P58**

Career progression

K2P57

There are lots of settings that provide for children's care, learning and development. These include:

- day nurseries
- children's centres
- pre-schools
- childminders
- nannies
- after-school clubs
- schools
- nursery schools.

As already mentioned, opportunities for support, feedback and the development of your skills and knowledge are available to you. It is also important to consider how you wish to progress within the sector. In order to progress, it will help if you know how the sector is structured.

It might help first if you consider how your own setting is structured. You could do this by looking at an organisational chart. If you do not have a chart, you could ask your supervisor to help you to draw one. Looking at the structure will help you to understand what you will need to do in order to progress. You may need to increase your experience and gain more qualifications. Once you have considered how you want to progress, you can set some career goals and targets that will help you to work towards your goal.

It is important to set professional goals and targets, as these will help you to develop your practice and knowledge and define your career path. Goals and targets will help you to maintain a focus and purpose. Goals and targets will also ensure that you make the best use of the opportunities that are available to you.

For example, you want to progress within your setting therefore your goals might look like this:

1   Complete the CCLD NVQ level 2 within a specific period of time.

2   Follow on with CCLD NVQ level 3.

3   Progress further into a room senior position.

Alternatively, you might decide that you want to move to a home setting and become a nanny. Your goals might look like this:

1   Complete CCLD NVQ levels 2 and 3.

2   Complete first aid and food hygiene training.

3   Learn to drive.

If you already have a particular career pathway in mind, you can find out about the time-scale, resources and level of personal commitment involved by talking to someone who is already in such a position. Your local college or careers adviser will also be able to help.

The diagram below outlines possible long-term progression routes.

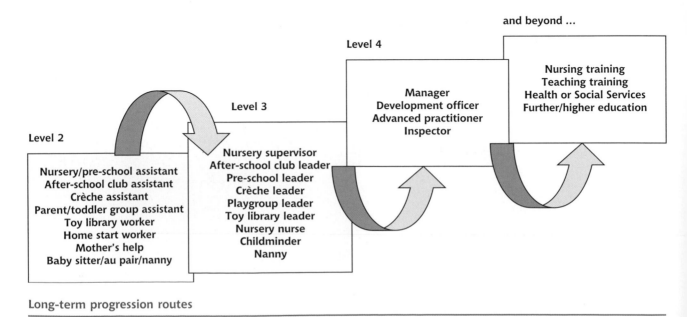

Long-term progression routes

Element 204.2

Are you ready for assessment?

Use new knowledge and skills to improve your practice

You need to show that you use new knowledge and skills to improve your practice. To do this you will need to be directly observed by your assessor and present other types of evidence. The amount and type of evidence you need to present will vary. You should plan this with your assessor.

Direct observation by your assessor

Observation is the required assessment method to be used to evidence some part of each element in this unit. Expert witnesses could supply additional evidence. Your assessor will observe you in real work activities and this should provide most of the evidence for the performance criteria for the elements in this unit.

Preparing to be observed

You need to show your assessor that you have gained new knowledge and skills. You will also need to show your assessor that you have used these skills to develop your practice. Observation for this element could be carried out during a supervision session (with the prior agreement of your workplace supervisor).

You should plan with your supervisor to discuss:

- the opportunities that you have used to develop new knowledge and skills
- the knowledge and skills that will be useful in your work

- how to use the knowledge and skills to improve your practice.

It might also help to ask your assessor to observe you using the knowledge and skills within your work.

Read the performance criteria carefully before your assessment. Try to cover as much as you can.

Other types of evidence

You may need to present different types of evidence in order to show that you have the required knowledge, understanding and skills. Such evidence could include:

- evidence of the development of new knowledge and skills – such as reflective accounts, diary entries
- copies of any written reports about your progress and development that have been made during supervision times – identify the development and use of new skills and knowledge on the report.

Reflecting on your practice

- Make a list of the strengths and weakness of your practice. Look at each weakness and decide what you could do to improve and develop your practice. Work with your assessor or supervisor to set some goals and targets. **K2P52**

- Why is it important to set career goals and targets? **K2P56**

- What are your career goals?

- What development routes are open to you in your setting both for obtaining qualifications and for in-service staff training and development? Are there any obstacles to you achieving these? **K2P57, K2P58**

Prepare and maintain environments to meet children's needs

This unit is about the importance of the environment in which children are cared for. Environments which have been well thought out can provide children with positive development opportunities.

This unit has close links with Units CCLD 202 and 206. It contains four elements:

⌒ *CCLD 205.1 Prepare and maintain the physical environment*

⌒ *CCLD 205.2 Prepare and maintain a stimulating environment*

⌒ *CCLD 205.3 Maintain an environment that builds children's confidence*

⌒ *CCLD 205.4 Support routines for children.*

The national standards for this unit include a list of key words and explanations that you need to understand. You should read this carefully as you plan the activities for your assessment. Your assessor can help you to make sure that you are interpreting the standards correctly.

⌒ Introduction

The environment is the place, setting or service where you work with children. The environment includes everyday living areas and play areas, indoors and outdoors.

Children should have a say about what happens in their environment. They can do this by talking to practitioners about what they would like and by helping to make things happen. All children should be able to use the environment and should not be prevented from doing so because of disability or a particular need. The environment should be attractive and stimulating. It should also present positive images of people and reflect the wider community. Caring routines should provide a balance of activities and quiet periods as well as supporting children's health and hygiene.

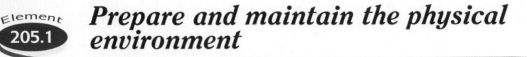

Element 205.1

Prepare and maintain the physical environment

You should aim to help plan and create an environment that is stimulating and attractive to children and one that meets their needs at different ages.

There are many things involved in creating a stimulating and caring environment for children. These include:

- providing a range of equipment and resources
- ensuring the children's safety
- good teaching skills
- a caring approach.

National standards

K2S65
K2D48
K2D49

Standards and regulations relating to the care and education of children are laid down by each of the four countries in the United Kingdom: England, Wales, Scotland and Northern Ireland. In England these are the National Standards for Under Eights Day Care and Childminding (2003) The standards cover aspects of childcare such as safety and the physical environment. This includes heating, ventilation, hygiene and outside play spaces. Regulations also cover the amount of space needed for each child and the number of adults required to care for the children. You should make sure that you know what regulations apply to your setting.

Arranging the area

Childcare settings may be in different kinds of accommodation. Some may be purpose-built, for example, a day nursery or nursery school. Others could include:

- a village hall, for a pre-school, playgroup, toddler group or children's clubs
- school buildings for after- and before-school provision.

Choosing furniture and equipment and planning the layout is important to make any setting welcoming, safe, secure and reassuring for the children.

Using the available space

The national standards lay down the requirements for the minimum space that is to be provided for each child. The minimum spaces for day care in England are shown in the table below.

Minimum spaces for day care, England

Age	Space
Under 2 years	3.5 square metres for each child
2 years	2.5 square metres for each child
3–7 years	2.3 square metres for each child

Provide a
welcoming
environment

Safety in the environment

K2S65
K2D48
K2D49
K2D50
K2D51

It is the responsibility of the adults to enable children to play and learn safely.

Health and safety policies

All childcare settings should have a health and safety policy. There is detailed information about this and other important safety measures in Unit CCLD 202.

Organising the environment meeting the children's needs and encouraging children to participate

K2D59
K2D60
K2D61
KS73
K2D70
K2D48
K2D49
K2D50

The environment needs to be organised so that there are different areas for different types of play and learning. There should be room to use large bricks, make bigger models and to use road and rail layouts. These activities should be situated away from other quieter activities. Smaller, quieter areas should be provided for some types of activities, such as sand, water, painting, imaginative play area and the book area. Messy activities like painting, sand and water may need to be placed where the flooring can be swept and washed. Messy activities also need to be near the sinks for hand-washing and drying racks for the paintings.

Activities can be provided at small tables with the right number of chairs. This will encourage the children to concentrate more easily and to work with a partner or in small groups. A carpeted area is good for bringing the children together for registration, sharing news and at story time. A larger area that can be used for drama and music and movement should be available. This may be outside the main room or perhaps shared with other groups.

Resources for activities should be positioned where the children can select them. This will help them to choose which materials they are going to use. In some settings, such as a nursery, the toys and equipment can be kept in cupboards and on shelves that are labelled with a picture as well as the written word. This will help the children to be tidy and to replace and care for the things they use. However, in some settings, such as a playgroup or after-school club, everything will need to be put into storage at the end of each session. In this case, equipment may be put into large storage boxes before being locked away. However, it is still important that the children help with the packing up.

Involving the children

K2D61

Children can be encouraged to help in putting equipment away and tidying areas of the setting. They should be encouraged to value and care for their environment. Time should be allowed as part of the routine of the setting for putting away all the equipment. You can encourage even the youngest children to take part by letting them help. Be prepared for the fact that this may take longer than doing it yourself. Check the equipment for any damage as you put it away so that the children can see that it is important to care for things. Remove anything damaged and report it so that repairs can be made or the item thrown away.

Meeting children's needs

K2D70
K2D48
K2D49
K2D50

Activities and areas of the setting must meet the needs of all the children. Children should not be left out of activities because they cannot physically get to them. Wider doorways ramps and larger toilet areas will be needed. This could be difficult in some buildings that are not purpose-built. However, simple changes like moving the furniture to provide better access will help. It may be possible to use special equipment including adjustable chairs, tables, painting easels, large print books and additional lighting. There is more information about this in Unit CCLD 202.

Acorn Pre-school

Acorn Pre-school uses a community hall. The hall is large and airy and has easy access to an outside play space. The practitioners provide a range of activities. They encourage the children to move freely between them. However, they noticed that very few of the children settled into the activities for any length of time. The room seemed very noisy and the children were frequently being reminded not to race around.

K2D60

The practitioners decide to set up the hall in a different way and to make sure that each staff member had a particular role to play at each session, as well as generally supervising the children.

> How would you arrange the hall? Say what activities you would have and how you would set about arranging the space. How does your new layout meet the children's needs? **K2D59**

> What would you want the practitioners to do during the session? Think about safety and security. **K2S65**

KST3

Comfort

The temperature of the setting should be kept at 16–24° C (60–75° F). Ventilation should allow fresh air to circulate. Opening the windows can usually do this. Check that children cannot climb out. Lighting in each part of the setting should be adequate for the activities provided. Natural light from windows is always best, but on duller days or in dimmer areas additional lighting will be needed. From a safety point of view, always use the main room lights rather than smaller table lamps that may get knocked or pulled over. A quiet area with books and comfortable seating will encourage children to pick up books and look at them, and engage in quieter activities. Where possible furniture should be child-sized. Attractive curtains and soft furnishing will add to the general attractiveness and comfort of the setting. Any soft furnishing must meet the safety and fire regulations. There is more information about this in Unit CCLD 202.

Playing outside

The outdoor play space should be safe and secure. The area and the toys and equipment should always be checked *before* the children use it. This is called risk assessment and there is more information about this in Unit CCLD 202. A variety of surfaces on the ground will provide for different types of play and learning, for example hard surfaces such as concrete for the wheeled toys and bikes, and grassy areas or soft surfaces for sitting and running games. It is very useful to have some outside play space that is covered for when the weather is wet, shady areas to provide cover on hot days, and space to run around and use the wheeled toys safely. Trees and plants and an area for planting and growing things will add to the children's learning experiences.

Changes to the layout of the environment

Introducing changes to the layout will help to stimulate children's ideas and support creative play. Some of the most common changes made are in the imaginative play areas. For example, staff may set up a shop or hospital, often to support a current theme or topic. Changes of this kind should be discussed in advance with the children so that they can share ideas and contribute to the project. Changes to the outdoor area may be made because new equipment has been bought, changes in the weather or for safety reasons.

**Provide a shady
area outside**

Element
205.1

Are you ready for assessment?

Prepare and maintain the physical environment

You need to show that you can competently prepare and maintain the physical environment. To do this you will need to be directly observed by your assessor and present other evidence. The amount and type of evidence you will need to present will vary. You should plan this with your assessor

Direct observation by your assessor

Observation is the required assessment method to be used to evidence some part of each element in this unit. Expert witnesses could supply additional evidence. Your assessor will observe you in real work activities and this should provide most of the evidence for the performance criteria for the elements in this unit.

Preparing to be observed

You will need to arrange to take part in the preparation and setting up of activities in your area. You should be able to show your assessor how the temperature, ventilation and lighting are controlled and know the required room temperatures. You should know where the exits are, particularly the fire exits, and be able to show that you know

▶

about the health and safety rules for your setting.

You will need to show that responsibility for caring for the environment is shared with the children by, for example, encouraging them to be tidy and to help put toys and equipment in their proper places.

You could prepare for your assessment by drawing a floor plan of your setting showing the indoor and outdoor play space. Mark the following on your plan:

- exits
- fire exits
- layout of the furniture
- where equipment and resources that are accessible to the children are placed
- activities.

Look at your plan and write about how the physical layout of the activities helps the children's learning.

Read the performance criteria carefully before your assessment. Try to cover as much as you can.

Other types of evidence

You will need to present different types of evidence in order to:

- cover criteria not observed by your assessor
- show that you have the required knowledge and understanding.

Element 205.2 *Prepare and maintain a stimulating environment*

K2D12
K2P14

How to display children's work

Displays and interest tables are an effective way of creating a stimulating and attractive environment for children.

The values of display

Display has many values. It can:

- be used as a stimulus for learning
- encourage children to look, think, reflect, explore, investigate and discuss
- act as a sensory and imaginative stimulus
- encourage parental involvement in their children's learning, and reinforce links with home
- encourage self-esteem by showing appreciation of children's work
- encourage awareness of the wider community, reflect society and reinforce acceptance of difference
- reflect the values and principles of the setting.

Display encourages children's interest

The length of time a display remains should be considered and planned. Any display that has become old or faded should be replaced.

Where to display

Displays should be placed where they can be seen easily, or touched if appropriate. Try getting down to a child's eye level and viewing the surroundings from that position.

What to include in a display

Variety makes displays interesting. Displays can include:

- children's painting and other individual work
- children's co-operative efforts
- natural materials and plants
- objects of interest, photographs, pictures, collage, real objects
- use of different colours, textures and labelling
- items that the children have brought in from home. This will make the display more personal to the children in the group. These can be familiar items or things that will show aspects of different cultural backgrounds, for example different items of clothing or material.

Recognising children's efforts and achievements

K2D63

All children should be able to contribute to the displays in their environment. When looking around their room, every child should have at least one piece of their work displayed, or have taken part in a group display. This will help the children to feel they are part of the setting and that their work is valued. Children should be involved in the choice of work that will be displayed. They should also help in the mounting of work and the creation of the display.

Positive images

K2D62

Displays that include people should reflect positive images of black people, women and people with disabilities, for example showing them working as politicians, doctors or lawyers and taking part in sporting activities. Children should be given the opportunity to represent themselves accurately. Practitioners should provide mirrors, paints and crayons of suitable colours. This will enable children to see and match their own skin tones.

The entrance to a setting gives the first impression that parents, children and visitors gain of your work. A welcoming entrance with displays of children's work will contribute to giving a positive impression.

Planning displays

It is important to plan displays, thinking everything through first. Think about the position, appropriate colours, backing, drapes and borders. Good presentation is

Good planning and presentation are essential

essential. This includes good mounting, backing and well-produced lettering. Staples and adhesive materials should be used discreetly.

The use of colour should be carefully considered. There are no rules – bright colours can be effective, but black and white may also be appropriate.

Mounting

Mounting involves putting children's work onto a background of card or paper to provide a framework. This can be a single or a double framework, and can enhance children's work. When you do this, it is important to make sure that you cut the mount accurately. A cutting machine will help to make sure that the edges are straight and level.

Mounting children's work provides a framework

Backing

The backing and borders around a display should complement the children's work. Choose the background colour carefully and avoid fancy borders that will detract from the children's work.

Labels and captions

Any labels and captions must be clear and of an appropriate size. Lower case letters should be used except at the beginning of sentences and proper nouns. (Proper nouns are people's names or place names.) Include the home languages of the children in the setting. If labels and captions are hand-written they should be carefully printed. It is important to practise printing using guidelines to help you until you are confident enough to print free-hand.

**Practise printing
using guidelines
to help**

**Displaying work
effectively**

What do you need to make a display?

It is always useful to keep all the things that are required to make a display together in a box. These items will be useful but can be added to:

- adhesive-tack (Blue-Tak or something similar)
- drawing pins – use carefully to avoid accidents
- craft knife, for example, a Stanley knife with a safety cap fitted
- glue, glue sticks
- pencils
- rubbers – make sure they are of good quality
- rulers and tape measures of different lengths
- pens – a good selection in different colours and sizes
- scissors – a selection of different sizes
- tape – single and double-sided
- spirit level.

If younger children are helping with the display, then rigorous supervision will be needed if they are using the tools.

Interest tables

Interest tables can be used to follow a theme or topic, or to display work/collections from a recent outing. They should be at a suitable height for the age of the children. If possible, you should put them in a quieter area of the setting. The table should be covered and any objects that are not intended to be touched should be placed in a protective container, such as a plastic tank. Babies and younger children can also examine interesting objects. Look at Unit CCLD 208 to find out more about this.

Helping children to learn about the natural world is important. Seeing how things grow and develop is part of learning about the world. Children can collect and display natural objects such as leaves, plants, and berries. Be aware of the dangers of poisonous plants. If you are in any doubt about anything you are going to use on a display, use a good reference book to identify it. Put the items in a container that will prevent the children handling them. It is important to help the children to learn how to care for any plant or cut flowers and foliage. Regular watering and removing any dead leaves and flowers will ensure that the display remains fresh and attractive. Children should be supervised when examining plants and berries. They should be taught not to taste or put objects in their mouths. Reference books can be put out on the table. These will help children and adults find out more about the things on display.

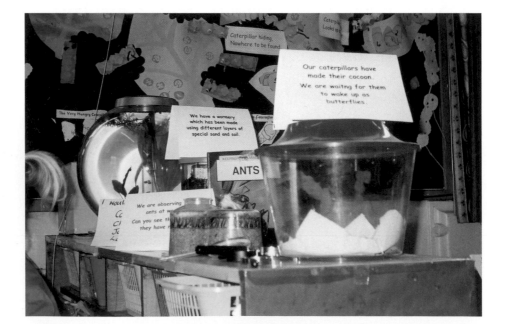

Interest tables can be used to display collections

Using the senses

A stimulating environment is one where the children can use all their available senses. Look at Unit CCLD 206 for more information about this.

Smell and taste

You can provide a selection of foods that can be smelt and tasted. You could do this at group times or provide them as part of snacks or meals. The things you display on the interest table could also be safe to taste and smell. Other things like plants, flowers and spices could be smelt with supervision.

Touch

Many of the items you display on the interest table can be handled. Circle time provides another opportunity to explore items. There is more about objects of interest in Unit CCLD 206.

Hearing

Make listening to music part of every day. Introduce a wide range of musical styles to the children. You should choose music that is culturally diverse, classical and contemporary. Encourage the children to request music and bring in music from home. You could provide a listening centre using CD and cassette players.

Sight

You can provide a colourful environment with well-chosen furnishings and displays. Use the natural and local environment to stimulate the children's learning. Children can:

- plant seeds, and watch and measure growth
- observe wildlife in its natural habitat, for example bird tables can be set up where children can see them
- study the weather – measure rainfall, find out the wind direction
- observe the neighbourhood on a local walk – look at shop and road signs, architectural features of new and old buildings.

Adding interest to displays

Interest can be added by good use of:

- colour – a co-ordinated backing and border can be used to display the children's work to its best advantage
- texture – include things that are interesting to touch and contrast with each other, for example smooth, shiny pebbles and rough sandpaper
- movement – consider hanging displays and objects that move
- sound – shakers and musical instruments made by the children
- familiar characters from books read at story time
- people they have met on a trip or who have visited the setting.

Benefits to child development of display work

Creating work for displays and taking part in putting a display together will benefit all areas of the children's development and learning, as shown in the table below.

Benefits of display work

Area of development/learning	Skills
Physical, fine motor	Placing, cutting, sticking, drawing
Physical, gross motor	Co-ordination, stretching, bending, balancing
Cognitive	Thinking, problem-solving, decision-making, using memory
Language and literacy	Discussion, negotiating, describing, communicating ideas, learning new vocabulary, developing writing
Mathematics	Measuring, estimating, creating patterns, using shape, angles, working in three dimensions
Personal, social and emotional	Team work, co-operation, sharing, concentration, and pride in their environment, awareness of wider environment and society. Sense of achievement, increased self-esteem, appreciating an attractive environment
Creative	Explore colour, shape and texture, use imagination, express ideas, and use a variety of materials

Element 205.2 — Are you ready for assessment?

Prepare and maintain a stimulating environment

You need to show that you can competently prepare and maintain a stimulating environment. To do this you will need to be directly observed by your assessor and present other types of evidence. The amount and type of evidence you will need to present will vary. You should plan this with your assessor.

Direct observation by your assessor

Observation is the required assessment method to be used to evidence some part of each element in this unit. Expert witnesses could supply additional evidence. Your assessor will observe you in real work activities and this should provide most of the evidence for the performance criteria for the elements in this unit.

Preparing to be observed

During your work with children you will be involved in preparing and maintaining displays and it is important to keep a record of what you do as evidence. You could take a photograph of your displays or draw a diagram and write a description. Your assessor will need to see your display work

►

and if possible see this in progress with the children involved in the preparation.

Make sure that your displays use the children's work and that you display the work attractively. Labels should be neat, clear and suitable for the children's age and stage of development.

You need to show your assessor that you can provide an environment to stimulate the children's senses. You will be able to do this by using group times or interest tables. In this way, children will be able to handle and experience a range of objects of interest. You should always pay attention to safety rules.

Read the performance criteria and range carefully before your assessment. Try to cover as much as you can.

Other types of evidence

You will need to present different types of evidence in order to:

- demonstrate the performance criteria
- show that you have the required knowledge and understanding.

Element 205.3
Maintain an environment that builds children's confidence

A positive environment

K2D64
K2D48
K2D49
K2D50

Providing a positive environment for children will depend on your commitment to the needs and rights of children. If the achievements of each child are to be recognised, practitioners should acknowledge that:

- children's well-being is paramount
- children are individuals and have different needs and abilities
- working in partnership with parents is of major importance
- good practice can promote all areas of development
- children and young people learn best through exploration and experience.

A positive environment will recognise children's achievements. You should ensure that children's work is valued. You should discuss the work (a painting, model or a piece of writing) with the child. You may then save it carefully for the child to take home. A positive environment will display many examples of all the children's work. You should make sure that all work is carefully labelled with the child's name. Encourage parents to look at the work displayed and talk about it with their child.

Children will achieve in other ways. For example they may do a difficult jigsaw or go down the slide for the first time. You should always give individual praise when it is deserved. However, these achievements can also be discussed at group times or in assemblies and golden times. Children will become more confident if their achievements are acknowledged. They will begin to see how they are able to achieve more. This will build their confidence. It will also enable them to cope with minor setbacks when things do not turn out as they hoped.

Promoting self-esteem, confidence and resilience

K2D64

A child's self-image and identity is their view of who they are and what they are like. Children who think well of themselves have a positive self-image. This means that they will have confidence and high self-esteem. Having high self-esteem is not the same as being conceited. Conceit involves one person comparing him or herself to another. Having high self-esteem does not involve comparisons; it is having an assurance about yourself that you are good and worthwhile.

It is very healthy for children and adults to have high self-esteem. People with high self-esteem are resilient. They tend to

- be happier and more successful in life
- make better and more secure relationships
- have better mental health
- be more able to cope with difficulties and frustrations in life.

The role of the adult

To help children to develop self-esteem practitioners should:

- listen to children carefully – encourage them to say what they need and help them to express their thoughts and ideas
- set goals at the right level for the child, which challenge the child but allow them to achieve with as little help as possible
- praise children's efforts and achievements. This will increase their self-confidence and self-esteem. Praise and rewards are very effective. They can be the words that adults use, looks such as smiles and nods, gestures or material rewards
- give children assistance when it is needed to overcome difficulties
- be aware that children's level of confidence and their skills may vary from one day to another. A child may not be as confident when tired, unwell or unhappy
- treat children with care and respect – they should not be hurried beyond their capabilities or feel inadequate if they cannot achieve a task without assistance
- have expectations of children that are appropriate to their age and stage of development
- avoid assuming that a child is or is not capable of something
- be aware that parents differ in their expectations of children. Some will expect them to be independent in their personal skills at a younger age than others. Accommodate parents expressed wishes when possible

High self-esteem is about having an assurance about yourself that you are good and worthwhile

K2D69
K2D48
K2D49
K2D50
K2D51

- show that they value what children do
- ensure that the children's safety is maintained at all times

These positive responses towards children are likely to encourage them to develop appropriate levels of high self-esteem, confidence and resilience.

Feeling secure

Welcoming children into an attractive and thoughtfully arranged environment will help to reassure them and help them settle in. Childcare settings for younger children should be geared to the needs of the children with child-sized equipment, attractive displays and a quiet, calm atmosphere. Cloakrooms, washbasins and lavatories should be easily accessible. For younger children, these fittings should be child-sized. For older children (12–16 years), there should be adult fixtures and fittings. For children with disabilities, special adaptations will be needed. Examples of these include:

- wide doorways to accommodate wheelchairs
- extra lighting to help children with restricted sight
- staff who can use British Sign Language to help children who are deaf and sign
- special equipment such as mobility aids.

This will promote security and growing independence. Providing a routine to the day will help children to feel secure. They will become familiar with the structure of the day and will become more confident as they recognise familiar routines and begin to know where they fit in.

Children need to know about the physical layout of their environment, for example, where the toilets are and where things are kept. They also need to know about the routine, for example, when snack time and story-time take place. This knowledge helps children to feel secure. It is important to discuss any proposed changes with the children before they happen. This will help them get used to the idea that changes are going to be made.

Children that feel secure in their environment will make best use of the play and learning opportunities provided. They will usually separate happily from their parent, join in and participate well. They will progress in their development and in their ability to share and make relationships with other adults and children. Children who feel insecure may not like being left by their parent. They will be reluctant to join in with play and activities. They may cling to one particular person at the setting and have difficulty in relating to the other children and adults.

A sense of belonging

Children need to develop a sense of belonging. They will feel more at home in a setting that contains things that are personal, familiar to them and reflect their own experiences and culture.

- Each child should have a coat hook labelled with their name and perhaps a picture. Older children may have their own locker.
- Other equipment, such as work trays, work books, bags, lunch boxes, should be named.
- The imaginative play area should contain a range of equipment. A selection of different dolls should represent different facial features and skin tones, as well as male and female body parts. Cooking equipment and play food need to reflect different cultural preferences.
- The dressing-up clothes should be varied; hats, uniforms and different forms of dress should represent male, female and different cultures.
- The selection of books should show positive images of different races, cultures and sexes and reflect equality of opportunity.

Each child should have a coat hook labelled with their name

- The displays should contain the children's work and reflect their interests.
- Music should contain a selection that is suitable for the age of the children and be culturally diverse.

Predicting and recognising common stages of fear and anxiety

K2D71
K2D48
K2D49
K2D50
K2D51

It is common for babies and young children to develop fears and anxieties and change, as they grow older.

- Around the age of 6 months, babies show a preference to be with their parent/main carer and they begin to develop a fear of strangers.
- Babies can also develop fears of noisy objects, especially if they have been startled by them, for example a vacuum cleaner or telephone.
- Between 1 and 2 years of age, they may become frightened of things they previously enjoyed, for example the bath or having their hair washed.
- By 3 or 4 years of age, children begin to put themselves in the position of others. They can picture dangers that they have not actually experienced. It is common for young children to begin to develop imaginary fears and worries linked to their growing awareness of the world around them. These may include fear of the dark, dogs, or other animals.
- Older children may be anxious about coming into new situations. They may worry about whether they will be accepted and make friends. They may be anxious about the physical changes that they experience around puberty.

The effects of separation from their parent/main carer on children's behaviour

K2T67
K2D48
K2D49
K2D50
K2D51

Sudden change and separation that is not handled well by adults can have a powerful effect on children's behaviour.

- Babies and toddlers may protest by crying, screaming and other expressions of anger at being left. If their carer does not return, they may become listless and refuse to play.
- Children of 3–5 years may not want to play or explore their environment. They may become more demanding, unhappy and clingy.
- At 5–7 years, children may go back (regress) in their behaviour to earlier more childish behaviour. They may show stress by being overactive and unable to concentrate, or they may become quiet and withdrawn.
- Older children will not find separation so stressful. However they may be anxious and show this by becoming withdrawn or by being aggressive and refusing to participate.

Comforting children

K2D70
K2D71
K2D48
K2D49
K2D50
K2D51

Most young children who are afraid will cry and seek comfort from a caring adult. Some fears are shown in more subtle ways and a child may show signs of being generally anxious. Children in an unfamiliar environment may react in a variety of ways. They may show their fears by crying, clinging to their parent, being unwilling to try new experiences, loss of appetite, sleeping problems. As children cannot always tell the adult what is worrying them, the practitioner must try to identify the cause.

Dealing with the problem depends on the cause of the anxiety. Some children, including those with disabilities or special educational needs, may need more reassurance. So it is important to know about any special methods for helping individual children. Listening to what parents and carers tell you about this will help. Generally children will respond positively to:

- a clear and honest explanation about what is going to happen. You may need to repeat these explanations, as young children may not remember or understand what you have said

- a clear explanation of what has just happened, in the case of an unexpected incident

- stress-reducing activities like looking at books, painting, listening to music

- having their preferred comfort objects, such as a special blanket or soft toy. This is especially important for the under 2s. Young children should not be discouraged from having their preferred comfort objects as they help to bridge the gap between the home setting and the care environment. They also play an important part in helping children to become more confident and independent in new situations. Comfort objects should be readily available to children. It may be advisable to keep all comforters, labelled with the children's names, in a central place until they are needed. A list of comforters and particular remedies will be useful if this can be displayed where staff can see and readily refer to it

- talking things through. Older children will need opportunities to discuss their anxieties in confidence.

Changes and unexpected events

K2T67

Children can easily become unsettled and upset if there are changes to their routine or environment. This can be more upsetting if the changes are unexpected or not explained. It is important that children have advance warning of any changes that you know about. Practitioners can tell the children what is going to happen in simple and understandable terms. This will help to prevent anxiety. It is important that practitioners are positive and cheerful about any changes. This will be reassuring for the children. It will also be necessary to repeat and remind the children about what is going to happen.

One of the most upsetting changes for children can be when their key person leaves or is absent because of sickness or holiday. Whenever possible, children should be prepared for changes, but it is not possible to plan for unexpected events so the children will need to be reassured and comforted if they become distressed.

Offering reassurance

K2D71

Practitioners should be warm, caring and responsive. Children easily recognise those who value and appreciate their company and those who have no real interest in them. The following points can help if you are not confident and will give positive messages to the children in your care.

- Be calm and try to speak softly. Do not shout.
- Maintain eye contact when speaking to children and try to get down to their eye level, sit with them or squat down to them if they are playing on the floor.
- Meet their needs quickly. Pick up the non-verbal clues and anticipate their needs. For example, the child hopping from one foot to another may need the toilet.
- Encourage conversation and give children time to speak. Ask open questions that will encourage a child to answer with more than a yes or no.
- Make time for children and young people to talk with you.

Offer reassurance

Are you ready for assessment?

Maintain an environment that builds children's confidence and resilience

You need to show that you can competently maintain an environment that builds children's confidence and resilience. To do this you will need to be directly observed by your assessor and present other types of evidence. The amount and type of evidence you will need to present will vary. You should plan this with your assessor.

Direct observation by your assessor

Observation is the required assessment method to be used to evidence some part of each element in this unit. Expert witnesses could supply additional evidence. Your assessor will observe you in real work activities and this should provide most of the evidence for the performance criteria for the elements in this unit.

Preparing to be observed

You will need to show your assessor that you can support children coming into the setting, that you provide an environment that recognises children as individuals and recognises their achievements. You should show that you can encourage them to participate by helping them to become familiar with the setting. Explain routines to the children and explain any changes that may take place.

You should know about any comfort objects that the children in your setting have and that they are readily available as

appropriate to the child's stage of development and the parent's wishes. You should ensure that you provide items labelled for individual children, for example pegs, trays.

Equipment and materials should reflect cultural diversity. Check the imaginative play area for different cooking utensils, the range of dressing up clothes. Use examples of other languages from the children's own backgrounds on displays and in the selection of books provided.

Read the performance criteria and range carefully before your assessment. Try to cover as much as you can.

Other types of evidence

You will need to present different types of evidence to:

- cover criteria not observed by your assessor
- show that you have the required knowledge and understanding.

Support routines for children

K2D75
K2D48
K2D49
K2D50

Routines

Routines provide a structure to the day that the children can learn and recognise. For example, they will quickly learn about what happens when they arrive at the setting and other things that happen each day like snack time and group times. Providing a routine to the day will help children feel secure. As they become familiar with the structure of the day, they will become more confident as they recognise familiar routines and they will begin to know where they fit in. It is particularly important to young children that their familiar routines are not changed.

Exercise and physical play

K2D76

Children need to have the opportunity to exercise regularly each day. This may be planned exercise, such as physical activities at school or nursery, or naturally occurring opportunities, such as walking to nursery or school.

Physical play in childcare settings

All childcare settings provide opportunities for regular physical exercise and activities as part of the daily routine. It is important that these are planned with the child's age, stage of development and safety in mind.

At nursery, outdoor play with tricycles, prams, trolleys, large building blocks, dens, tyres and climbing frames may create an environment for imaginative physical activity. Using music to encourage movement by using the body to interpret the sounds will improve co-ordination and balance. Group activities may encourage children who lack confidence.

At primary school and secondary school, opportunities for exercise could include using the apparatus, dance, music and movement, football and other team games, throwing and catching activities, and swimming.

Children will sometimes have separate clothing to wear when doing physical activities. However, during outdoor play at nursery the children will be wearing their own outdoor clothes. It is important to make sure that clothing does not get in the way or make play dangerous. It may be necessary to adjust long skirts or tie up trailing scarves to avoid accidents. Some children may need to keep their limbs and bodies covered for cultural reasons, so it is important to be aware of this and enable the child to take part in activities safely.

There is more about physical play in Unit CCLD 206.

Children with limited physical play opportunities

When caring for children, it is important to remember that every child is an individual with specific needs. Some children may not achieve the level of physical ability expected for their age group, so they may need an individual programme that will help them to progress at their own pace. They may spend longer at each stage of development before moving on to the next. Special/individual needs should be viewed positively and each achievement should be encouraged and praised.

Fresh air

All children need regular exposure to fresh air and preferably an opportunity to play outside. The indoor play area should be well ventilated to provide fresh air. Fresh air provides oxygen and helps to prevent infections being spread.

Safety

When supporting children's exercise, it is very important to pay close attention to the safety of the children. Every setting will have health and safety procedures and you should make sure that you follow these in your work with the children. Look at Unit CCLD 202 for more information.

Accidents

Any accidents should be dealt with promptly. Look at Unit CCLD 202 for more information on first aid. Always follow the procedure of your setting. Seek help from a senior member of staff and remember to complete the accident form or accident book carefully.

Rest, sleep and quiet periods

K2D77
K2D48
K2D49

Children often have very busy lives and their days are filled with activity. Although children will be able to join in with stimulating activities for a period of time, they must also be allowed to rest. Whether the rest periods involve sleeping or just more restful and less demanding, quieter activities will depend on the age and stage of development of the child. It may also be important to take into account the parents' wishes especially where daytime sleeping is concerned. When planning for the children, practitioners should provide opportunities for rest and/or sleep as part of the routine of the day.

Give children the opportunity to play outside

Restful activities

Restful activities should be planned as part of the daily routine of the setting and a suitable area chosen where the children can relax. Quiet activities could include:

- story time in a suitable area perhaps in a curtained-off area of a bigger nursery or playgroup with some soft cushions to sit on
- a quiet time to look at books
- quiet conversation
- listening to suitable music in a quiet area
- play with small world toys in a quiet area.

Story time should be an opportunity for quiet relaxation

Children need not be stimulated all the time; it is sometimes useful for them to be given toys or activities that are relaxing and relatively easy to do.

Sleep

Everyone needs sleep but everyone has different requirements. Children need different amounts of sleep depending on their age and stage of development, and the amount of exercise taken.

Babies and young children will need a daytime sleep. There is more information about this in Unit CCLD 208.

The requirements of a balanced diet

K2S79
K2S81

Nutrients are different kinds of food. To be healthy, the body needs a combination of different nutrients. These nutrients are:

- protein
- fat
- carbohydrates
- vitamins
- minerals
- water
- fibre.

Protein, fat, carbohydrates and water are present in large quantities in the foods we eat and drink. Vitamins and minerals are only present in small quantities, so it is much more common for those to be lacking in a child's diet.

Vitamins and minerals

Vitamins and minerals are only present in small quantities in the foods we eat. They are essential for growth, development and normal functioning of the body. The tables on pages 165 and 166 show the main vitamins and minerals, which foods contain them and what they do in the body.

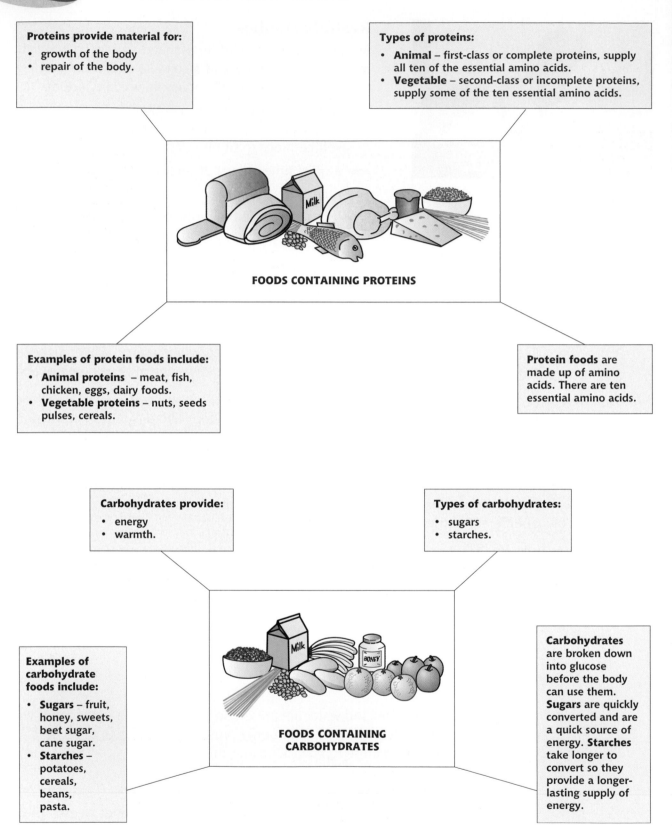

Proteins provide material for:
- growth of the body
- repair of the body.

Types of proteins:
- **Animal** – first-class or complete proteins, supply all ten of the essential amino acids.
- **Vegetable** – second-class or incomplete proteins, supply some of the ten essential amino acids.

FOODS CONTAINING PROTEINS

Examples of protein foods include:
- **Animal proteins** – meat, fish, chicken, eggs, dairy foods.
- **Vegetable proteins** – nuts, seeds pulses, cereals.

Protein foods are made up of amino acids. There are ten essential amino acids.

Carbohydrates provide:
- energy
- warmth.

Types of carbohydrates:
- sugars
- starches.

FOODS CONTAINING CARBOHYDRATES

Examples of carbohydrate foods include:
- **Sugars** – fruit, honey, sweets, beet sugar, cane sugar.
- **Starches** – potatoes, cereals, beans, pasta.

Carbohydrates are broken down into glucose before the body can use them. **Sugars** are quickly converted and are a quick source of energy. **Starches** take longer to convert so they provide a longer-lasting supply of energy.

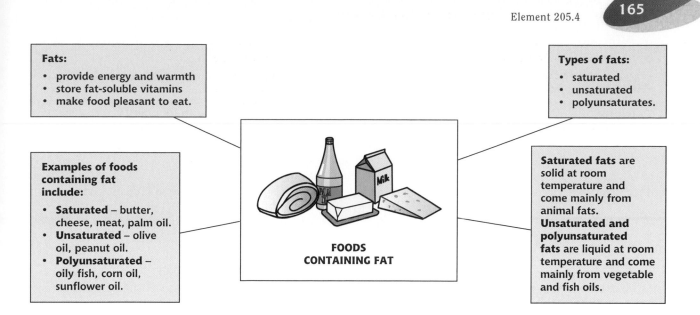

Fats:
- provide energy and warmth
- store fat-soluble vitamins
- make food pleasant to eat.

Types of fats:
- saturated
- unsaturated
- polyunsaturates.

Examples of foods containing fat include:
- **Saturated** – butter, cheese, meat, palm oil.
- **Unsaturated** – olive oil, peanut oil.
- **Polyunsaturated** – oily fish, corn oil, sunflower oil.

FOODS CONTAINING FAT

Saturated fats are solid at room temperature and come mainly from animal fats.
Unsaturated and polyunsaturated fats are liquid at room temperature and come mainly from vegetable and fish oils.

The main vitamins

Vitamin	Food Source	Function	Notes
A	Butter, cheese, eggs, carrots, tomatoes	Promotes healthy skin and good vision	Fat-soluble; can be stored in the liver. Deficiency causes skin infections, problems with vision. Avoid excess intake during pregnancy.
B	Fish, meat, liver, green vegetables, beans, eggs	Healthy working of muscles and nerves. Active in haemoglobin formation	Water-soluble, not stored in the body so a regular supply is needed. Deficiency results in muscle wasting, anaemia.
C	Fruits and fruit juices (especially orange and blackcurrant), green vegetables	Promotes healthy skin and tissue. Aids healing processes	Water-soluble, daily supply needed. Deficiency means less resistance to infection; extreme deficiency results in scurvy.
D	Oily fish, cod liver oil, egg yolk; added to margarines and to milk	Aids growth and maintenance of strong bones and teeth	Fat-soluble; can be stored by the body. Can be produced by the body by the action of sunlight on skin. Deficiency results in bones failing to harden and dental decay.
E	Vegetable oils, cereals, egg yolk, nuts and seeds	Promotes healing, aids blood clotting and fat metabolism	Fat-soluble; can be stored by the body.
K	Green vegetables, liver, whole grains	Needed for normal blood clotting, aids healing	Fat-soluble; can be stored by the body. Deficiency may result in delayed clotting, excessive bleeding.

The main minerals

Mineral	Food Source	Function	Notes
Calcium	Cheese, eggs, fish, pulses	Essential for growth of bones and teeth	Works with Vitamin D. Deficiency means that bones fail to harden (rickets) and leads to dental decay.
Fluoride	Occurs naturally in water or may be added to water, tooth-paste, drops and tablets	Makes tooth enamel more resistant to decay	There are arguments for and against adding fluoride to the water supply.
Iodine	Water, seafoods, vegetables, added to salt	Needed for proper working of the thyroid gland	Deficiency results in disturbance in the function of the thyroid gland.
Iron	Meat, green vegetables, eggs, liver, dried fruit, (esp. apricots, prunes, raisins)	Needed for the formation of haemoglobin in red blood cells	Vitamin C helps the absorption of iron. Deficiency results in anaemia, causing lack of energy.
Phosphorus	Fish, meat, eggs, fruit and vegetables	Formation of bones and teeth, helps absorption of carbohydrate	High intake is harmful to babies.
Potassium	Meat, milk, cereals, fruit and vegetables	Helps to maintain fluid balance	Deficiency is rare as potassium is found in a wide range of foods.
Sodium chloride	Table salt, fish, meat, bread, processed foods	Needed for fluid balance, formation of cell fluids, blood, sweat, tears	Salt should not be added to food prepared for babies and young children.

Fibre

Fibre is found in plants and adds bulk, or roughage, to food and stimulates the muscles of the bowel. This encourages the body to pass out the waste products left after digestion of food.

Water

Water is an important part of diet. It contains some minerals, but its main role is to maintain fluid in the cells and blood stream.

A balanced diet

A well balanced diet means that the food eaten provides all the nutrients that the body needs in the right quantities. To do this, a variety of foods should be eaten every day so that there will be no deficiency of a particular nutrient. A balanced diet gives children the opportunity to choose foods that they like and to taste new foods.

Proportions of nutrients

Children are growing all the time, so they need large amounts of protein to help them grow. They are also using a lot of energy, so they need carbohydrate in the form of starches. In addition, they will need adequate supplies of vitamins and minerals.

Suggested daily intakes are as follows:

- two portions (helpings) of meat, fish or other vegetable protein foods, such as nuts and pulses
- two portions of protein from dairy products such as milk, cheese, yoghurt (for vegans substitute two other protein foods from plant sources)
- four portions of starchy carbohydrate foods, such as bread, pasta, potatoes, sweet potatoes, breakfast cereals
- five portions of fruit and vegetables
- six drinks of fluid, especially water.

Begin with small portions. The size of the portions will get bigger as the child grows and can eat more.

Select the best quality food that you can. For example, choose wholemeal bread rather than white and select fresh fruit and vegetables.

Look at Unit CCLD 208 for information about feeding babies and younger children.

Diets of different groups

K2S81

Each region or country has developed its own local diet over many years. Diets are based on available foods, which in turn depend on climate, geography and agricultural patterns, as well as social factors such as religion, culture, class and lifestyle. Each diet contains a balance of essential nutrients.

Diet is a part of peoples' way of life and the importance of familiar food should never be overlooked.

Religious aspects of food

For some people, food has a spiritual significance. Certain foods may not be eaten. Respecting an individual's culture and religious choices is part of respecting that individual as a whole. Talking to parents and carers about food requirements is important for practitioners, especially when caring for a child from a cultural or religious background different from your own.

Religious restrictions may affect the diets of Hindus, Sikhs, Muslims, Jews, Rastafarians and Seventh Day Adventists. Members of other groups may also have dietary restrictions.

People are individuals and will vary in what they eat and what restrictions they observe; you should be aware of this when discussing diet with parents. It is not possible here to make blanket statements about the diets of different groups, only to suggest things that may be important and which practitioners may find useful to know about.

Dietary principles of different groups

Group	Dietary Principles
Hindus	Many devout Hindus are vegetarian. Hindus eat no beef and drink no alcohol.
Muslims	May not eat pork or pork products. Alcohol is not permitted.
Jews	May not eat pork or shellfish. All other meat must be Kosher. Milk and meat are not used together in cooking.
Rastafarians	Mainly vegetarian. Whole foods are preferred. No products of the vine are eaten.
Christians	May avoid eating meat at certain times. Some foods may be given up in Lent.

It is very important to take account of these points when preparing activities involving food. If you are setting up a baking activity, for example, it would be best to make sure that you use vegetable fats. These are generally more acceptable. Many more people today are moving towards a vegetarian diet or a diet that includes fewer animal products.

Food allergy and dietary deficiencies

K2S82

Food allergy and food intolerance may be caused by a number of factors including an **allergic response** or an **enzyme** deficiency, such as coeliac disease or diabetes. These children will need a special diet.

Children may be allergic to some foods, for example nuts or milk. It is very important that staff are fully informed about any allergies to food that the children have. **Always check before giving food and drinks to babies and children.** If children are not allowed certain foods or drinks, this should be made clear to all staff. Notices in the kitchen and in the room where the children are cared for should clearly display this information. Information about children's allergies to food or drink must be regularly updated. This must be discussed with the parents when a child is admitted and at regular intervals afterwards to keep staff fully informed about any changes.

There is more about feeding younger children in Unit CCLD 208.

Social interaction at mealtimes

Mealtimes are a good opportunity for families and other groups to tell each other their news and ideas as they eat together. It is good if adults and children sit together at the table without other distractions.

Illness

Children who are not feeling well may not have much appetite and may refuse food, or not eat very much. This is quite usual and appetite will return when the child feels better. However, it is important that the child drinks plenty, so encourage drinking, preferably water and clear fluids, such as water-diluted fruit juices, and as much as the child will take.

Food refusal

Refusing to eat food provided and making a fuss about food at mealtimes is common. It is important to check that the child is of normal body weight and height and that the doctor has identified no medical condition. It is important that mealtimes should not become a battleground so practitioners should:

- offer food at mealtimes only
- avoid snacks between meals
- encourage children to take part in family and group mealtimes
- allow the child to eat independently
- not fuss about any mess when children are learning to eat independently
- remove any remaining food without fuss
- make mealtimes a pleasant experience.

Allow children to eat independently

Food additives

Additives are added to foods to add colour, give flavour or preserve the food. Permitted food additives are given an E number and are listed on the label. For some children different behaviour may be associated with additives in food.

To reduce additives in the diet:

- use fresh foods as often as you can
- make your own pies, cakes, soups
- look at the labels: the ingredients are listed.

Practical Example

Looking at the labels on food

Marian looks after Laurie and Anna. She needs to give the children lunch and, as she hasn't got time to shop, she will be using food from the fridge and freezer. Laurie's family is vegetarian and Anna is allergic to food colourings. Marian finds some fish fingers in the freezer and some chocolate puddings in the fridge. This is what the labels say:

Fishfingers:
Nutritional information

Protein   3.9 g
Carbohydrate   4.0 g
Fat   2.2 g
Fibre   0.3 g
No artificial colouring or flavouring

Chocolate pudding:
Ingredients:
Skimmed milk
Sugar
Chocolate
Vegetable oil
Beef gelatine

➤ *Will Marian be able to give the food to Laurie?*
➤ *Will Marian be able to give the food to Anna?*
➤ *Explain the reasons for your answers.*

Preparing food

K2S78

Food must be handled and prepared hygienically. Always:

- wash your hands well before touching food
- cover any cuts with a waterproof dressing
- wear an apron and tie hair back when preparing food
- avoid touching your nose and mouth, or coughing and sneezing in the food preparation area
- disinfect and replace kitchen cloths and sponges often
- disinfect all work surfaces regularly and especially before preparing food
- teach children these rules.

Cooking

To keep food safe it is very important to cook it properly. Always:

- defrost frozen food thoroughly before cooking
- cook foods like chicken and meat thoroughly – make sure that it is cooked through to the middle.
- prepare raw meat separately – use a separate board and knife
- ensure cooked food is cooled quickly and then refrigerated or frozen
- cover any food standing in the kitchen
- keep raw foods and cooked foods separate in the fridge
- ensure eggs are thoroughly cooked before eating – for babies and small children, cook the eggs until the white and yolk are solid
- remember that cooked food should only be reheated once – reheat until very hot all the way through
- reheat cooked chilled meals all the way through.

It is important that children learn the basic rules about handling food. Always make sure that they wash their hands before eating. If children prepare food as part of a learning activity, the food safety rules should always be followed. Children need to understand why this is important, so explain why they need to follow these rules.

Care of children's skin and hair

Personal hygiene

K2S83

Personal hygiene is all about keeping clean and includes washing, bathing, hair washing and teeth cleaning. All children need adult help and supervision as they learn to keep themselves clean. Good standards of hygiene in childhood are important because they help to:

- prevent disease and the spread of infection
- prepare children for life by teaching them how to care for themselves and become independent.

The routines in any childcare setting should maintain good standards of hygiene. There will be routines to encourage children to use the toilet regularly and to wash their hands after using the toilet and before eating, drinking or touching food.

To support hygiene routines always:

- check the bathroom and toilet area before the children use it to make sure that it is safe and clean
- check that there is enough soap and towels and that the hand driers are working
- supervise the children and give help when needed
- check the water in the hot tap is not too hot to be used safely
- provide steps to help children reach the sink if necessary
- ensure each child has sufficient time and privacy to use the toilet
- make sure that children wash their hands properly and dry them thoroughly
- encourage the children to put paper towels in the correct bins and that bins are properly covered
- leave the area clean and tidy
- use the protective clothing provided, for example aprons, gloves, if you are handling any bodily waste.

Caring routines for children's skin and hair

- Wash the hands and face first thing in the morning.
- Keep the nails short. This will prevent dirt collecting under them.
- A daily bath or shower. Dry the skin thoroughly, especially between the toes and in the skin creases to prevent soreness and cracking.
- If a daily bath is not possible, a thorough wash is good enough. Remember to encourage children to wash their bottoms after the face, neck, hands and feet.
- Observe the skin for rashes and soreness.
- Black skin and other dry skin types need moisturising. Putting oil in the bath water and massaging oil or moisturisers into the skin afterwards helps to prevent dryness.
- Hair usually needs to be washed two or three times a week. More often if parents wish.
- Rinse shampoo out thoroughly in clean water. Conditioners may be useful for hair that is difficult to comb.
- Black curly hair may need hair oil applying daily to prevent dryness and hair breakage. Use a wide toothed comb with rounded ends on the teeth. Take care to comb carefully without pulling.
- All skin types need protecting from the sun. Use a sun block or high factor sun cream and keep a close eye on the length of time children spend in the sun. Make sure that children wear sun hats.

A daily bath is good for active toddlers

Teeth

Teeth may appear at any time during the first two years of life. They usually begin to appear during the first year and come through in the same order as shown in the illustration, but this may vary.

The first 20 teeth are often called the **milk teeth**, and they will usually be complete by the age of 3 years. From 5–6 years, these teeth begin to fall out as the adult

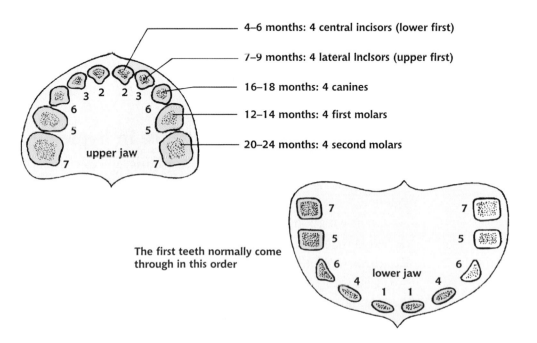

4–6 months: 4 central incisors (lower first)

7–9 months: 4 lateral incisors (upper first)

16–18 months: 4 canines

12–14 months: 4 first molars

20–24 months: 4 second molars

upper jaw

The first teeth normally come through in this order

lower jaw

(permanent) teeth come through. There are 32 **permanent teeth**, and the care they are given in childhood will help them to last a lifetime.

Care of the teeth

Provide a soft toothbrush for a baby to use and become familiar with. Give them the opportunity to watch adults and other children clean their teeth. When the first tooth does appear, try to clean it gently with a small, soft brush. Ensure that cleaning the teeth becomes a habit: in the morning after breakfast and after the last drink or snack before bed. Cleaning the teeth after meals should be encouraged, but this may not always be possible.

Ensure that cleaning the teeth becomes a daily habit

Encourage healthy teeth and prevent tooth decay by providing a healthy diet that is high in calcium and vitamins and low in sugar. Avoid giving sweet drinks to babies and children, especially in a bottle as this coats the gums and teeth in sugar and encourages decay. Sugar can also get into the gum and cause decay before the teeth come through. If you need to feed a child between meals, avoid sugary snacks. Provide food that needs to be chewed and improves the health of the gums and teeth, like apples, carrots and bread.

Visit the dentist regularly. A child who attends with an adult, and then has their own appointments, will feel more confident about this. Prepare children for their dental appointments by explaining what will happen and introducing play visits to the dentist. Never pass on any adult feelings of worry about the dentist.

Encouraging independence in hygiene

Children need to be able to learn to keep themselves clean. There are several ways in which practitioners can encourage a child to develop independence in personal hygiene:

- Provide a good example yourself.
- Have routines that encourage cleanliness from early babyhood.
- Make bath-time fun: use toys in the bath, cups and containers, sinkers and floaters.
- Provide children with their own flannel, toothbrush, hairbrush, etc. that they have chosen themselves.

Hygiene is important

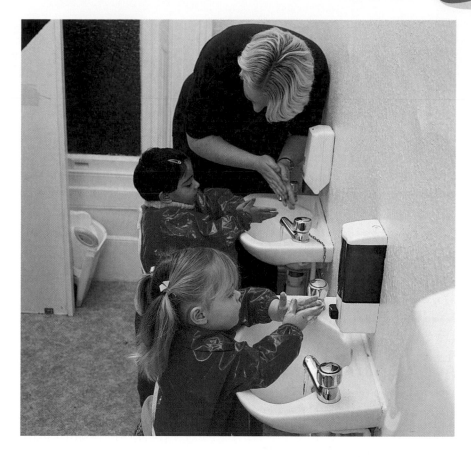

- Encourage children to wash themselves and participate at bath time. Let them brush their hair with a soft brush and comb with rounded teeth.
- Provide a step so that they can reach the basin to wash and clean teeth.
- Allow time for the children to complete the tasks without rushing.

Health education

Children need to learn about their bodies and why it is important to be clean and healthy. Some children will need help as they carry out personal hygiene routines like bathing, hand washing, teeth cleaning. This gives you time to discuss why these activities are important to keep children healthy and safe from infection. This is also a good opportunity to talk about parts of the body and bodily functions with the children. How much you can talk about will depend on the age and development of the children.

Observation

Supporting children's personal hygiene routines will also give practitioners opportunities to observe the children for any signs of infection or abuse. Any sign of injury or infection, such as rashes, sore patches, bruising, blood in children's pants or knickers, should be reported promptly to your senior staff member. The accident/incident book should be completed promptly and accurately.

Element 205.4

Are you ready for assessment?

Support routines for children

You need to show that you can competently support routines for children. To do this you will need to be directly observed by your assessor and present other types of evidence. The amount and type of evidence you will need to present will vary. You should plan this with your assessor.

Direct observation by your assessor

Observation is the required assessment method to be used to evidence some part of each element in this unit. Expert witnesses could supply additional evidence. Your assessor will observe you in real work activities and this should provide most of the evidence for the performance criteria for the elements in this unit.

Preparing to be observed

You will need to arrange to take part in organising the daily routines in your setting. This will include physical play, indoor and outdoor activities and children's quiet periods.

You will need to arrange to take part in indoor and outdoor activities that provide opportunities for children's physical exercise. It will help with your assessment if you write a plan for the physical play session beforehand so that you know what equipment you will need to provide and what you will be doing during the session. Drawing a plan of the equipment and where it will be placed may also help you. Make sure that the equipment and activities you select are suitable for the ages of the children involved. Check and set out any equipment carefully, and make sure you use the space you have effectively. For example, you may wish to restrict the wheeled toys to a certain area well away from any ball games. During the session you should supervise the children carefully. This is usually a team effort, but make sure that you know what your responsibilities are. Support and encourage the children so that they get maximum benefit from the session and that they move on and develop their skills. For example, a child using the balancing beam for the first time may well need help or for you to be nearby, but after a few successful attempts may feel confident enough to try by themselves.

Quiet periods are likely to be planned as part of the routine of the day or session. You will need to ensure that you can show your assessor how quiet periods are planned as part of the day and show how they meet the children's developmental and physical needs. You should be aware of how your setting takes account of any of the parents' wishes. Find this out if you don't already know. While you are supporting the children when they are sleeping or during quieter activities, you will need to ensure that a relaxed atmosphere is maintained and keep distractions to a minimum. Check that any equipment you use is safe and that ventilation and temperature are correctly maintained.

►

Your assessor will need to see you supporting children's personal care. This will include taking children to the toilet or supervising them at this time. This may be before snack or lunch-time. Make sure that you have checked the toilet area to make sure that it is clean and that there are enough towels and soap. Give help to the children if they need it and use the opportunity to talk to them about personal hygiene and why it is important. Avoid rushing the children, but make sure that they wash and dry their hands thoroughly. Check that the area is left clean and tidy and that bins are properly covered.

You will need to arrange to help children when eating and drinking at a mealtime or snack time. Ensure that you prepare the area where children will eat and drink by making sure that all the tables and utensils are clean and that there are enough suitable aprons and bibs if needed. Provide enough chairs of a suitable size and height for the children to be seated comfortably. Make sure that suitable cups, plates, bowls are provided so that the children can feed and help themselves. Create a relaxed atmosphere so that this is an enjoyable time.

Read the performance criteria and range carefully before your assessment. Try to cover as much as you can.

Other types of evidence

You will need to present different types of evidence in order to:

• cover criteria not observed by your assessor

• show that you have the required knowledge and understanding.

Reflecting on your practice

- How do you help children to manage change in your setting? Think of some examples of how you have helped children when changes were made. **K2T67**

- What are the rules in your setting that make sure you handle food safely? **K2S78**

- How do you encourage children to take part in making decisions and taking responsibility in your setting? **K2D61**

- Think of an example to show how activities are arranged to meet the children's needs in your setting?

- How are children's efforts and achievements recognised in your setting? **K2D63**

Support children's play and learning

This unit is about supporting children's learning through play. It explores the value of play in helping children learn. It identifies your own role within play activities and experiences. The scope of this unit is broad and you will find references to other units in this book to give you further information.

This unit contains five elements:

⌒ *CCLD 206.1 Participate in activities to encourage communication and language*

⌒ *CCLD 206.2 Provide opportunities for children's drama and imaginative play*

⌒ *CCLD 206.3 Encourage children to be creative*

⌒ *CCLD 206.4 Support physical play and exercise*

⌒ *CCLD 206.5 Encourage children to explore and investigate.*

This unit will also provide underpinning knowledge for CCLD 203, as follows:

⌒ *K2D49.7, K2D49.8, K2D49.9, K2D49.10, K2D49.11, K2D49.13, K2D49.15*

⌒ *K2D50.7, K2D50.8, K2D50.9, K2D50.10*

⌒ *K2D51.7, K2D51.9, K2D51.11.*

The national standards for this unit include a list of key words and explanations that you need to understand. You should read this carefully as you plan the activities for your assessment. Your assessor can help you to make sure that you are interpreting the standards correctly.

⌒ Introduction

K2D89

All elements of this unit require an understanding of the importance of play in promoting children's development. Play is the most appropriate medium to provide for all aspects of children's learning and development.

Why is play important?

- Play occurs naturally in children. It is a way for children to acquire and practise knowledge, skills and concepts in situations that are open-ended and enjoyable.

- Play cannot be wrong. It therefore provides a safe situation for the child to try out new things without fear of failure. This is important in promoting positive self-esteem.

- Play provides the opportunity for repetition. One of the important ways that learning takes place is through repetition.
- Play provides an opportunity for extending learning. A carefully structured play environment allows for learning across a wide ability range. For example, exploring sand may provide a soothing sensory experience but can also provide an opportunity to learn about capacity and volume.
- Play is always at the child's own level, so the needs of all children within the group can be met.

The development of social play

How children play within the group follows a developmental pattern. As children learn and develop social skills, these are taken into account in their play. It is difficult to link these stages directly with ages as progress through the stages will depend upon having the opportunity to play with other children.

- *Solitary play* This is an early stage of play. Children play alone and take little notice of other children.
- *Parallel play* A child plays side-by-side with another child but without interacting. They may share space, possibly equipment but their play remains independent of each other.
- *Associative play* Here play begins with other children. Children make intermittent interactions and/or are involved in the same activity although their play remains personal.
- *Co-operative play* Here children are able to play together co-operatively. They are able to adopt a role within the group and to take account of others' needs and actions. At this stage, they will begin to understand and keep to simple rules.

The development of social play

Curriculum frameworks

K2D88

Planning for play will need to take into account any statutory requirements for the curriculum. Any setting receiving public funding (nursery grant) for the education of 3- and 4-year-olds must follow the Curriculum Guidance for the Foundation Stage (QCA, 2000), which focuses on children's progress towards the Early Learning Goals. These goals are across six areas of learning:

- personal, social and emotional development
- communication, language and literacy
- mathematical development
- knowledge and understanding of the world
- physical development
- creative development.

In maintained schools, including maintained special schools, the National Curriculum must be followed. The Foundation Stage curriculum is applied in reception classes, and key stage 1 of the National Curriculum is followed in Years 1 and 2 of primary school.

Birth to Three Matters: A Framework to Support Children in their Earliest Years (DfES/Sure Start, 2002) was published with the intention to inform and develop the practice of those who work with the youngest children. The framework focuses on four aspects as a way of approaching and understanding how to provide for the growth, learning and development of very young children. These aspects are:

- a strong child
- a skilful communicator
- a competent learner
- a healthy child.

For more about *Birth to Three Matters*, see Unit CCLD 208.

Working with children when English is not their first language

K2D86

So much of what a child learns comes from his or her interactions and communications with the adults and other children in your setting. Therefore, where children have difficulty interacting because they are **bilingual** (use two languages) or **multilingual** (use more than two languages), you must make extra efforts to make sure that play and learning is available to them. Some children will learn English alongside another language, or languages. Others may have heard very little English. It is an important part of your role to show respect for every child's cultural background, and this includes giving children the opportunity to develop and use their home language as well as English. Some points to remember:

- Just as you would for any child in your setting, find out about the child's home life and language by speaking to the family. Use an interpreter if necessary. Your line manager will be able to contact the Children's Information Service for advice.

- Use the settling in time to work with the parent. Use gestures and positive body language to show both child and adult that you want to interact with them. Build a relationship with the child so that you can fully support his/her play and learning. Encourage the parent to explain routines and activities to the child in his/her home language.

- Learn key words from the child's main language and use them often. Children need to develop their home language as well as English and they should be encouraged in this. Teach key words to the other children in the setting. This will encourage an interest in languages from an early age.

- Many children using more than one language will go through 'quiet phases', while they begin to understand the differences between different language systems. During this time you should be celebrating the smallest efforts to communicate, talking to them as usual and not trying to force them into speaking aloud. Rest assured that they will be 'taking it all in'!

- Children learn best through talking and listening with others, so make sure the child is playing with other children and joining in with a wide range of activities.

The adult's role in play

K2D85
K2D108
K2D109

Adults have an important role in children's play to ensure that the maximum benefit is gained from it. The adult needs to plan and set up the activities carefully, interact with the children during the activity and monitor what is happening through observation.

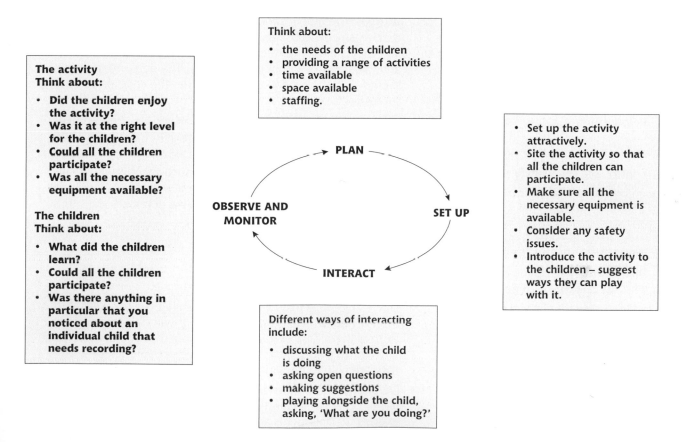

The activity
Think about:

- Did the children enjoy the activity?
- Was it at the right level for the children?
- Could all the children participate?
- Was all the necessary equipment available?

The children
Think about:

- What did the children learn?
- Could all the children participate?
- Was there anything in particular that you noticed about an individual child that needs recording?

Think about:

- the needs of the children
- providing a range of activities
- time available
- space available
- staffing.

- Set up the activity attractively.
- Site the activity so that all the children can participate.
- Make sure all the necessary equipment is available.
- Consider any safety issues.
- Introduce the activity to the children – suggest ways they can play with it.

PLAN

SET UP

OBSERVE AND MONITOR

INTERACT

Different ways of interacting include:

- discussing what the child is doing
- asking open questions
- making suggestions
- playing alongside the child, asking, 'What are you doing?'

The adult's role in play

What you need to do/think about Plan	Why this is important
• The needs of the children	• Different children will need different activities and experiences to help them learn. The activities provided must meet the needs of the children in the group.
• Providing a range of activities	• Children need to participate in many different activities to develop all the different skills/concepts and attitudes necessary. All activities and experiences will need to be repeated many times so that the children have the opportunity to practice and develop their emerging skills.
• Time available Space available Staffing	• For activities and experiences to be successful the appropriate time space and staffing needs to be considered. This will be different for each activity/experience. Children need a balance between free play and adult directed play.
Setting up the activity • Set up the activity attractively.	• Children are more likely to participate in an activity that looks inviting.
• Site the activity so that all children can participate	• All children should be able to participate in all activities. Careful consideration needs to be given to where and how activities are provided so that children who have particular needs can participate in the usual way.
• Make sure all the necessary equipment is available	• Children will need to be able to participate in the activity without searching for tools and equipment. They will learn more easily because their concentration will be encouraged and they will feel satisfied at having completed a task if they are able to work without distractions. The equipment provided should also be of a good quality so that the children can use it successfully.
• Consider any safety issues	• Safety issues need to be considered before the children begin the activity. You are responsible for the children's health and safety.
• Introduce the activity to the children – suggest ways in which they can play with it	• Many activities will need some introduction. This will mean that the children are aware of different ways to play with the activity. They will also have been shown necessary skills to be successful at the activity.
Interaction during the activity Different ways that you can interact with the children include: • Discussing the activity with the children	• Discussing the activity will enable the children to think carefully about what they are doing. It will help them to express their ideas verbally. It will show that you are interested in what they are doing and it will give you an idea of what they are able to do and not do.
• Asking open ended questions	• Open-ended questions are questions that require more than a yes or no answer. Questions like this encourage children to express their thoughts and ideas.

- Making suggestions of different ways to play with the activity

- Playing alongside the children and describing what you are doing

- Children need to play at the same thing over and over again because repetition will help them to learn. However, they will eventually need to move on to the next stage of learning.
- Joining in their play, and either making suggestions or playing alongside them to show them what to do, will encourage children to develop their skills and concepts further.

Observation and monitoring

The activity

- Did the children enjoy it?

- Was it at the right level for the children?

- Could all the children participate?

- Was all the necessary equipment available?

The activity

- It is important that the activities that are provided enable the children to practice their existing skills and develop new skills/concepts.
- Observing and monitoring exactly what children learned at an activity will mean that the activities planned are always appropriate for the children's level of understanding.
- Were there any reasons why certain children couldn't participate? It is vital that children who have particular needs are able to join in all the activities provided. This may mean very careful consideration of where and what to provide.
- Children will quickly lose interest if they have to keep stopping to find tools and equipment. So that they can concentrate and learn and develop all the necessary skills and concepts things need to be readily available and in good condition.

The children

- What did the children learn?

- Could all the children participate?

- Was there anything that you noticed about an individual child that needs recording?

The children

- It is important to know what individual children learned and also what the children learned from the activity (this may not be what you intended them to learn) so that future activities are appropriate for them. It is also important to monitor the progress that individual children are making.
- All children need to participate in a wide range of activities so that they have the experiences necessary to learn. Some children's needs may limit their ability to participate in certain activities, for example, physical or learning difficulties, lack of confidence. The staff in the setting must observe when this is happening and make sure that changes are made to give all children equal access to the activities.
- Individual children's learning needs to be noted and sometimes recorded so that further activities and experiences can move them onto the next step. Where there are issues around children's behaviour these too will need to be observed and perhaps recorded.

Participate in activities to encourage communication and language

K2D110

Language and communication are perhaps the most important skills that children need to develop. Children will not be able to become independent, confident people if they are unable to explain their thoughts, feelings and ideas. They will learn how to use language by listening to you and the other adults and children around them. You are therefore a very important role model and every time a child hears you talking, they will be learning from you.

It can be quite daunting to think about this. Everything you do or say will have an impact. It is not just while you are sitting down at an activity with children that you need to be aware of this, because you cannot separate the 'play and learning' from the 'caring and supervising'. You will be communicating with children while they eat, attend to their personal hygiene, move between activities – all the time, from the moment they arrive until the moment they leave.

The main points to remember when communicating with children are:

- Don't just talk – remember to listen.
- Stop what you are doing in order to give children your undivided attention.
- Use what you know about the child and the family to maintain and extend conversation.
- Don't just ask questions. Give something of yourself to the child – it's OK to chat.
- When you do ask questions, show that you are interested in the answer through your body language, eye contact and voice.
- If you want to extend children's language and communication skills, you will need to use new vocabulary in the correct way so that children will understand and learn from you.
- Questions should be 'open' – not yes/no answers.
- Make sure you are a good role model for language skills.
- Take every opportunity to communicate with children – not just during activities, but during the normal daily routines as well.
- Choose the most appropriate method of communication for the individual child.
- Provide opportunities for children to see words and make their own written communications. You can do this by labelling the environment, using name cards, sharing big books and having a well-stocked book corner. Mark-making can be encouraged by having a writing corner, leaving pencils and paper in the home corner and letting the children see you writing in context – making lists and writing letters, for example.

You will find more information about the way you should communicate with children in Unit CCLD 201. This includes information about your body language, how to talk to children and using questions and language to extend children's understanding.

Communicating together in play

K2D90
K2D107
K2D108

It is important that practitioners frequently provide activities and experiences that encourage children to play co-operatively and purposefully with others. Play is very effective in helping children to communicate and use language.

Between 1 and 3 years of age, children need increasing social contact with adults and children. By the time they are 3 years old, many children are capable of taking account of other people's actions and needs. They are able to co-operate with others by taking on a role in a group. They are becoming confident and competent communicators and will continue to develop these skills with the support and encouragement of the adults in the setting.

As they get older, they need to be given more responsibilities within the setting. They can make choices, not only about their own activities, but also about routines. Children's input into the setting's plans will be invaluable in helping you to meet their needs and develop their interests. Practitioners should know which activities, both indoors and outdoors, encourage children to play and communicate. They should encourage children by praising and rewarding them for positive behaviour. They need activities that promote the use of all their senses. They should have access to resources and equipment that stimulate every area of development. These activities include:

- imaginative play experiences, sometimes in role play areas such as a home corner, shops, a hospital, vets or garden centre
- games that involve working in pairs or in a group, which help children to share and take turns, including board, dice, card and computer games

Play is very effective in helping children to relate to each other

Games that involve working in a group help children to communicate

- children helping to prepare activities, for example they can help to put resources out and clear them away, prepare and share meals and snacks

- using resources co-operatively, for example, collage and making models, sand and water play and using a computer

- the exploration and investigation of objects and events in a group, including group discussions, looking at natural and made objects. Some of these may be brought from home.

- opportunities for children to talk and listen to each other and to share their experiences, including having agreed codes of conduct when taking turns, speaking and listening to each other.

Music and movement

K2D90

Children need many opportunities to listen and respond to music, and to make their own music. For most children, the aim of these early musical experiences is to develop an interest in music and to become aware of music as a means of communication and self-expression.

Songs, rhymes and music for young children include:

- listening to music
- moving to music
- learning and enjoying songs and rhymes
- making music.

Listening

- Make listening to music part of every day. Introduce a wide range of musical styles to the children. Choose music that is culturally diverse, classical and contemporary. Encourage children to request music and to bring in music from home. Choose pieces that are not too long and repeat them often so that the children become familiar with them. Identify the characteristics of the music – pace, tone, pitch – and listen for repeated phrases.

- Provide a listening centre using cassette/CD players. Again, provide a range of music for the children to listen to. Taped stories and poetry are also very enjoyable, and encourage careful listening.

- Invite people in to play musical instruments or to tell stories, possibly a parent or older child. Include a range of instruments and stories from different cultural and music traditions.

Give children an opportunity to make their own music

Moving to music

- Create a mood with music. Choose sad music, cheerful music, frightening music, etc. and get the children to respond.
- Set a scene with music. A mixture of sounds and tunes can represent, for example, the sea or a rainforest.
- Use music to tell a story. Different pieces of music can be associated with characters and events in a story. Favourites include *Peter and the Wolf* (Prokofiev) and *The Carnival of the Animals* (Saint-Saëns).
- Give children an opportunity to respond physically to music. They need time and space to develop confidence in dance. Involve all children but be sensitive to less confident children.
- Introduce children to different styles of dance. Community dance groups will often perform for children.

Learning and enjoying songs and rhymes

- Teach children rhymes and songs.
- Include actions with the rhymes and songs. This will help the children to learn them.
- Choose many different types of rhymes and songs – traditional, funny, number, rhyming and not rhyming – from all over the world.
- During song time, try to balance traditional songs and rhymes with newer ones. Leave time for requests so that the children can choose their favourites.
- Show children the rhythm in songs and rhymes through clapping and simple percussion accompaniment.
- Get children to use their voices musically, high and low voices, long and short, loud and soft.

Making music

- Encourage children to make simple instruments – to shake, pluck, blow and scrape. Provide a range of materials for the children to use so they can recreate the sounds they have heard instruments make.

- Provide commercially-made instruments for the children to use alongside their home-made ones. Try to represent all musical traditions.

- Explore music made from body sounds – clapping, clicking, tapping – and listen carefully to different voice sounds.

- Provide opportunities for children to experiment and discover how to make sounds, and then to change them. For example, a bottle half-filled with water will make a different sound when tapped to one that is half-filled with sand.

- Use music to accompany stories – create a mood from music.

- Hold musical conversations where children respond to each other with instruments or clapping. Get them to repeat and then create musical patterns, taking turns as in a conversation.

- Let children tape their music to listen to, to play to parents or to use at storytime or in their play.

Using specific language to support learning

K2D85
K2D92

There will be times in your setting when there is an opportunity to use new language when working with children. This might be during specific activities or during daily routines. For example, snack time provides lots of opportunities for maths – *how many cups*, *more* or *less*, *full* or *empty*. You should use these words and ask questions to encourage the children to use them. It is much more valuable to children's understanding to use real-life situations because they will have the direct experience and will therefore understand the concept and vocabulary better. A routine such as snack time is also repeated daily, allowing the children to reinforce the learning daily.

Developing children's curiosity and encouraging them to ask questions, experiment and draw their own conclusions provides the basis for scientific understanding. By providing activities for children to investigate, experiment and ask questions, you will be encouraging this learning. Take part in it yourself, ask questions aloud, such as 'I wonder why . . .?', 'What happens if . . .?', 'How can I . . .?'. This will encourage the children to think in this way too.

Practical daily activities and routines

K2D107
K2D110

Involving children in practical daily routines and activities, such as cooking or gardening, will help children to develop a sense of responsibility for each other and their environment. It will also provide opportunities for them to develop and learn. These activities can be linked to the setting's theme, to stories and rhymes or to celebrations and festivals. For example, planting bulbs in the spring, baking currant buns for snack time or making Khatai (Indian sweets) to celebrate Diwali when sweets are traditionally exchanged – the recipe for this is below.

Learning through cooking activities

Darren was making Khatai in the cooking area, using the recipe card below. He had mixed the ingredients together and was dividing the mixture into the small cases.

Nursery nurse:	How many sweets are you going to make?
Darren:	(touching each case as he counts) Twelve.
Nursery nurse:	Have you made some already?
Darren:	Yes, five.
Nursery nurse:	How many more do you have to make?
Darren:	(counts empty cases) Seven.

He continued to fill the cases until the mixture was all gone. He noticed that some of the cases contained lots of mixture while others contained very little.

Darren:	No one will want those little ones.

He moved some of the mixture from the full cases to the less full cases.

➤ *What did Darren show that he knew about counting and size?* **K2D107**

➤ *What was the role of the nursery nurse here?* **K2D108**

➤ *How could you have developed this activity to enhance other aspects of Darren's learning?* **K2D92, K2D108**

➤ *What other routines occur in your setting and how do they help children's learning?* **K2D110**

Simple recipe cards can be used with children

Element 206.1

Are you ready for assessment?

Participate in activities to encourage communication and language

You will need to show how you competently encourage children's communication and language through play activities in your setting. These activities will include music, movement, rhymes, games and role play. To do this you will need to be directly observed by your assessor and present other types of evidence.

The amount and type of evidence you will need to present will vary. You should plan this with your assessor.

Direct observation by your assessor

Observation is the required assessment method to be used to evidence some part of each element in this unit. Expert witnesses could supply additional evidence. Your assessor will observe you in real work activities and this should provide most of the evidence for the performance criteria for the elements in this unit.

Preparing to be observed

Read through the key words section at the front of your unit to make sure that you fully understand what is needed. You should then plan carefully with your assessor to make sure that you are able to demonstrate the national standard required. Think about activities and experiences where the children can participate and use their language and communication skills. Think about your own role and choose activities where you encourage children to communicate. Make sure that the activities you choose are suitable for the children in your setting. By planning carefully with your assessor, you should be able to gather more evidence for other units, for example CCLD 201 and CCLD 203.

Read the performance criteria carefully before assessment. Try to cover as much as you can.

Other types of evidence

You will need to present different types of evidence in order to:

- cover criteria not observed by your assessor
- show that you have the required knowledge understanding and skills.

Provide opportunities for children's drama and imaginative play

Supporting learning through drama and imaginative play

**K2D93
K2D94**

There are likely to be many activities provided in your setting to encourage children's drama and imaginative play. These may include:

- dressing up
- home corner/role-play area
- small world play
- water or sand tray
- puppets
- books and props.

Imaginative play and drama provide opportunities for children to practise and refine many skills and concepts. Children can:

- express creative and imaginative ideas
- express and experiment with many different feelings
- experience what it feels like to be someone else
- experience playing in a group of children
- develop symbolic play – that is using one thing to represent another, for example, a box for a spaceship, a doll as a baby. This skill is important when learning to read and write. Think about words written down. They are only squiggles on a page that represent speech
- use reading and writing in a real way, for example reading a menu in a cafe or writing it down, addressing an envelope in a post office
- use numbers and counting in a real way, for example putting five pieces of fruit in a bag for a customer in a fruit shop, working out how many plates will be needed when setting a table
- use gross motor skills to build and change areas
- use fine motor skills, for example to set up play with small world activities, to dress and undress themselves and dolls
- learn and develop their ideas about the world that are beyond their own experience, for example working on a farm or in a shop, sailing on a boat, camping.

Role play

**K2D96
K2D95
K2D105**

Through imaginary play, children have the opportunity to explore their feelings and the opportunity to experiment with responses to their feelings. Role play is a particularly good way for children to express positive feelings openly and begin to develop ways of expressing difficult feelings in acceptable ways. They can experiment with being someone else, for example a parent, a teacher, a powerful captain or a princess. They are in charge, in control. They can direct what happens. In this way, children can begin to understand what it feels like to be someone other than a small child.

Play can also build a positive self-concept. Our self-concept is the way that we feel about ourselves. It has a large impact on all aspects of our lives. It is therefore important that children develop a positive self-concept. Play is familiar and natural to them and so is not a threatening experience – play cannot be wrong. This is particularly true of pretend play. Children play at their own level and so the risk of constant failure is minimised. This familiar positive environment gives them the opportunity to develop a positive sense of their achievements and to begin to feel good about themselves. By providing equipment, materials and props from children's own lives and communities, you can support them in exploring their own backgrounds. This will have a positive impact on their self-concept, which will in turn affect their later development.

Practical Example

Expressing and exploring emotions in imaginary play

Amelia's mother had just had a new baby. Initially Amelia was excited and spoke a lot about the baby and what she did to help look after her. Once this initial excitement had died down, the staff noticed how she would role-play being her mother over and over again.

In the home corner, with a friend, Amelia would be the mother and her friend became Amelia. They looked after the baby together. However, in role, Amelia would tell her friend that she was too tired to play and that they could not go to the park now because the baby needed to be fed. During this play, Amelia instructed her friend to cry when she was told that she could not do something that she wanted to do. Amelia responded by sighing a lot, putting her arm around her friend and kissing her, and sitting her on her knee to comfort her.

➤ *Why do you think Amelia wanted to play like this?* **K2D93**
➤ *What are the benefits of this role play?* **K2D95**

⌐ Setting up activities

K2D94
K2D95

As children will often play more freely when an adult is not directing the activity, your role is to ensure that they have the equipment they need in order to express their imaginations. You will need to ensure that they have access to a wide range of materials, equipment and props that will support this area of play. You will need to check that what you provide allows all the children to act out their own experiences. You will need to promote **anti-discriminatory** ideas – those that recognise and value individuals without prejudice.

Sometimes children's play will reflect what they have learned or heard from the important adults in their lives, from the television or from older siblings. This may include stereotypical ideas, such as 'Girls can't be policemen' and 'Boys don't play in the home corner'. These comments limit children's play because they may stop some children from participating in certain activities. You therefore need to challenge these comments. You should explain to the children that the activities are for *all* the children. You should make sure that the equipment, materials and props you provide promote positive images of all kinds of people. You should avoid using words such as 'policeman' and 'fireman', instead using words such as 'police officer' and 'fire-fighter'.

K2D93
K2D105
K2D108
K2D109

Setting up activities: some questions to consider

Take a look at your own setting and ask yourself:	
Can the children see the different outfits on offer?	When dressing-up clothes are not displayed well, children's choices are often limited to what they can see or reach.
Can the children put on the outfits with a minimum of help, to encourage their independence?	Encouraging independence in this area will help children to develop their own ideas without interruption, as well as developing their self-help skills.
Are the outfits clean and in a good state of repair?	When was the last time the equipment was cleaned? Young children will often put play food up to their mouths, or 'drink' from pretend cups. It should also be checked for damage daily.
Are accessories provided?	This will allow children to develop their ideas freely.
Can the children 'admire' themselves in a mirror?	An important part of dressing-up is being able to see yourself in another role. Having a full-length safety mirror near the dressing-up clothes will allow this to happen.
Do the outfits and equipment reflect the children's own culture, and that of others?	Children need to be able to act out experiences in their own lives, and to 'try out' the lives of others. This will encourage the development of respect and **empathy** (being able to understand another person's feelings).
When the children use the area, do they seem to act out stereotypical roles for example, the boys dress up as fire-fighters, and the girls as brides?	If this seems to be the case, you should be thinking about why this is happening. What choices of outfits are there for the children? Are you promoting stereotypes by, for example, providing only nurses' dresses and cowboy outfits?
Is there enough space for the children to access the equipment and play freely?	A small home corner or a dressing-up box hidden underneath other activities will not encourage children to play freely with the equipment.
Is this area for **child-initiated** play (led by the child's ideas), or is it **adult-led** (adults decide and direct the activity)?	Children's imagination will be much better supported when they are in control of their own play, and not acting out an adult's ideas.
Is there enough equipment for the children to develop their own ideas?	You may notice that some children will share the equipment, but they have completely different ideas about how the game is played. As they get older, they begin to play together, negotiating the boundaries of their game and developing their ideas. They learn to adapt their own ideas to take account of those of others.

Practical Example

Creating a pretend play area

As part of a playgroup's topic on transport, the staff decided to create a street in the playground to use with the bikes and trucks. The children had been out to look at the street outside and staff had made a note of all the different things that they had seen.

With boxes and tubing, they made traffic signs including traffic lights, stop signs and bus stops. They labelled the bikes and trucks as cars, buses, ambulances, fire engines and lorries. Finally, they drew the street markings on the playground with chalk, including roundabouts and junctions.

The staff introduced the area to all the children, pointing out simple driving rules. The children were then free to play.

➤ *Why is it important that the staff encourage both girls and boys to play in this area?* **K2D95**

➤ *List the different ways in which the children are learning.* **K2D94**

➤ *List other things that the staff could add to the play area to extend the play.* **K2D94**

➤ *Why was it important that the adults left the children to play freely? Describe why it may be necessary for sensitive adult intervention.* **K2D96**

Element 206.2

Are you ready for assessment?

Provide opportunities for children's drama and imaginative play

You will need to show how you competently help children express themselves through drama and imaginative play in your setting. To do this you will need to be directly observed by your assessor and present other types of evidence.

The amount and type of evidence you will need to present will vary. You should plan this with your assessor.

Direct observation by your assessor

Observation is the required assessment method to be used to evidence some part of each element in this unit. Expert witnesses could supply additional evidence. Your assessor will observe you in real work activities and this should provide most of the evidence for the performance criteria for the elements in this unit.

Preparing to be observed

Read through the key words section at the front of your unit to make sure that you ▶

fully understand what is needed. You should then plan carefully with your assessor to make sure that you are able to demonstrate the national standard required. Think about activities and experiences where the children can participate in drama and imaginative play. Think about your own role and choose activities where children's play can flow freely without adult intervention. Make sure that you set these activities up carefully, avoiding stereotypes and extending children's awareness of their own and others' cultures. Make sure that the activities you choose are suitable for the children in your setting. By planning carefully with your assessor, you should be able to gather more evidence for other units, for example CCLD 203.

Read the performance criteria carefully before assessment. Try to cover as much as you can.

Other types of evidence

You will need to present different types of evidence in order to:

- cover criteria not observed by your assessor
- show that you have the required knowledge, understanding and skills.

Element 206.3

Encourage children to be creative

K2D97

The value of creative play in promoting learning

Being creative is a uniquely human characteristic involving the expression of ideas and feelings in a personal way. Children do not need to be taught to be creative but if we want to develop these abilities we must provide them with opportunities to explore and experiment with a wide range of materials, encouraging confidence to express ideas and to respond in their own ways.

Creative play and development

- Creative play supports children's *emotional development* giving them opportunities to express what they are thinking and feeling. It can help them to deal with negative as well as positive feelings. Their confidence and self-esteem will be encouraged by an approach that is not concerned with a 'right' or 'wrong' way.
- Creative play encourages children's *intellectual development* by introducing them to a wide range of materials. A 'hands-on' approach will enable them to discover the different properties of the materials they are using and encourage problem-solving. This experiential learning stimulates the senses and the imagination.
- Using tools and other equipment promotes children's *physical skills*. Their fine motor skills are encouraged through handling brushes, glue spreaders, dough cutters, etc. As these skills develop, more challenging tools and techniques should be introduced. Building with large 'junk' materials and moving buckets of water or sand provides opportunities to develop gross motor skills too.

- Children's *social development* is encouraged as they work alongside one another at creative play activities, sharing equipment and space. Older children will work as a group at an activity or collaborate on a project. Planning and completing a task will give children a sense of achievement and develop independence too.

- Creative play provides all kinds of opportunities for children's *language development*. They will talk with adults and with other children about what they are doing. Younger children, concentrating on a task, will often talk this through to themselves, accompanying their play with a commentary. As unfamiliar tools and materials are introduced into their play, children will learn the new vocabulary associated with these.

Children work alongside one another sharing equipment and space

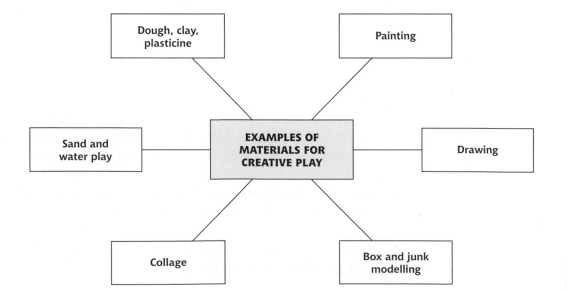

Dough, clay, plasticine		Painting
Sand and water play	**EXAMPLES OF MATERIALS FOR CREATIVE PLAY**	Drawing
Collage		Box and junk modelling

Some principles of providing for creativity

- To avoid frustration, children should be provided with materials and tools that are enjoyable to use and appropriate for their stage of development.
- Adults should support and encourage children's creative play, but not dominate it.
- Something to take home is not so important to a child. For them, the process is more important than the product.
- All children should have the opportunity to participate in creative play. Practitioners will need to consider the individual needs of all children in the group.
- Health and safety should always be a consideration, but this need not stop children enjoying creative play.

Adults should support and encourage children's creative play

Stifling creativity

Luke, aged 3, had lots of drawing and painting experience before he went to nursery. He loved these activities and was eager to join in with them. Luke was looking forward to making a Mother's Day card for his mum. He was pleased when he'd finished his card and he took it proudly to his keyworker. She told him that he hadn't followed her instructions and that his mum wouldn't want a messy card like his. He would have to start again, this time copying her. He made another card, closely supervised, but didn't seem so pleased with it this time. Later, staff noticed that he didn't seem so eager to join in with sticking and painting any more and was now constantly looking for reassurance that he was doing the right thing.

> ➤ *What effect do you think this had on Luke's confidence and enthusiasm? Why is it important for children to have their own attempts accepted and valued?* **K2D99**
>
> ➤ *How can you make it clear to children that you value their work for its own sake?* **K2D99**

Activities, equipment and materials for creative play

A wide range of activities and materials can be used to provide for children's creative play. The table below shows a range of materials, and some of the issues involved in using them.

Materials for creative play

Material	Benefits for creative play	Issues to consider
Water	Familiar, enjoyable, absorbing, cheap, available, therapeutic Versatile – can be used with a range of equipment and additions	Could irritate some skin conditions Spillage can be hazardous Clothing needs protection
Sand	Inexpensive and available Enjoyable, relaxing, therapeutic Less familiar than some other materials Can be used wet or dry in a variety of ways	Not all types are suitable for play Must be kept clean Can get in eyes and hair Floor becomes slippery if sand is spilt
Malleable materials	Clay, dough and plasticine can be used many times, with different tools and implements Materials are readily available, soothing and pleasurable	Issues concerning freshness when stored Should not be eaten Protection of clothing
Food	Peas, beans, lentils and pasta provide different textures, shapes and colours Are easy to handle Useful for collage	Ethical issues over use of food, especially if not past 'sell-by' date Possible allergies need consideration (especially nuts) Choking could be an issue with very young children Dried beans must not be eaten raw
Plants and wood	Fresh or dried leaves, berries and flowers, wood and bark are readily available and children enjoy collecting them Provides a stimulus for learning, particularly aesthetic awareness and an understanding of the natural world	Care should be taken that poisonous plant material is not used Storage needs care

Paint	Can be used in many ways with fingers or tools Helps manipulative skills, gives a sense of pride and achievement, valuable for self-expression, enjoyable	Must be non-toxic, protection of clothing and surfaces required Over-emphasis of outcomes to be avoided
Pencils, crayons and drawing materials	Encourage concentration, experimentation and expression Materials can be used in combination with each other Provide range for different age groups Inexpensive, easily stored and readily available for use	Must be non-toxic Any sharp points need supervision
Collage and construction	Paper, magazines, fabric, wool, cards, boxes, food containers and other discarded materials are ideal for two- or three-dimensional play Stimulates ideas, design and technology Very enjoyable Stimulates fine motor skills	Hygiene might be an issue with recycled materials Organised storage of a range of materials will be required Use of scissors must be supervised closely Children will become frustrated if tools are inadequate for the task

Water is versatile and can be enjoyed in a variety of ways

Storing and using materials safely

The safe use and storage of any materials available for play must always be an important consideration for the practitioner. Some of these issues have been identified in the table above. Whenever children have opportunities to play with water, they must always be closely supervised. Hygiene is an important consideration with sand, water and dough as contamination could present a risk.

Protection of surfaces and clothing

For some creative play activities, it will be necessary to protect surfaces. If surfaces are not able to be wiped clean, then covering will be needed for activities which use glue, paint and malleable materials, such as dough and clay. Some flooring, for example polished wood or parquet, will need protecting if water or sand are used. (In some settings these activities may be prohibited inside as a condition of the lease and will need to be offered outside.) Plastic sheeting is useful for this purpose and old newspapers can also be used. Care will be needed to anchor these securely if used on floors.

Children's clothing will need to be protected for some messy activities. They should be encouraged to select and put on aprons that are appropriate for the activity chosen. Aprons should be laundered regularly and fastenings checked so that they are easy for children to manage. Sand hats are provided in some settings to protect children's hair. Any policy regarding wearing aprons and hats should be discussed with the children and encouraged. Consideration should also be given to whether any of the materials provided are likely to provoke allergic reactions in children. Children with eczema may be sensitive to some materials; in this case it may be better to avoid the substance and provide an alternative to offer to all the children.

Painting is an absorbing activity

How to display children's work

K2D98
K2D99

Creating displays of the children's work will help you to make your environment attractive to children and their families. But it will do much more than that. When children's work is on display, they will feel very proud of themselves. They will feel that you value their efforts – even the less than 'perfect' ones. Drawing parents' attention to the displays will further enhance the children's self-esteem and will strengthen the bond between parent and child.

How you display the children's work is very important. This is explored in more detail in Unit CCLD 205.

Notice boards and displays

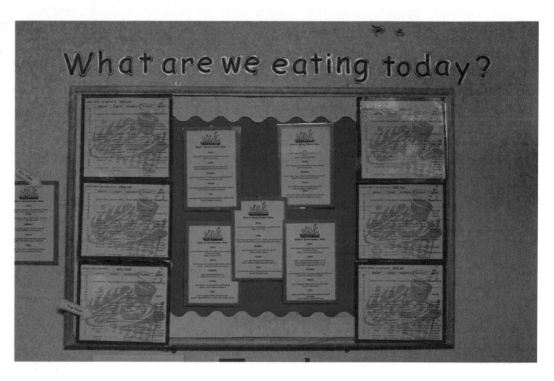

What are we eating today?

Are you ready for assessment?

Encourage children to be creative

You will need to show that you competently encourage children to be creative. To do this you will need to be directly observed by your assessor and present other types of evidence.

The amount and type of evidence you will need to present will vary. You should plan this with your assessor.

Direct observation by your assessor

Observation is the required assessment method to be used to evidence some part of each element in this unit. Expert witnesses could supply additional evidence. Your assessor will observe you in real work activities and this should provide most of the evidence for the performance criteria for the elements in this unit.

Preparing to be observed

You will need to make sure that the activities you provide in your setting to encourage children's creativity are suitable for the children's age, needs and abilities. ▶

Choose to be observed at an activity that truly enables the children to express their own ideas. Be aware that your role is to provide the right kinds of materials, equipment and props to enable this to happen. You might like to show your assessor how you have planned what to provide, being careful that you are not encouraging stereotypes. Planning carefully with your assessor will enable you to gather evidence for other units, for example CCLD 201, 202, 203 and 205.

Read the performance criteria carefully before your assessment. Try to cover as much as you can.

Other types of evidence

You will need to present different types of evidence in order to:

- cover criteria not observed by your assessor
- show that you have the required knowledge, understanding and skills.

Element 206.4

Support physical play and exercise

⌒ Physical development

K2D102

Physical development is about the growth, development and control of the movement of the body.

Children need to have the opportunity to exercise regularly each day. This may be planned exercise, such as physical activities at school, nursery or play setting, or naturally-occurring opportunities, such as walking to nursery, school or play setting.

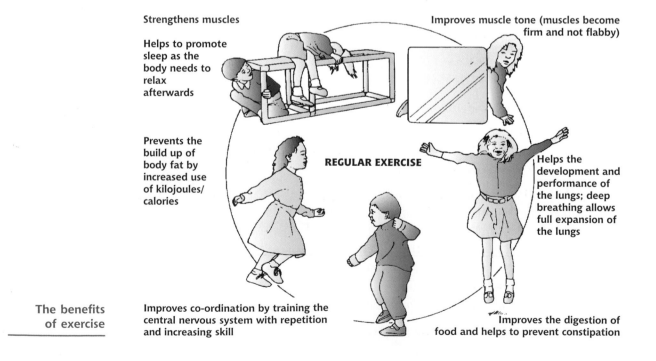

Strengthens muscles

Helps to promote sleep as the body needs to relax afterwards

Improves muscle tone (muscles become firm and not flabby)

Prevents the build up of body fat by increased use of kilojoules/calories

REGULAR EXERCISE

Helps the development and performance of the lungs; deep breathing allows full expansion of the lungs

The benefits of exercise

Improves co-ordination by training the central nervous system with repetition and increasing skill

Improves the digestion of food and helps to prevent constipation

Physical development at nursery and school

K2D100

All childcare settings provide opportunities for physical exercise and activities. It is important that these are planned with the child's age, stage of development and safety in mind.

At nursery, outdoor play with tricycles, prams, trolleys, large building blocks, dens, tyres and climbing frames may create an environment for imaginative physical activity. Using music to encourage movement by using the body to interpret the sounds will improve co-ordination and balance. Group activities may encourage children who lack confidence. Fine motor development can be encouraged through a range of table-top activities – threading, peg boards, puzzles, mark-making, cut and paste. The development of fine motor control is particularly important for the future development of writing. Finger rhymes and playing instruments will also help.

At school, opportunities for exercise could include using the apparatus, dance, music and movement, football, team games, throwing and catching activities, swimming.

Children will sometimes have separate clothing to wear when doing physical activities. However, during outdoor play at nursery the children will be wearing their own outdoor clothes. It is important to make sure that clothing does not get in the way or make play dangerous. It may be necessary to adjust long skirts or tie up trailing scarves to avoid accidents. Some children may need to keep their limbs and bodies covered for cultural reasons, so it is important to be aware of this and enable the child to take part in activities safely.

Supporting children's exercise

Physical play on large equipment helps children to develop:

- agility
- co-ordination
- balance
- confidence.

It allows them to get rid of surplus energy and to make noise. This is particularly important for children who spend a lot of time in smaller spaces. It is also important for children who are learning how to behave in a quiet, controlled indoor environment such as nursery or school.

The equipment provided should give opportunities for children to:

- climb
- slide
- bounce
- swing
- crawl
- move around.

Climbing

Equipment

- Match the size of equipment to the size of the children.
- Climbing up is often easier than climbing down – climbing frames with slides attached give children a safe way down.

Safety

- Climbing should always be closely supervised, but children should also be given the opportunity to test their boundaries and assess risk themselves.
- Safety surfaces underneath the equipment are important – mats inside, safety surfaces outside.
- Equipment should be regularly checked for strength of joints, bolts, etc.
- Care should be taken when moving large equipment – you could injure yourself or the children.

Sliding and bouncing

Equipment

- There is a huge range of slides in different materials and sizes. Before buying or using a slide, think about who will be using it and where it will be put.
- Bouncing equipment includes trampolines, hoppers, bouncy castles, etc.

Climbing equipment

Safety

- Children need to be taught basic safety rules when using this equipment, for example only one child at a time on the slide or trampoline.
- These activities should be supervised at all times. Children will be excited, which is good, but when they are excited they may need gently reminding of how to use the equipment safely.

Swings

Equipment

- There is a wide range available – the type of swing needs to be matched to the stage of physical development of the children in the group.
- Home-made swings are popular with older children, for example a tyre, a piece of wood on a rope, a large knot in a rope.

Safety

- Walking in front of swings is dangerous. Children need to be taught about this danger and reminded to be careful before playing outside.

Crawling

Equipment

- Rigid concrete tunnels can be installed outside.
- Collapsible plastic tunnels can be used outside and inside.
- Other equipment such as climbing frames can be used for crawling through, under and over.

Tunnels can be used outside

Safety

- Make sure that outside tunnels are kept clean; dogs and cats making a mess can be a problem.
- Make sure that the children know the rules about using the tunnels, for example no jumping on to collapsible tunnels or rolling them around the floor.

Moving around

Equipment

- A variety of bikes, cars, trucks, trikes, carts and trailers will be needed to meet the range of abilities and needs.

Safety

- Wheeled toys need plenty of space to avoid collisions. It is sensible for these toys to be used in an area set aside for their use.
- Regular maintenance will be necessary.

Wheeled toys need plenty of space

Avoiding stereotyping in physical play

It is important to make sure that all children can use the activities. The activities provided should be suitable for the range of abilities in the group and be managed by the staff to ensure that all children can join in. Activities should not be taken over by children who are physically very able. It may, therefore, be necessary to limit time on popular toys or at popular activities to make sure that everyone can have a go.

Adults should challenge any stereotyping linked to physical play. Comments such as 'Girls can't run fast' or 'Cars are for boys' are unacceptable and are likely to limit what children will try to do or play with. Therefore, not all children will have an equal opportunity to develop good physical skills.

Adults must also be aware of their own language and attitudes when supervising physical play. Comments or worries about whether certain children, for example girls or children with special educational needs, are capable of boisterous physical play, is likely to limit their physical play. Similar comments or a negative attitude towards less physically capable boys is not acceptable.

Outside play

Staff had noticed that a number of children were reluctant to go outside to play. They decided to observe the play over a week to see how they could improve provision, so all children could take part happily in outdoor play. Each day a member of staff was given time to observe the play outside and to record what they saw. At the next staff meeting, the staff were informed of results of these observations. The staff had observed that a small group of boisterous children were taking over the space. They enjoyed playing on the bikes and would use the whole of the playground area in their game. This meant that the other children played at the edges of the playground and would sometimes be anxious about crossing the playground. Also, the boisterous children used the bikes all the time. They were the first children outside and raced to get to the bikes. Other children didn't get a chance to play on the bikes.

The staff discussed how they could improve the outdoor play. They decided to create areas in the playground for different activities. Their plans included:

➤ *marking out a section of the playground for the bikes with chalk marked roads, junctions, etc.*
➤ *sometimes selecting the quieter children to go on the bikes first*
➤ *creating an area with hoops, skipping ropes, juggling balls and stilts*
➤ *creating an area with large construction activities*
➤ *creating a pretend play area*
➤ *looking into acquiring or buying small benches and tables for table-top activities.*

The staff's observations and the changes that they made ensured that all the children were able to participate in all activities. It means that all children have an equal opportunity to develop the necessary skills and concepts. The boisterous children became involved in a wider range of activities and the other children were able to use the bikes and to play outside happily.

➤ *Why did the staff decide to observe the outdoor play before making changes?* **K2D102**
➤ *Why was it important to allow the quieter children sometimes to go on the bikes first?* **K2D102**
➤ *Why was it important to have a range of boisterous and quieter activities planned for outdoors?* **K2D102**

Children with disabilities

When caring for children with disabilities, it is important to remember that every child is an individual with specific needs. Some children may not achieve the level of physical ability expected for their age group, so they may need an individual programme that will help them to progress at their own pace. They may spend longer at each stage of development before moving on to the next. Special/ individual needs should be viewed positively and each achievement should be encouraged and praised. However, you must not forget that all children need opportunities for physical development, and it is the responsibility of the setting to ensure these needs are met.

Safety and risk

K2D101

When supporting children's exercise it is very important to pay close attention to the safety of the children. Every setting will have health and safety procedures and you should make sure that you follow these in your work with the children. All settings that care for children outside their own home are regularly inspected by the Office for Standards in Education (Ofsted) to ensure that positive steps are taken to promote safety within the setting to comply with the National Standards for Day Care, Sessional Care, Out of School Care, Crèches and Childminding.

Before the children start any indoor exercise or outdoor play, the area and equipment should be thoroughly checked for any hazards. Equipment should always be carefully and correctly assembled following the manufacturer's instructions. Any safety mats should be in place.

Children must always be carefully supervised to ensure their safety. However, it is also important to let the children develop their physical skills by joining in with more challenging activities or using more advanced equipment. This will help them to learn to assess risks for themselves in a controlled environment where you are on hand to help and guide. Good supervision will mean that you are there to support them and to make sure that what they are trying to do is realistic. Give help where needed to support these attempts and to help the children achieve their goals. You can alert children to risks beforehand through warnings and discussions. This will help you avoid over-protecting the children in your setting.

Giving children the opportunity to play outside will help them develop their physical skills

Are you ready for assessment?

Support physical play

You will need to show that you competently support children's physical play. To do this you will need to be directly observed by your assessor and present other types of evidence.

The amount and type of evidence you will need to present will vary. You should plan this with your assessor.

Direct observation by your assessor

Observation is the required assessment method to be used to evidence some part of each element in this unit. Expert witnesses could supply additional evidence. Your assessor will observe you in real work activities and this should provide most of the evidence for the performance criteria for the elements in this unit.

Preparing to be observed

You will need to make sure that the activities you provide in your setting to encourage children's physical skills are suitable for the children's age, needs and abilities. You will also need to balance the need for children to carry out challenging activities. You need to be encouraging them to assess and take reasonable risks, whilst supervising carefully. Pay attention to the way you set out the equipment. Planning carefully with your assessor will enable you to gather evidence for other units, for example CCLD 201 and 203.

Read the performance criteria carefully before your assessment. Try to cover as much as you can.

Other types of evidence

You will need to present different types of evidence in order to:

- cover criteria not observed by your assessor
- show that you have the required knowledge, understanding and skills.

Encourage children to explore and investigate

K2D106

Children learn most effectively through first-hand experiences. They take in information through all of their senses; the younger the child, the more important it is to provide opportunities for sensory learning. Play with objects is known as **heuristic play**. This type of play is sometimes provided for babies and toddlers in treasure baskets, which contain a selection of interesting objects for the child to handle and explore. These would not be familiar toys but everyday items that the child could experiment with. Obviously, safety must be considered when selecting these items. Remember that babies and toddlers explore with their mouths as well

Exploring the washing basket

as with their hands and their eyes. Appealing to all the senses should also be a consideration. A good selection will offer the chance to explore interesting and contrasting textures as well as including items that stimulate the senses of hearing and smell.

How handling objects of interest promotes development

K2D106

Holding and handling objects will promote children's *physical development*. A range of differently sized and shaped objects should be provided. Fine manipulative skills and hand–eye co-ordination will be practised when picking up and holding and also when opening and closing fastenings, for example on boxes, jewellery, etc.

Introducing children to unfamiliar objects will provide them with an opportunity to develop their *language skills.* Naming the objects and describing their features will introduce new vocabulary in a meaningful way.

Giving children interesting objects to explore will promote their natural curiosity and widen their horizons. Older children will be able think about where the object comes from, who owns it and what it might be for. They will be able to group objects together by recognising their similarities and differences, sorting and classifying them. This stimulates their *intellectual development.*

When children are encouraged to explore and investigate objects together as a group, their *social skills* will be practised. They will learn to take turns and be considerate of others. Children can begin to learn about other people and cultures through examining and exploring objects. For example, handling a collection of

special lamps (divas) would be a good starting point for children to find out about the Hindu and Sikh celebration of Diwali.

Handling beautiful and unusual objects will enable children to experience and show a range of feelings such as wonder, joy and fascination. This contributes to their *emotional development*. When children bring in items from home for others to examine and explore, this is likely to have a positive effect on their self-esteem.

Encouraging children to handle objects and cultural artefacts with care and respect

Small children will need to be shown how to handle objects that are fragile and delicate. It is part of the role of the practitioner to help children to handle objects with respect, showing them how to hold and touch. If you have borrowed objects for your circle time or interest table, it is likely that these are special or precious to someone. Children need to know about this. If children are examining living things, plants or small animals, such as minibeasts in bug boxes, it is particularly important to ensure gentle handling.

Enabling children with particular needs to explore and examine objects

K2D103

All children should be provided with opportunities to explore and examine objects. When planning an activity and selecting items, the practitioner must ensure that all children can participate fully. If there are any children with a visual impairment, objects that can be explored through the senses of touch, sound and smell, as well as sight, should be selected. Children who have a hearing loss will not appreciate the 'noisy' aspects of objects, but can explore with their other senses. Some children may have difficulty picking up and holding on to objects, so items that are easy to grasp should be included, perhaps on trays close to the child.

Choosing objects of interest and cultural artefacts for children to explore

K2D103

Many settings have interest tables where a selection of items, sometimes linked to a theme, are set out for children to handle. Circle time provides another, more structured, context for children to explore items. Children are naturally curious and will be interested in most items that are presented to them. However, care and thought needs to be given to choosing objects so that children's enjoyment and learning is maximised and their safety ensured.

Providing a range

These are some suggestions of general categories of items to offer to children:

- natural materials with interesting features, for example pine cones, cork, bark, sponges, pumice, rocks and pebbles, fossils, etc.
- items associated with animals, for example feathers, nests and eggs (abandoned), a chrysalis, shells of all sorts, wool from sheep, fur, etc.
- manufactured items, particularly unfamiliar and unusual items, for example a sundial, barometer, metronome, chiming clocks, timers, etc.
- objects that reflect people and their culture, for example cooking utensils, music (tapes and instruments), fabrics, clothes, games and 'special' items such as candlesticks, prayer mats, statues
- things from the past, for example photographs, toys, household equipment, clothes and, for older children, printed material such as ration books, certificates, newspapers.

Where to find them

- Ask parents, friends and families, but remember that items might be precious and you would need to be sure that you could look after them. Do not borrow anything that is irreplaceable.
- Make your own collection from car boot sales, your cupboards, your travels.
- Make contact with local community groups. They may have items to lend or can suggest sources.
- Many local museums have collections that can be borrowed for use with children.

Conservation

Remember to emphasise conservation. Children should be encouraged to care for and protect the natural environment. Wildlife must not be disturbed to provide objects for interest tables!

Safety

You must make sure that any objects are safe for the children to handle:

- Remember that babies and toddlers will explore by sucking and chewing, as well as in other ways. Check that objects are made of non-toxic materials, are clean and have no loose, small pieces.
- Older children can be warned about sharp edges or any other concerns. Make sure you look for possible hazards beforehand.
- Many plants have poisonous berries. As these are very attractive to small children, you should make sure that children do not come into contact with them.
- If any of the children in the group are allergic to certain substances, for example feathers or fur, you should avoid providing these.

Using the natural and local environment to promote children's learning

K2D106

Children can learn a great deal from the outside environment. Most settings give children regular opportunities to play outside either on the premises or using facilities in the local environment. This experience can provide children with many relevant and worthwhile opportunities for learning. Here are some examples:

- Children can plant seeds and bulbs and watch and measure growth. Caring for a pet can help children to understand about life cycles and develop a sense of caring and responsibility.

- Observing wildlife in its natural habitat can be very rewarding. Bird tables can be set up where children can see them easily. Minibeasts can be found and examined in a garden area, perhaps using magnifying glasses and bugboxes. Pond dipping can help children to understand a different type of habitat.

Children can learn a great deal from the outdoor environment

- Studying the weather can be fascinating for small children. They can watch puddles form and evaporate, measure rainfall and find out the direction of the wind. Children love to feel snow, to experience its texture as they build with it and to watch it melting away. Icy puddles and icicles provide interesting experiences too.

- On a walk in the neighbourhood, draw children's attention to street furniture such as signposts, letter boxes, lamp posts and shop and road signs. They can look for architectural features such as doorways, roofs and chimney pots too.

Using ICT to support play and learning

K2D91

Children learn best from the adults and children around them. Using ICT (Information and Communication Technology), including computers, software packages and the internet, can support play and learning. There is a wealth of information that can be accessed from a PC (Personal Computer). However, it is not a substitute for real experiences and interactions. ICT activities tend to be very popular among children and often the children are more able to use the equipment than the adults in the setting! It can be tempting to use ICT as an easy activity where adult input is not required. Although children's independence can be encouraged in this way, you should make sure that children are offered a broad range of activities and experiences. ICT should play only a small part in the overall plans for children's play and learning.

Software packages should be carefully chosen to ensure that they are appropriate for the ages of the children. You will find that many packages will show links to the National Curriculum (Foundation Stage or Key Stages 1–4), which will help you to judge whether or not they are appropriate. Children should not be left unsupervised to surf the internet. An adult should always be aware of what children are doing on a PC, as it is very easy for unsuitable material to be accessed quickly, by accident or otherwise.

Use ICT to help children investigate further

Element 206.5

Are you ready for assessment?

Encourage children to explore and investigate

You will need to show that you competently encourage children to explore and investigate. To do this, you will need to be directly observed by your assessor and present other types of evidence.

The amount and type of evidence you will need to present will vary. You should plan this with your assessor

Direct observation by your assessor

Observation is the required assessment method to be used to evidence some part of each element in this unit. Expert witnesses could supply additional evidence. Your assessor will observe you in real work activities and this should provide most of the evidence for the performance criteria for the elements in this unit.

Preparing to be observed

You will need to make sure that the activities you provide in your setting to encourage children's exploration and investigation are suitable for the children's age, needs and abilities. You should plan to use both the indoor and outdoor

environment if possible.

Planning carefully with your assessor will enable you to gather evidence for other units, for example CCLD 201, 202, 203 and 205.

Read the performance criteria carefully before your assessment. Try to cover as much as you can.

Other types of evidence

You will need to present different types of evidence in order to:

- cover criteria not observed by your assessor
- show that you have the required knowledge, understanding and skills.

Reflecting on your practice

- Why is play so important to children's learning and development? **K2D89**
- What activities do you provide to support (a) children's communication, (b) children's intellectual development and (c) children's learning in your setting? **K2D85**
- How do you use everyday routines to support children's learning? **K2D110**
- How do you, or would you, support children's play and communication development in bilingual or multilingual settings? **K2D86**

Contribute to the effectiveness of teams

This unit considers ways that you as a practitioner contribute to your team. It encourages you to think about your role as a team member and to think about the way that your effectiveness and behaviour affects the team that you work with.

The term 'work team' refers to a group of people who work together to meet the needs of children.

Your performance in your work team should help to support the effectiveness of the setting. You should be prepared to work hard, be helpful and offer ideas and information to other members of the team. If other members of your team make suggestions, you in turn should accept them positively and use them constructively to improve your practice with the children.

This unit contains two elements:

⌒ *CCLD 207.1 Agree and carry out your role and responsibilities within the team*

⌒ *CCLD 207.2 Participate as a team member.*

There are clear underpinning knowledge links within this unit to Units CCLD 201 and 204. It will help you to revise the relevant content of both of these units as you work.

The national standards for this unit include a list of key words and explanations that you need to understand. You should read this carefully as you plan the activities for your assessment. Your assessor can help you to make sure that you are interpreting the standards correctly.

⌒ Introduction

Effective teams

K207H05

In most work settings, practitioners work with colleagues as part of a team. You may have thoughts and feelings about the team of people that you work with. Do you feel happy and fulfilled in what you are doing? Are you all working well and providing the best possible environment for the children in your care? If the answer is yes, it probably means that you are working in an effective team.

To be effective any professional team should have:

- clearly defined aims and objectives that all members can put into words and agree to put into practice
- flexible roles that enable individuals to work to their strengths, rather than in roles where they must conform to expectations

- effective team leaders who manage the work of the team, encourage and value individual contributions and deal with conflict
- team members who are committed to:
  - developing self-awareness
  - building and maintaining good working relationships
  - demonstrating effective communication skills
  - expressing their views assertively rather than aggressively
  - understanding and recognising their contribution to the way the group works
  - carrying out team decisions, irrespective of their personal feelings
  - accepting responsibility for the outcome of team decisions.

Responsibility and accountability

K207H02

In order to work well within any organisation, you need to be clear about your own role and the role of other team members.

Be clear about team roles

Your own role, including:	The role of other team members, including:
what your responsibilities are	their role and responsibilities
to whom you are accountable	to whom they are accountable
what your job description includes	what their job description includes
who your line manager is (this is the person who is immediately responsible for your work)	the line management structure of the setting

In your job description, you should be able to locate a list of your responsibilities. This will help you to understand what is expected of you and how your role fits into the structure of the team.

Roles within the team

Lines of management and reporting

A line manager is the first person that you and others should expect to report to and be guided and managed by.

This is an example of a line management structure in a private day nursery:

Owner

⇑

Officer-in-charge

⇑

Deputy officer-in-charge

⇑

Nursery officers – room leaders

⇑

Nursery officers – qualified

⇑

Nursery officers – working towards qualifications

Legislation and regulations

**K207H01
K207H02**

Legislation and regulations are in place to provide a framework of practice that is acceptable. Lots of laws, legislation and regulations exist and are intended to protect you, your colleagues, and the children and parents that you work with. The laws outline rights and responsibilities and tell you what is expected of you and how you should behave at work.

The legislation relating to the four countries of the United Kingdom (England, Wales, Scotland and Northern Ireland) includes some differences. Make sure you know about the regulations that apply to the area where you are working. The table on page 219 gives some examples of the legislation concerning children in each of the four countries.

Legislation linked to employment in children's care, learning and development is vast. It is often reviewed and updated. It is important that you are aware of this. You can keep up to date with legislation through research in your workplace and on-line.

Legal and organisational requirements when working with teams

K207H01

In order to contribute to the effectiveness of your team you need to ensure that you adhere to your legal responsibilities and the policies and procedures of your setting in relation to:

- equality
- diversity
- discrimination
- rights.

Equality of opportunity is about recognising differences and enabling people to have the opportunity to participate in every area of life to the best of their abilities.

Examples of legislation concerning children in England, Wales, Scotland and Northern Ireland

England	• The **Children Act 1989** (came into force in 1991; revised 2004) aims to protect children in every situation, whether in their own homes, in day care or full-time care. It provides extensive guidance on the regulation of services for children and their families
	• The **National Standards for Under Eights' Day Care and Child Minding 2001** (revised 2003) applies to all childcare providers in England. The Standards relate to the Children Act 1989. There are 14 standards, which are regulated by Ofsted.
Wales	• The **Child Minding and Day Care (Wales) Regulations 2002** arises from the Children Act 1989. Regulations and national minimum standards cover such matters as planning for individual needs and preferences, quality of life, staffing and management, concerns, complaints and protection and the physical environment.
	• The **Care Standards Inspectorate of Wales (CSIW)** inspects and aims to ensure that services meet the standards set out in the regulations.
Scotland	• The **Children (Scotland) Act 1995** is the major piece of legislation for children in Scotland. It provides guidance on the regulation of services for children and their families.
	• **National Care Standards** for childcare cover services for children and young people up to the age of 16 years. These standards are regulated under the **Regulation of Care (Scotland) Act 2001** and are inspected by the Scottish Commission for the Regulation of Care.
Northern Ireland	Northern Ireland operates a separate jurisdiction to England, Wales and Scotland.
	• The **Children (Northern Ireland) Order 1995** is a major piece of legislation relating to children. It provides extensive guidance on the regulation of services for children and their families.
	• The detailed regulations and standards relating to day care services for children under 12 are contained in the **Children (Northern Ireland) Order 1995: Regulation and Guidance Volume 2: Family Support, Childminding and Day Care**. The standards set the regulations for services in day care in nurseries, playgroups and childminders.

Equality can be promoted at government level by passing laws, at organisational level through working practices and codes of conduct, and at a personal level through increased awareness and skills in meeting needs.

Understanding and accepting diversity is essential for all practitioners. All team members can benefit from an environment that embraces cultural and linguistic diversity. Discrimination within a team must be actively opposed. A positive working environment is achieved primarily through attitudes and behaviour. In order to adopt anti-discriminatory approaches to team work, it is essential for practitioners to accept diversity within the team. This means that team members should value the contributions of all personnel and the different ideas and practices that such diversity produces.

Negative attitudes and assumptions based on stereotypical ideas about people can lead to discrimination. Our attitude to people affects the way we act and behave towards them.

Attitudes can be positive or negative:

+ A positive attitude towards a person based on knowledge, understanding and respect enables that person to feel good, valued and have high self-esteem.

− A negative attitude towards a person, based on poorly informed opinion and stereotypical assumption, can lead to low self-esteem and feeling unwanted or rejected.

As team members, practitioners can make a personal commitment not to discriminate against people by:

- examining their own attitudes and practices
- increasing their knowledge and understanding of people who are different from themselves
- undertaking training and awareness-raising courses to increase their ability to provide for the needs of all
- always looking for up to date information and resources.

Your legal responsibilities in relation to equality, diversity, discrimination and rights are contained in legislation, including:

- Race Relations Act 1976, which has been strengthened by the Race Relations Act (Amendment) 2000
- Sex Discrimination Act 1975
- Disability Discrimination Act 1995
- Special Needs and Disability Act 2001
- Employment Rights Act 1996.

Your responsibilities in relation to equality, diversity, discrimination and rights within your setting are contained within your setting's policies and procedures, including:

- equal opportunities policy
- anti-bias/anti-discrimination policy
- staff handbook
- code of conduct/code of practice.

Codes of practice and codes of conduct

As an employee, you are expected to behave in a professional manner; the expectations for this behaviour are laid down in your contract, staff code of conduct, policies and procedures. Further information about conduct, and behaviour should be available in the staff handbook or policy manual. For example, you should be able to find out:

- how you are expected to behave if you have a disagreement with a colleague in the staff behaviour policy
- whether you can wear shorts in the summer in the staff dress code.

You should be able to locate up to date policies and procedures at your setting. Most of these are reviewed and dated. It is important that you check to make sure that you are performing in line with the current policies and procedures. If you are not sure, it is always best to check with the manager.

Keeping and accessing records

K207H03

Recording information

Your role is likely to involve recording information for a variety of purposes. The table below indicates what information you may need to record for and about the children in your care and for whom.

Records that must be kept

Record of what?	For whom?
• Attendance • Health • Progress • Accidents/incidents • Child protection • Planning • Child observations	• Yourself • Parents/carers • Team members • Line manager • Other professionals

The way in which you need to record information will vary according to your role, the purpose of the information and who the records are for.

The Data Protection Act (1998)

Personal information about children, parents and staff is held at your setting. Whether this information is held in manual files or on computer, it is subject to the Data Protection Act (1998). The Act says that such information must:

- be correct
- not be used for any reason other than the reason it was collected for (unless permission has been given)
- not usually be passed on without permission
- not be kept for longer than necessary
- be secure.

The Act also allows everyone to see the information that is held about them, to correct it if necessary and to know how it is being used. Therefore, parents are able to ask to see records that are held about their children.

Access to any records in your setting should be managed through a procedure. Your employer will probably have registered as a Data Controller and must have policies in place to make sure that they are not breaking the law. It is therefore very important that, as part of your team, you follow the procedures for your setting.

Jenny experiences data protection

Jenny is an assistant at an after-school club. On Thursday evening, a parent came to collect his child. He is going to help with a fun day at the weekend and asks Jenny for the contact number of a colleague who is organising the event. He explains that he needs to speak to the person urgently as he is having problems with some of the activities he volunteered to organise.

Jenny is worried that if she cannot put the parent and her colleague in touch, the fun day may be affected. She is also unsure whether she is permitted to give this information.

Jenny decides to ask the parent if he would wait whilst she asks her manager. Her manager advises her that she is not permitted to give out information without her colleague's permission. The manager suggests that if the parent leaves his telephone number; Jenny could then phone her colleague with the message. The parent agrees to leave the number and Jenny's colleague contacts him later that evening. The fun day goes well.

➤ *Was Jenny right to ask for her manager's support in this situation?* **K207H03**

➤ *Do you think that the manager's advice was in line with the Data Protection Act?* **K207H03**

➤ *Where could Jenny find information about data protection in your setting?* **K207H02, K207H04**

Confidentiality

All practitioners have a responsibility to maintain confidentiality at all times. Maintaining confidentiality means that any information given to you should not be passed on to others unless it is in the best interests of the child and their family.

Although the idea of confidentiality may be easy to understand, the practice can be complex. Maintaining confidentiality will require self-control and a commitment to your organisation, your team, the welfare of the children and their families. You will often hear confidential information about children and their families. You will also become aware of information about your organisation and colleagues. You are in a position of trust. Breaking confidentiality is a serious matter and could lead to you losing your job.

Agree and carry out your role and responsibilities within the team

Working with others in a team

You need to know who manages your team and what their expectations are of you as a team member. You may be part of a team of people who have the same professional background, for example nursery officers working together in a day nursery. Or you may be part of a **multidisciplinary team**. A multidisciplinary team has members from a number of professional groups, for example family workers, teachers and health visitors working together in a Sure Start area.

What makes a team effective?

Co-operation	The children see the benefits of people working together and co-operating with each other.
Consistency	All team members adopt the same approach to the task of caring for children and working with their families.
Encouragement	Members of the team stimulate, motivate, praise, encourage and support one another.
Respect	Team membership satisfies a need to belong and to be respected and to have ideals and aims confirmed and shared by others.
Efficiency	The skills of all members are used to arrive at the best solutions.
Belonging	Individual staff feel a sense of belonging and can share problems, difficulties and successes.
Sharing	Responsibility and insight is shared by all.
Innovation	Individuals become more willing to adopt new ways of thinking and working.
Balance	The strengths and weaknesses of one person are balanced by the strengths and weaknesses of others.

Assisting others in the team and carrying out instructions

When you work in a team, it is important that you:

- offer help to others in the team when they need it
- do this willingly in a friendly, positive and helpful way
- take responsibility for what you do. This means taking care to do everything you are asked to do, not assuming others will do it for you and understanding your role, if you are the person who is in charge of the activity. The activity can be anything from sharpening the pencils to being responsible for collating key person notes for a specific child.

You may need to make a note of instructions you are given to make sure that you are able to follow them accurately. You should then carry out the tasks to the

Effective teams value
the contributions of
team members

standard required and in the time allocated, making sure that you are aware of the policies and procedures of your workplace for any of these activities.

You may need to ask your line manager or someone in a supervisory role if you do not understand what to do or if you think the task is not your responsibility. You may need to delay some tasks until someone in a supervisory role has shown you what to do or until you have received appropriate training.

If you have any suggestions for changing things, make them to an appropriate person, at the appropriate time, rather than grumbling or gossiping behind their back. Opportunities such as staff meetings or supervision meetings are appropriate times to discuss your suggestions and ideas. Open communication of positive and negative issues helps staff to develop positive relationships with each other. You should put your point of view, but also be open to the views of other people. It is important to remember that others might not be as excited or enthusiastic about your ideas and that it might be necessary to compromise.

Feedback, support and professional development

Detailed information about receiving and responding to feedback, accessing support and identifying professional development is included in Unit CCLD 204 .

Element 207.1

Are you ready for assessment?

Agree and carry out your role and responsibilities within the team

You need to show that you can competently agree and carry out your role and responsibilities within the team. To do this you will need to be directly observed by your assessor and present other types of evidence. The amount and type of evidence that you need to present will vary. You will need to plan this with your assessor.

Direct observation by your assessor

Observation and/or Expert Witness Testimony is the required assessment method to be used to evidence some part of each element in this unit. If your assessor is unable to observe you s/he will identify an expert in your workplace who will provide testimony of your work-based performance. Usually your assessor or expert witness will observe you in real work activities and this should provide most of the evidence for the performance criteria for the elements in this unit.

Preparing to be observed

You will need to plan your assessment carefully, so that you are observed at a time when you are agreeing and carrying out your role and responsibilities within your team. The amount and type of evidence that you need to present will vary. You should plan this with your assessor.

Read the performance criteria carefully before your assessment. Try to cover as much as you can.

Other types of evidence

You will need to present different types of evidence in order to:

- cover criteria not observed by your assessor
- show that you have the required knowledge and understanding.

Other types of evidence to show that you can competently agree and carry out your role and responsibilities within your team could include:

- evidence of your ability to carry out agreed responsibilities
- evidence of your ability to evaluate and use feedback constructively
- evidence that you have used support to develop.

Element 207.2

Participate as a team member

Keeping others informed

When you are working with others in a team, it is important that other members of the team know what you are doing. You can do this:

- *verbally* – face-to-face with an individual person or during a small team meeting or a whole staff meeting
- *in writing* – recording what you do. This may mean using an agreed format. Records and plans should be kept in a place where others can easily refer to them.

Professional confidentiality should be maintained at all times when exchanging and recording information.

You could use an opportunity such as a staff meeting to keep your colleagues informed about your activities.

Participating in team meetings and groups

In a work setting, groups meet both formally and informally, for example:

- staff team meetings
- meetings with groups of parents and carers
- meetings with other professionals.

Groups can find meetings effective in stimulating new ideas, managing projects, making decisions, monitoring and reviewing progress and supporting group members.

It helps if group members consider their behaviour and think about how they can establish and develop constructive relationships with others in the workplace. You should think about how positive and negative your behaviour is and how it may help or prevent the team in achieving its aims.

Interactive styles

K207H06

You will find more information about interacting and communicating with others in Unit CCLD 201.

Positive interaction and communication within a team is essential. You will be expected to interact and communicate with your team members on a regular basis. The way that you do this will depend on the tasks and activities that you need to complete.

Whatever you are asked to do and however you feel about doing it, you need to ensure that you perform to the best of your ability and with the best interests of your team in mind. However, it is fair to say that the way that we are asked to do things can affect our willingness and effectiveness. We interact in different ways and sometimes individuals do not realise that the way that they interact and communicate with others can be seen as domineering or overbearing. Such behaviour might cause a request to feel more like an order. Similarly, the way that we respond to a request can give the impression that we are not interested or lack enthusiasm or commitment to our team.

Practical Example

Interacting with others

Charlie

Charlie is working in a day nursery. There is a team rota for settling children at rest time. It is not Charlie's day to carry out this task. He is just about to go for his lunch break when he is asked to cover for a colleague and go into the rest area. He does not respond to the request verbally, but stomps off in the direction of the rest area. He settles the children and goes for his lunch 20 minutes later.

Nikki

Nikki is responsible for putting up a display in the school hall. The display is supposed to include the work of children from Year 1 and Year 2. Her colleague comes to tell her that he has forgotten to gather the work together.

Nikki responds calmly and suggests that he could help her to put up the work they have. They decide that rather than leave the display unfinished, they should put up a cartoon style 'work in progress' sign.

The colleague and Nikki work together that afternoon to complete the display work with the children. Once it is complete, they both receive recognition for the display.

➤ *Think about the situations above. How do you think the interactive styles of the individuals affect the team?* **K207H06**

Time management

If you agree to do something within your work team, it is very important that you do what you agreed. You need to manage your time well to achieve all the tasks that you are responsible for. This means **prioritising** them. Prioritising means putting tasks in an order of importance; you should decide which must be done first and allow the right amount of time to get it done. You should arrive at work at the right time and not leave before your finishing time, unless you have permission or have been instructed to.

You may also find it helpful to:

- make lists and add dates/times by which the task needs to be done. If you do this then you should be more able to cope with the busy and stressful times that occur within any work setting
- observe and learn from experienced staff. Watch them to see how they manage to do their tasks within the time that is available to them
- ask your line manager for feedback about how well she thinks you manage your time

- avoid interrupting people while they are working with children or talking with parents or other colleagues. This could make them negative in their response to you. Unless it is urgent, choose a time when they are free to speak with you
- observe others in your team and, if you can, offer them help and support if they are very busy.

Stress and conflict within teams

K207H07
K207H08

Within any team there is likely to be conflict or clashes at some time. Conflict usually happens when people do not understand what others are doing or why. It can also happen when everyone is particularly busy and feeling stressed. Practitioners should try to be aware of this and be sensitive to other people. You can then avoid causing further stress to others at busy times. It is important to deal with conflict constructively and positively rather than to try to ignore it.

If you disagree with someone, you should:

- try to settle differences of opinion in a way that avoids giving offence
- never be rude or impatient
- remain calm, positive and polite.

If you do this, you are more likely to maintain respect between you and your colleagues. You may need advice from your line manager about the best way to deal with the problem. Conflicts that are not sorted out become a barrier to good working relationships.

You should also get advice from an appropriate person, such as your line manager, if you experience interpersonal problems that include clashes of personality, bullying, harassment and discrimination.

It is important to deal with conflict constructively and positively

The following guidelines for behaviour will help you to handle and minimise interpersonal conflict:

- Join with the other person so that you can both 'win'. People in conflict often tend to be against rather than with each other. Keep a clear picture of the person and yourself, separate from the issue. The issue causing the conflict may be lost by the strength of bad feeling against the other person. You need to be committed to working towards an outcome that is acceptable to both people.

- Make clear 'I' statements. Take responsibility for yourself and avoid blaming the other person for how you feel and what you think.

- Be clear and specific about your view of the conflict and what you want. Listen to the other person's view.

- Pool your ideas for ways of sorting out the conflict: make a list of all the possible solutions and go through them together.

- Deal with one issue at a time. Avoid confusing one issue with another and using examples from the past to illustrate your point. Using the past or only telling part of the story to make your own point can lead to a biased version of what happened. The other person is likely to have forgotten or may remember the incident very differently.

● Look at and listen to each other: deal directly with each other and the difficulty.

● Ensure that you understand each other. If you are unclear and confused about the issue, ask open questions and paraphrase back what you think you hear.

● Choose a mutually convenient time and place. It is useful to agree on the amount of time you will spend.

● Acknowledge and appreciate one another. Think of the other person's attributes separately from the conflict issue and acknowledge and appreciate them.

Strengths and weaknesses

K207H09

Information about strengths and weaknesses is included in CCLD 204. As part of your team, you might already be aware that you have strengths and weaknesses.

The table on page 231 identifies the characteristics that make a team effective. The table below considers the strengths and weaknesses of team members in relation to those characteristics.

Balance is possibly the most important characteristic. A good and effective team consists of a range of people. The strengths that these people bring to the team will complement each other. One team member might be particularly keen to share a skill or talent, such as drawing or sign language. This can be a positive experience for other team members, as they will have the opportunity to develop a new skill, and this might help members to build on a personal weakness. Interactions like this will help the team to be more effective.

A word of caution: a team that relies solely on its members' strengths may become less effective.

Strengths and weaknesses of team members

Team characteristic	Strong team members	Weak team members
Co-operation	Able to work with others Accept tasks willingly	Prefer to work alone Dislike being told what to do
Consistency	All team members adopt the same approach to tasks	Find it difficult to adopt the same approach as others
Encouragement	Members of the team stimulate, motivate, praise, encourage and support one another	Find it difficult to accept or to give praise Unsure when to ask for support
Respect	Team membership satisfies a need to belong and to be respected and to have ideals and aims confirmed and shared by others	Find it difficult to belong Unsure of the need to have ideals and aims confirmed by others
Efficiency	The skills of all members are used to arrive at the best solutions	Inefficient particularly when working to a timescale Poor organisational skills
Belonging	Individual staff feel a sense of belonging and can share problems, difficulties and successes	Find it difficult to share difficulties and problems
Sharing	Responsibility and insight is shared by all	Tend to take the burden of responsibility oneself
Innovation	Individuals become more willing to adopt new ways of thinking and working	Inflexible Not keen to try new things
Balance	The strengths and weaknesses of one person are balanced by the strengths and weaknesses of others	

Practical Example

Team tactics

Asling is a member of the toddler room team at a day nursery. The team had a meeting to prepare for parents' evening. Asling was given the task of collating photographs of the children and presenting them in an album. It was a busy month, Asling had taken lots of pictures but she had not had time to type and print the captions. There was a panic in the toddler room as none of her colleagues was able to use the computer.

Asling talked to her room leader and it was decided that the only way to get the job done was for Asling to leave some of her other tasks and work through her lunch break. Later in the day, a colleague told Asling she would stay after her shift to help her. Another colleague said that he would come in before the parents' evening just in case they had not finished. Asling really appreciated the support of her team members. The photograph album was ready just in time.

➤ *How did Asling's colleagues prove to be effective team members?* **K207H05**

➤ *What does this example tell you about Asling's strengths and weaknesses?* **K207H09**

➤ *What could Asling's colleagues do to improve their performance within team activities that involve using computers?* **K207H10**

Further information about identifying strengths and weakness and professional development can be found in Unit CCLD 204.

Element 207.2 Are you ready for assessment?

Participate effectively as a team member

You will need to show that you can competently participate effectively as a team member. To do this you will need to be directly observed by your assessor and present other types of evidence. The amount and type of evidence that you need to present will vary. You should plan this with your assessor.

Direct observation by your assessor

Observation and/or Expert Witness Testimony is the required assessment method to be used to evidence some part of each element in this unit. If your assessor is unable to observe you s/he will identify an expert in your workplace who will provide testimony of your work-based performance. Usually your assessor or expert witness will observe you in real work activities and this should provide most of the evidence for the performance criteria for the elements in this unit.

Preparing to be observed

You will need to plan your assessment carefully, so that you are observed at a time when you are participating effectively as a team member. This might be during a team meeting or whilst you are preparing tasks or participating in activities.

Read the performance criteria carefully before your assessment. Try to cover as much as you can.   ▶

Other types of evidence

You will need to present other types of evidence in order to:

- cover the criteria not observed by your assessor
- show that you have the required knowledge and understanding.

Such evidence could include:

- evidence that your behaviour supports the effectiveness of your team
- evidence that you have offered support to others within the team
- evidence that you have dealt with difficulties within your team in line with policy and procedure
- evidence of your understanding of barriers to developing relationships and how you can overcome these.

Reflecting on your practice

- Why is it important to carry out your role and responsibilities within your team?
- Reflect on your experiences as a team member. What do you think are the key characteristics of your work team? **K207H05**
- Use the table on page 231 to identify your strengths and weaknesses as a team member. Consider how you could work to develop your weaknesses, including professional development activities. **K207H09, K207H10**
- Consider the ways that you and your team members interact. How do you think these interactions affect the way that you work as a team? **K207H06**

UNIT 208

Support the development of babies and children under 3 years

This unit is about observing babies and children under 3 years, providing appropriate physical care and supporting the development of babies and young children. This includes, the accurate recording of developmental progress following the procedures of your setting, communicating with babies and children under 3 years old, and taking their needs and preferences into account.

This unit contains four elements:

⌒ *CCLD 208.1 Observe babies or children under 3 years as part of your everyday work*

⌒ *CCLD 208.2 Provide safe physical care for babies and children under 3 years*

⌒ *CCLD 208.3 Provide play activities to encourage learning and development*

⌒ *CCLD 208.4 Communicate with and respond to and interpret the needs of babies or children under 3 years.*

The national standards for this unit include a list of key words and explanations that you need to understand. You should read this carefully as you plan the activities for your assessment. Your assessor can help you to make sure that you are interpreting the standards correctly.

⌒ Introduction

K2P111

Practitioners who work with children aged 0–3 years have a very significant influence on children's self-concept and learning. Practitioners need to have knowledge of child development. They also need to have an understanding of the development of each individual child in their care. Professional updating plays an important part in this (see Unit CCLD 204). Observing the babies and young children in your care will help you to gain this understanding. Observation will also help you to recognise and understand their needs. Using what you learn from your observations will help you to provide safe physical care, to plan and provide activities and to communicate with and respond to babies and young children.

This unit has close links with Units CCLD 202, 203, 205 and 206.

'Children's experiences in the earliest years of their lives are critical to their subsequent development.'

Birth to Three Matters: A Framework to Support Children in their Earliest Years (DfES/Sure Start 2002)

Birth to Three Matters

Birth to Three Matters was published with the intention to develop the practice of those who work with the youngest children. The framework focuses on four aspects as a way of approaching and understanding how to provide for the growth, learning and development of very young children. These aspects are:

- a strong child
- a skilful communicator
- a competent learner
- a healthy child.

Four broad stages of development are identified:

- Heads up, Lookers and Communicators (0–8 months)
- Sitters, Standers, and Explorers (8–18 months)
- Movers, Shakers and Players (18–24 months)
- Walkers, Talkers and Pretenders (24–36 months).

You will find it helpful to use *Birth to Three Matters* as you work on this unit. You will find it an essential guide as you work with children 0–3 years.

Element 208.1 Observe babies or children under 3 years as part of your everyday work

Why do we observe babies and young children?

Observation is a vital professional tool for practitioners. They observe babies and young children so that they can:

- check a baby's development
- collect information to see if a baby is progressing in relation to normal development
- learn about any particular difficulties a baby may have
- meet the specific needs of babies
- understand babies and young children as individuals, their likes and dislikes
- assess what the baby has achieved and then plan for the next stage
- record and document anything that gives cause for concern
- provide information about the baby to parents and to others who have an involvement with the baby
- evaluate the effectiveness of the activities and routines.

You will find more information about the basic pattern of development and how to record observations in Unit CCLD 203. You must read this as you work on this element.

Informal observations

K2D112

Practitioners observe babies and young children and they act on these observations as part of their everyday practice. For example, you might observe that a young child has fallen over and quickly offer support and comfort. Notice that a toy is too far out of a baby's reach and move it to a better position. Look for signs that babies and children are enjoying activities, need support or have had enough of a particular activity. Notice that a baby or young child is looking tired and arrange for a rest or sleep.

Formal observations

K2D112

Practitioners also carry out more formal observations of babies and young children. These include:

- using prepared charts to record development
- recording weight or height on a chart
- keeping records of a child's day
- recording details of bottle feeds, weaning, food and drinks taken
- recording details of nappy changes
- recording details of when babies sleep.

Other observation methods are described in Unit CCLD 203 and can be used to observe how babies and young children under 3:

- move around and what they do with their bodies, for example gross motor skills, such as large body movements including head control, rolling over, sitting, crawling, pulling to stand, walking, running, climbing, and fine motor skills, such as hand–eye co-ordination, eye contact, focusing, grasping and manipulating objects
- communicate with adults and other children, for example responding to sounds, cooing, babbling, recognising familiar sounds and voices, understanding language (responding to 'no' and own name, using words, non-verbal language, listening to adults and others)
- play together and express their feelings, for example smiling, laughing, imitation, recognising people, relating to known and unknown adults, co-operating with others or not, playing alongside other children.

Using formal methods of observation will help you to observe for a purpose. For example, completing a development chart for a baby or young child will help you to:

- check her progress against normal development
- identify areas where there might be cause for concern

Gross motor development includes the development of head control

- provide information for parents and other professionals
- help you to plan suitable activities.

Records and confidentiality

**K2D114
K2D117
K2D119
K2D120**

If you are a practitioner in training, you must seek permission from the parents and your supervisor before you carry out an observation. Parents and supervisors will want to know what you will be observing and why you want to do this. They will also want to see what you have written. When making observations, you should conceal the child's identity. You should not identify your setting by name. If you observe something that causes you concern, you should raise this with your line manager or supervisor. They will take appropriate action.

If you are a member of staff, it is likely that you will make observations of children that will provide information for other professionals. These could include social workers, speech therapists, educational psychologists or health visitors.

Today it is considered to be good practice for children's records to be available for parents to see. The Data Protection Act states that anyone who keeps personal information on a computer must register with the Data Protection Registrar. Individuals have the right to ask for a copy of the information held.

Element 208.1

Are you ready for assessment?

Observe babies or children under 3 years as part of your everyday work

You need to show that you can competently observe babies and children under 3 years as part of your everyday work. To do this, you will need to be directly observed by your assessor and present other types of evidence. The amount and type of evidence you need to present will vary. You should plan this with you assessor.

Direct observation by your assessor

Observation and/or Expert Witness Testimony is the required assessment method to be used to evidence some part of each element in this unit. If your assessor is unable to observe you s/he will identify an expert in your workplace who will provide testimony of your work-based performance. Usually your assessor or expert witness will observe you in real work activities and this should provide most of the evidence for the performance criteria for the elements in this unit.

Preparing to be observed

You will need to show your assessor that you can make informal observations of children as you care for them. You may also undertake a range of formal observations of babies and children's development, play and responses. You should show that you could use your observations to help you contribute to planning activities and routines for the children. You must follow your settings procedure with regard to recording and confidentiality.

Other types of evidence

You may need to present different types of evidence in order to:

- cover criteria not observed by your assessor
- show that you have the required knowledge and understanding.

Element 208.2

Provide safe physical care for babies and children under 3 years

Safety

K2S123
K2S124
K2D48

It is very important to provide a safe environment for babies and young children. To do this, you will need to be familiar with their development. For example, babies walk at different ages, usually between 12 and 18 months. Once they can walk, they are very keen to use their new skill to explore the environment.

Children under 3 years are naturally curious. This means that ensuring their safety is very important. Fireguards and plug socket covers should be in place. Stair gates should be used to keep babies and young children away from dangerous areas. Reins can be used to keep the baby close to you when they start walking outside. Harnesses should always be used to keep babies and young children secure when they are in a high chair, pram or pushchair.

Constant careful supervision of babies and young children is crucial to ensuring their safety. Don't take your eye off them for a minute! Having said this, babies and young children do need to practise their new skills as they develop them. This means that you will need to provide a safe environment for them to do this. You can do this by providing activities and play materials that are safe and suitable for their stage of development. Always check the environment for potential hazards. You will find more information about providing a safe, stimulating environment in Units CCLD 202 and 205.

Exploring the environment

The nutritional needs of babies

All babies should be fed on milk only for at least the first six months of life. The decision to breast- or bottle-feed is a very personal one. Most women have an idea of how they will feed their babies before they become pregnant. This may be influenced by how their mother fed them or how their friends feed their babies. There are advantages and disadvantages to both methods, but breast milk is the natural milk for babies. It is the ideal source of food for the few first months of life.

Bottle-feeding (formula feeding)

K2S131

Most modern infant formulas (modified baby milks) are based on cows' milk. However some are derived from soya beans, for babies who cannot tolerate cows' milk. Manufacturers try to make these milks as close to human breast milk as possible. All modified milks must meet the standards issued by the Department of

Health. There are basic differences between breast and modified milks. Unmodified cows' milk can be difficult to digest as it has more protein and fat than breast milk. Unmodified cows' milk also has a higher salt content. Salt is dangerous for babies as their kidneys are not mature enough to excrete it. Making feeds that are too strong or giving unmodified cows' milk can be very dangerous. This may cause damage to the baby's kidneys and brain.

Cleaning and sterilising equipment for feeding

All equipment for bottle-feeding must be thoroughly cleaned and sterilised. The normal washing and drying methods are satisfactory for adults and older children. Equipment that is used to feed small babies, under 1 year of age, needs to be sterilised to kill germs that are not removed using normal washing methods. This includes feeding bottles, teats, teat caps, plastic spoons, bowels and feeding cups. Equipment can be sterilised using cold water sterilising solutions. These come in tablet or liquid form, a steam steriliser can also be used.

Equipment must be washed and rinsed before it is sterilised. Do not use salt to clean teats, as this may increase the salt intake of the baby. Use a proper teat cleaner, which is like a small bottle-brush. When it has been thoroughly washed, the equipment is ready to be sterilised. Follow the manufacturer's instructions on the sterilising solution bottle, packet or steam steriliser.

Cleaning and sterilising feeding equipment

Rinse the equipment with cold water, then wash in cold water and detergent. Use a bottle brush for the inside of bottle and teat cleaner for teats

Rinse everything thoroughly in clean water. Check that the holes in the teats are clear by squeezing water through them. Fill the steriliser with clean, cold water and the tablets or solution. Follow manufacturer's instructions.

Place the equipment into the solution and ensure that everything is completely covered and there are no air bubbles. Do not put metal equipment into the solution. Cover and leave for the stated time.

Making a formula (bottle) feed

Feeds should be made up according to the guidelines on the milk container. The following equipment will be needed:

- bottles (some have disposable plastic liners)
- teats
- bottle-covers
- bottle brush
- teat cleaner

- plastic jug
- sterilising tank, sterilising fluid or tablets, or steam steriliser.

These are the important points to remember:

- Always wash your hands before and after making up feeds or weaning foods.
- Wipe down the work surface before preparing feeds using hot soapy water or anti-bacterial spray.
- Rinse the feeding equipment with boiled water after it comes out of the sterilising fluid.

When making up a feed, *always*:

- use the same brand of baby milk; do not change without the advice or recommendation of the health visitor or doctor
- put the water into the bottle or jug *before* the milk powder
- use cooled boiled water to make up feeds.

Never:

- add an extra scoop of powder for any reason
- pack the powder too tightly into the scoop
- use heaped scoops.

These actions would result in the feed being too strong. This is dangerous for the baby.

If the feed is not being used immediately, cool and store in the fridge. Throw away any feed that has been stored in the fridge for 24 hours. If a feed has been taken from the fridge and warmed to feed a baby, it should be used within 45 minutes. The teat should always be covered when not in use.

If feeds have been stored in a fridge, they will need to be warmed before they are given to a baby. Put the bottle into a jug of hot water for a few minutes to heat through. You will need to shake the bottle to distribute the heat through the milk. Test the temperature of the milk before feeding. An easy way to do this is to drop some milk onto the inside of your wrist. It should feel just warm. Beware of using a microwave to heat up feeds as they can heat unevenly producing hot spots in the feed.

How much milk?

Bottle-fed babies should also be fed on demand and they usually settle into their own individual routine. New babies will require about eight feeds a day – approximately every three to four hours – but there will be some variations. A general guide to how much to offer babies is 150 ml per kg of body weight per day (24 hours). For example, a 3 kg baby will require 450 ml over 24 hours.

To work out how much milk to offer the infant at each feed, divide the daily amount by the number of feeds a day. When a baby finishes each bottle, offer more milk.

Preparing a feed

1 Check that the formula has not passed its sell-by date. Read the instructions on the tin. Ensure the tin has been kept in a cool, dry cupboard.

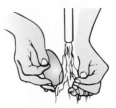

2 Boil some fresh water and allow to cool.

3 Wash hands and nails thoroughly.

4 Take required equipment from sterilising tank and rinse with cool, boiled water.

5 Fill bottle, or a jug if making a large quantity, to the required level with water.

6 Measure the <u>exact</u> amount of powder using the scoop provided. Level with a knife. Do not pack down.

7 Add the powder to the measured water in the bottle or jug.

8 Screw cap on bottle and shake, or mix well in the jug and pour into sterilised bottles.

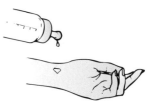

9 If not using immediately, cool quickly and store in the fridge. If using immediately, test temperature on the inside of your wrist.

10 Babies will take cold milk but they prefer warm food (as from the breast). If you wish to warm the milk, place bottle in a jug of hot water. <u>Never keep feeds warm for longer than 45 minutes</u>, to reduce the chance of bacteria breeding.

Note: whenever the bottle is left for short periods, or stored in the fridge, cover with the cap provided.

Choice of milks

There are many different kinds of formula milk available. Parents choose the type of milk for their baby and this should be continued when the baby is being cared for at nursery or in other situations. A decision to change the type of milk used may be made for medical or other reasons. Some babies have difficulty in digesting cows' milk products, so the baby's doctor may advise a soya-based formula. There are some medical conditions such as Phenylketonuria (PKU) that require the baby to be fed with very special formula milk.

Always check that you are giving the correct feed.

Storing expressed breast milk

K2S133

If a baby is breast-fed, milk expressed by her mother may be brought in to the nursery. It is important to store this milk safely until it is needed. Make sure that the milk is brought in a feeding bottle or other sterile container. The container or bottle, teat and cover must be sterilised in the same way as for formula milk (see above). The bottle must be stored in the fridge until it is needed. The milk can then be warmed in the bottle (as described above) before you feed the baby.

Feeding babies

K2S132
K2D48

When feeding babies:

- Check the feed chart to make sure that you prepare the correct amount of feed and that you are aware of any special requirements for the baby's feed.
- **Some babies are allergic to milk protein and other ingredients in baby milks and weaning foods. Always check that the feed you are preparing to give the baby is the correct one. Never give milk or food to a baby without checking first.**
- Ensure that you have everything ready before beginning to feed the baby.
- You should allow plenty of time to feed the baby without rushing.
- Wash your hands.
- Make sure that you are comfortably seated and that you are holding the baby securely.
- Fasten the baby's bib to protect her clothes.
- This is an ideal time to develop a close and loving relationship with the baby. Use this time throughout the feed to make eye contact with the baby and to talk to her. Make this a relaxed and enjoyable time. Feeding should never be rushed.
- Test the temperature of the milk. An easy way to do this is to drop some milk onto the inside of your wrist. It should feel just warm.
- Check the size of the hole in the teat: Tilt the bottle to allow the milk to flow. It should come out of the teat in steady drops. If the hole is too small the baby

will take in air as she sucks hard to get the milk. This will cause wind; if the teat is too large the feed will be taken too quickly and the baby may choke.

- Make sure that the bottle is held at an angle, so that the baby cannot take in air as she is fed.
- Wind the baby once or twice during a feed and at the end of the feed. To do this, sit the baby upright on your lap and gently stroke or rub her back. This should help the air in the baby's stomach to be brought up. The baby may also bring up a very small amount of the feed during this, so have a tissue or bib ready.
- Settle the baby, clean and wash her face, change the nappy if necessary.
- Clear away. Wash and re-sterilise feeding equipment.
- Record information about the amount taken and any other relevant points on the baby's feed chart so that you can give information to the parents at the end of the day.
- Ensure that any other information about any feeding difficulties is passed on to the relevant member of staff

Feeding a baby should be a one-to-one experience

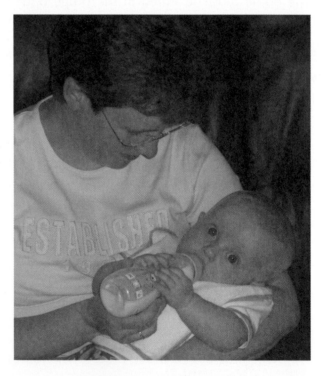

Special equipment for feeding babies

Some babies may need adaptations to the feeding equipment or specialised equipment for feeding. For example, some babies may require a larger or smaller hole in the teat or a softer or harder teat. In more specialised cases, such as babies with a cleft lip and palate, a special teat or spoon may be used and the baby may need to be fed in an upright position. These requirements should be clearly recorded on the baby's feed chart so that practitioners can follow parental and medical advice consistently.

Colic usually occurs between 2 weeks and 3 months of age

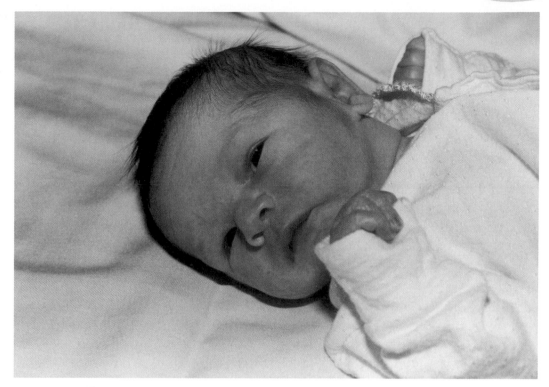

Colic

Whether breast- or bottle-fed, some babies may experience colic, which is caused by air taken in during feeding or crying. This wind passes through the stomach and becomes trapped in the small intestines resulting in painful contractions of the intestines.

Signs of colic

The signs of colic are the baby crying, a reddened face, drawing knees up and appearing to be in pain. It is common in the evenings. However, some babies are affected by colic in the day and night. Any concerns should be discussed with the parent, who may consult the health visitor or doctor.

Care of a baby with colic

- Comfort the baby.
- Lying the baby on the tummy on your lap and rubbing the back will help.
- Rocking movements may also help to relieve the pain.
- Some doctors advise breast-feeding mothers to monitor their diet to avoid foods which may cause colic.
- Bottle-fed babies should be winded regularly; check the teats for hole size and flow of milk.
- The GP may prescribe medicinal drops to be taken before a feed.

Weaning (introducing solid food)

K2S134

Current advice from the Department of Health is that exclusive breast-feeding until a baby is 6 months old provides the best nutrition for babies. Six months is the recommended age to start to introduce solid food for all healthy infants, whether they are breast-fed or bottle-fed. However, there may be individual circumstances when this might vary. You should always follow the advice given to the parents by their health visitor or doctor.

Why is weaning necessary?

Milk alone is not enough for a baby over the age of 6 months. The baby has used the iron stored during pregnancy and must begin to take iron in their diet. Starch and fibre are also necessary for healthy growth and development. Weaning also introduces the baby to new tastes and textures of food.

Weaning and development

Babies at around 6 months can actively spoon feed with the upper lip moving down to clean the spoon. They chew and use the tongue to move food from the front to the back of the mouth. This muscular movement helps the development of the mouth and jaw, and also the development of speech. At 6 months, a baby can also have finger foods and this helps to develop their hand–eye co-ordination. Babies at 6 months will be curious about other tastes and textures.

Mealtimes are sociable occasions and babies need to join in with this. As weaning progresses, they learn how to use a spoon, fork, feeding beaker and cup. They also begin to learn the social rules in their cultural background associated with eating. To do this, they need good role models. Rules may include using a knife and fork, chopsticks, chewing with the mouth closed or sitting at the table until everyone has finished eating.

How to wean

Once the baby can sit with support, it will be easier if the baby is in a high chair at mealtimes. There should be a relaxed atmosphere and no distractions. The practitioner should sit with the baby throughout the feed. It may take a few days of trying for the baby to take food from the spoon successfully.

Guidelines for weaning

- Try different tastes and textures gradually – one at a time. This gives the baby the chance to become accustomed to one new food before another is offered. If a baby dislikes a food, do not force them to eat it. Simply try it again in a few days' time. Babies of six months will be taking an interest in what others are eating. They will want to pick up and taste finger foods, and this should be encouraged.
- Gradually increase the amount of solids to a little at breakfast, lunch and tea. Try to use family foods so that the baby experiences foods from their own

culture. Offer lumpier thicker foods to encourage chewing. The baby may be offered food to hold and chew, such as a piece of toast or apple. A cup may be introduced. Three regular meals should be taken as well as breast or formula milk each day.

- As the baby becomes used to eating solid food, he or she should be having three minced or chopped meals each day plus breast or formula milk as the main drink.
- Babies that do not eat meat or fish should have two servings of split pulses, such as red lentils, beans, chick peas or tofu. This will ensure that they get the nutrients they need.
- Milk will still form the largest part of a baby's diet during the first year of life around 500–600 ml each day.
- Water may be offered in a feeding cup.

Cows' milk

After 6 months, babies may be given cows' milk in food. They should not be offered it as a drink until they are over 1 year old. Milk drinks should continue to be formula milk or breast milk.

Young children over 1 year can be given cows' milk to drink. Semi-skimmed milk should not be given until a child is 3 years old. Skimmed milk is not suitable for children.

Iron

By 6 months, the baby's iron stores are low, so foods containing iron must be given. These include:

- liver
- lamb
- beans
- dahl
- green vegetables
- wholemeal bread
- cereals containing iron.

Do not add salt to any food, as babies' kidneys cannot cope with it. Avoid adding sugar to food or drink as this can lead to tooth decay.

Remember:

- Weaning is a messy business. Babies love to touch their food and to try to feed themselves. Just make sure that the baby's hands are washed before feeding and that the floor is washable or covered to allow for spills.
- Encourage independence by allowing the baby to use their fingers and offering a spoon as soon as the baby can hold one.
- Offer suitable finger foods.
- Allow the baby to find eating a pleasurable experience.
- Babies are not conventional and may prefer to eat things in a different order. Never start a battle by insisting that one thing is finished before the next is offered. When the baby has had enough of one dish, calmly remove it and offer the next.
- Babies will normally want to eat so refusing food could be a sign that a baby is ill.

Feeding children after they are weaned

K2S135

After they are weaned, children will gradually take more solid food in their diet. As they increase the amount of solid food they eat they will need to drink less milk. This process will vary. Some children will accept a mixed diet more readily than others. It is important not to fuss or make food an issue. Children need to be encouraged to try new foods. This is all part of their experience of life. Children who regularly eat a range of foods will be most likely to be getting a balanced diet containing all the essential nutrients There is more information about what makes up a balanced diet in Unit CCLD 205.

Helping children when eating and drinking and ensuring their safety

Young children can learn the skills of feeding independently. They can share with others and learn about appropriate behaviour at mealtimes.

- The children should be comfortably and appropriately seated in a high chair or at the tables so that they can reach their food without difficulty.

- They should not be allowed to eat or drink while walking or running around, nor should they run around holding any feeding utensils.

- If the children are using adult sized furniture they will need a booster seat on the chair.

- Safety harnesses should always be fastened.

- Protective clothing such as aprons and bibs will protect the children's own clothes and allow them to have a go at eating independently.

If younger children are to manage to feed themselves they need to be able to practise the physical skills to enable them to do this. They should be provided with:

- suitable utensils such as cups with two handles

- small sized cutlery, and large rimmed dishes

- help to cut up their food if they need it.

Older children should be given the opportunity to use adult utensils and to manage their own food.

Social interaction at mealtimes

Mealtimes are a good opportunity for families and other groups to tell each other their news and ideas as they eat together. It is good if adults and children sit together at the table without other distractions, such as the television, which

Younger children need to practise feeding themselves

will stop the conversation. Adults can provide help and encourage acceptable behaviour by providing positive role models for the children.

Food allergies

Food allergies can be detected most easily if a baby is offered new foods separately. Symptoms of allergy may include:

- vomiting
- diarrhoea
- skin rashes
- wheezing after eating the offending food
- severe reactions such as convulsions, difficulty in breathing. Look at Unit CCLD 202 to see what to do if this happens.

Always check before you give a baby any food to make sure that it is safe to do so.

Peanut and nut allergy appears to be increasing among young children. For this reason, they are best avoided in the diet. Whole nuts should not be given to children under 5 as they could cause choking.

Signs and symptoms of illness in babies and children under 3

K2S136

Babies and young children will often become ill quite quickly. You may welcome a child in the morning who appears to be quite well. However, after a short time you observe signs and symptoms that tell you they are ill. The signs and symptoms that you see first are often general ones such as:

- crying
- diarrhoea
- vomiting
- irritability
- feeling hot
- different behaviour
- not eating
- not drinking
- not responding to friendly contact
- listless, not lively
- coughing
- runny nose.

You may see one or some of these signs. You must report your concerns to your line manager who will decide on the proper course of action. Make a record of what you have observed.

If the baby or child continues to be ill it is possible that you will see more signs of a particular illness. These could include rashes. There is more information about the signs and symptoms of specific illnesses in Unit CCLD 205.

Signs of illness are always more urgent and worrying in a baby. **You should never delay reporting your concerns.**

Bathing and washing babies

K2S137
K2S138
K2D48

Caring for a baby's skin and hair will ensure the child stays comfortable and free from infection. Most babies and small children will have a daily bath. However, this may not always be necessary and parents may not wish the baby to be bathed each day. An all-over wash may be enough. In most day care settings, you will only need to 'top and tail' babies (see below).

Safety while washing and bathing

Babies must be supervised at all times while in the bath or while being washed. Always hold a small baby securely while bathing and washing. As the baby gets older, she may feel more comfortable in a sitting position in the bath. Constant physical support must be given to prevent the baby from sliding under the water or from feeling insecure. A non-slip bath mat is essential for safety. Discourage older babies from standing up in the bath, as serious injuries could result from a fall.

Bath time is fun

K2D48

If the baby is safe in the bath, they will feel secure and begin to enjoy the experience of kicking and splashing. Once babies can sit up in the bath, there are many toys available or you can use household objects. For example, empty washing-up liquid bottles can be used to squirt water; plastic jugs will enable filling and pouring.

Bath time is fun

Topping and tailing

K2S138

Topping and tailing involves cleaning the baby's face, hands and bottom.

Preparation

Make sure that the room is warm, the windows are closed, there are no draughts, and the room and the equipment are clean and safe. Put on protective clothing such as an apron and gloves. It is standard practice in day care settings to use latex disposable gloves while washing and changing babies. In private homes, high standards of hygiene should be followed. Any cuts or grazes should be covered. You should always wash your hands before and after washing and changing a baby even if you wear gloves.

Collect all the necessary equipment:

- a bowl of warm water
- a separate bowl of cooled, boiled water for the eyes in the first month or so
- cotton wool balls
- baby sponge or flannel
- towel
- change of clothes
- nappies
- creams, if used
- blunt-ended nail scissors.

Method

1   Lay the baby on a towel or changing mat. While lifting a small baby it is important to support the baby's head. To do this, put one hand under the head and one under the body as you lift the baby.

2   Remove outer clothing, if the baby is to be changed. Leave the nappy in place.

3   Gently wipe each eye with a cotton wool ball, moistened with cooled boiled water. Wipe from the inner corner to the outer (nose to ear). Use a separate cotton wool ball for each eye.

4   Wipe the face, neck and ears with moistened cotton wool balls.

5   Dry with clean cotton wool balls. Pay attention to skin creases especially the neck creases.

6   Clean the baby's hands, using a sponge or flannel. Check that nails are short and that there are no jagged edges that may scratch.

7   Change the nappy. This is described in detail below.

8   Replace clothing.

9   Brush or comb the hair.

10   Settle the baby.

11   Dispose of waste materials and nappies in the designated bins.

Topping and
tailing

12   Put clothes ready for collection or laundering.

13   Clear away the equipment and wash your hands.

Remember bathing like this is a time when you can talk to the baby, communicate and have fun.

When washing, bathing and changing babies, it is important to know about any preferences the parents may have. For example, they may prefer certain skin creams, shampoos, oils or lotions. The baby may have a reaction to some skin products. Always check first.

Changing babies and small children

K2S138
K2S139

Small babies wet and soil their nappies frequently. So it is important to change them as often as necessary. Most settings will have a routine for doing this. The usual times will be at feed times and before settling the baby down for a sleep. Extra changes will often be needed to keep the baby comfortable, dry and clean. Nappy changing should suit the needs of the baby and the wishes of the parents.

The environment

Most settings will have an area set aside for changing babies. There may be a separate bathroom for the babies. It is important that this area is warm and free from draughts. All the equipment needed should be stored in this area so that it can easily be reached. This will include clean nappies, toiletries, clothes and bags and bins for disposing of wet and dirty nappies. In some settings, parents will provide nappies and toiletries for their baby. In other settings, these may be provided. Strict hygiene procedures must be followed. Changing mats and surfaces must be thoroughly cleaned after each baby has been changed.

Nappies and toiletries

There are two types of nappy available: reusable (terry) nappies and disposable nappies. The choice of nappy is based on personal preference. This is something that will need to be discussed with the parents so that their preferences are followed.

Both types of nappy are quite adequate if they are used with care. Whichever type is used, babies should be changed every three to four hours, at each feeding time, and between if they are awake and uncomfortable. Talk to the baby while you are changing the nappy, and let them enjoy some freedom without the restriction of a nappy.

Disposable nappies are available in a wide range of sizes. They are made to suit all ages and may be shaped for boys and girls. Terry nappies are either shaped or the standard rectangle. Rectangular nappies will need to be folded to fit each baby. Terry nappies are fastened with one or two nappy pins. These are large safety pins and have a safety cap that prevents the pin opening accidentally. Plastic pants are used with terry nappies. These are available in different sizes to suit each baby.

Folding terry nappies

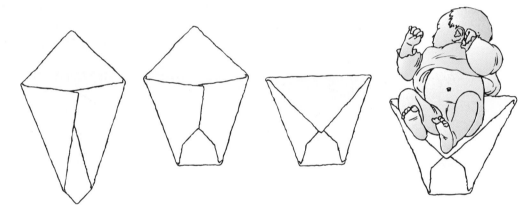

If one-way nappy liners and disposable nappy liners are being used with a terry nappy, arrange the layers like this.

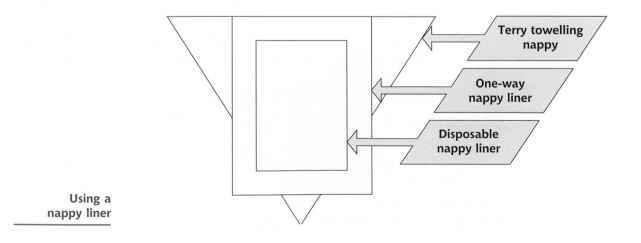

Using a nappy liner

One-way nappy liners help to keep the baby dry. They let the wetness through to the terry nappy but stay dry themselves. Disposable liners make dealing with dirty nappies easier as they can be flushed down the lavatory. Terry nappies are rinsed then put to soak in nappy sterilising solution. Use a bucket with a well fitting lid for this. Disposable nappies are well wrapped in a plastic bag and put into the correct bin. Some settings may have a special nappy unit that seals nappies into plastic bags.

In some cultures, nappies are not used and babies may simply have a piece of cloth placed under them. When they are bigger, clothing is designed to make using a potty quicker and easier.

Changing a nappy

K2S138
K2S139
K2D48

Ideally it should be the child's key person who regularly changes the nappy. This will help the child to develop a close relationship with that person. It is also better if babies and young children are changed as they need it, rather than adopting the conveyor belt approach of a mass changing time, where there is no time for talking and playing.

1   Prepare the changing area before you start. There should be a separate area for this, well away from the food preparation and eating areas. Make sure that the area is clean and that there are no draughts. Keep the other children away from this area.

2   Gather all the things you will need including:
    – changing mat
    – wipes or bowl of water for washing the baby's bottom
    – towel or cotton wool to dry the baby
    – clean clothes
    – clean nappy
    – a bucket with a lid for the soiled nappy.
    – a container for any dirty clothes

3   Put on an apron, wash your hands and put on gloves.

4   Fetch the baby from the cot or pram and lay her on the changing mat. The mat should be placed on a safe surface or on the floor. Very careful supervision is needed to ensure the baby's safety. **Never leave a baby for any reason, do not look away or get distracted.** It is best to keep one hand on the baby at all times.

5   Undress the baby so that you can get at the nappy. Remove the nappy and any soiled clothes and put them into the containers provided.

6   Clean the baby's bottom thoroughly using water, baby wipes or other chosen toiletries. Make sure her bottom is dry before applying any creams, oils or lotions chosen by the parents.

7   If the baby is happy, then give her time to kick free from the nappy. This is a good time to observe the baby's skin and note any marks or soreness.

8   Put on a clean nappy and dress the baby.

9   Place the baby back in her cot, pram or other safe place.

10   Dispose of the dirty nappy and clothes.

11   Wash your hands (with your gloves on) and clean the changing mat and area and leave it ready for the next user.

12   Remove and dispose of your apron and gloves.

13   Wash your hands.

This is an ideal time to talk to babies and small children. They are naturally in a situation of one-to-one care, so use this time for making eye contact, talking, laughing.

Always make time to play with the baby and talk to her while changing her nappy. Take your time and don't rush this and the baby will enjoy being free from her nappy for a while and having the full attention of her carer

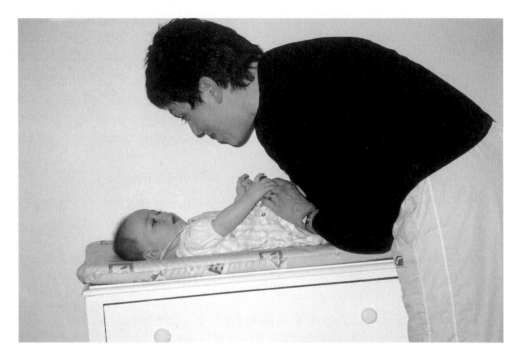

Reporting any concerns

This is a good time to observe a baby's skin. Any concerns should be recorded and reported to a senior member of staff for advice and guidance. For example, you may see:

- soreness

- a rash

- bruising.

When a baby dirties its nappy, the contents are often referred to as stools. A normal stool is usually of a soft consistency and yellow in colour. Variations may mean that the baby has a problem. For example:

- Streaks of blood may indicate an injury.
- Small hard green stools could mean that the baby is constipated.
- Very frequent stools (diarrhoea) may indicate an infection.

A baby's nappy is normally wet at each nappy change. If the nappy stays dry, there is a decrease in the amount of urine passed and this may be a sign of illness. A chart to record information about feeds and urine and stools is a helpful way of identifying any cause for concern.

Care of black skin

All babies may have dry skin, but it is especially common in babies who have black skins and this should be given special care. Always consult the parents about any special care that needs to be given to a baby's skin and hair. The following are general guidelines:

- Oil may be added to the bath water and do not use detergent-based products, as these are drying.
- Oil or cream may be massaged into the skin after bathing. Oil may also be massaged into the hair to help prevent dryness and damage.
- Observe the baby frequently for signs of dryness and irritation – scaly patches need treating with a moisturising cream.
- Beware of sunshine. Always use a sun block on a baby's skin in the sun, and a sun hat.
- Comb very curly hair with a wide-toothed comb.
- Avoid doing tight plaits in the hair as this can pull the hair root out and cause bald patches.

Toiletries

There are lots of toiletries that are specifically made for use with babies. These include:

- soap
- baby wipes
- lotions
- creams
- bath products
- barrier creams
- shampoo
- body powder
- sun protection creams and lotions.

There are some creams, oils and lotions that are specially made to use when changing a nappy. They help to protect the baby's bottom and prevent rashes and soreness developing. It is important to find out which toiletries are used for each baby. Parents will have particular preferences and will wish certain products to be used. Some toiletries may cause skin reactions. Babies with very sensitive skins may have special creams prescribed by their doctor.

Common skin problems

Cradle cap

Cradle cap affects the scalp. It is seen as a scaly, greasy or dry crust usually around the soft spot (fontanelle) on the baby's head. Prevent this by washing the hair once or twice a week, and rinsing it very thoroughly. If it becomes unsightly or sore, the crust can be removed using special shampoo.

Heat rash

Heat rash is caused by over-heating and appears as a red, pinpoint rash, which may come and go. Remove surplus clothing, bath the baby to remove sweat and to reduce the itching and make the baby feel comfortable.

Eczema

Eczema is fairly common in babies, especially if there is a family history of allergies. It begins with areas of dry skin, which may itch and become red. Scratching will cause the skin to weep and bleed. Cotton scratch mittens should prevent this. Avoid perfumed toiletries; use oil such as Oilatum in the bath and an aqueous cream instead of soap. Biological washing powders and some fabric conditioners may irritate the condition, so use an alternative. Cotton clothing is best, as it is absorbent and not irritating to the skin. The baby's doctor should be consulted if the condition is severe or causing distress.

Nappy rash

K2S136

Nappy rash usually begins gradually with a reddening of the skin in the nappy area; if this is not treated it will blister and become raw and sore. It is extremely uncomfortable for the baby, who will cry in pain when the nappy is changed. Causes of nappy rash are:

- a soiled or wet nappy left on too long – this allows ammonia present in urine to irritate the skin
- an allergy to, for example, washing powder, wet-wipes or baby cream
- an infection, for example thrush
- inadequate rinsing of terry nappies, and using plastic pants.

Treatment is as follows:

1   Remove the nappy.
2   Wash the bottom, rinse and dry thoroughly.
3   Let the baby lie with the nappy off as much as possible, to expose the bottom to the air.

4   Change the nappy as soon as the baby has wet or soiled it, at least every two hours.

5   Apply cream sparingly and make sure the baby's bottom is completely dry before putting on any cream.

Do not use plastic pants. If there is no improvement, consult the health visitor or doctor.

Helping with 'toilet training'

K2D140
K2D48

'Toilet training' is the normal development of bowel and bladder control (being able to be dry and clean).

Babies and young children do not have control over their bladder or bowels and will just wet or dirty their nappies at any time. This often happens after they have been fed. The ability to control the bladder and bowels so that children become clean and dry will gradually develop. This will happen when the child is able to understand when the **bladder** or **bowel** is full. Most children will usually be reliably clean and dry by the age of about 3 years. The age at which this happens will vary. There does not seem to be any point in rushing this. It is much easier if any 'training' is left until the child is at least 2 years old and is able to understand what is needed.

There are some general guidelines for deciding when a child is ready to be clean and dry:

- Wait until the child is ready. They may tell you they do not want to wear a nappy or be interested in other children using the potty or the toilet.
- The child must be aware of the need to use the toilet or potty and be able to tell that the bowel or bladder is full by recognising the feeling.
- Children must be able to tell their carer, verbally or with actions, that they need to go to the toilet.

Helping children become dry and clean

- Children need to be given the opportunity to visit the toilet or use the potty regularly. They may need reminding if they are playing.
- Be relaxed give praise for success. As children become successful, they will be more independent and they will feel pleased about their achievements, increasing their self-esteem. Do not show displeasure or disapproval about 'accidents' just accept them. Do any cleaning and provide clean clothes without any fuss.
- Provide good **role models**. Seeing other children without nappies and being clean and dry will help children to understand the process.
- Avoid sitting children on the potty for long periods of time.
- Remember that parents may have their own ideas about toileting. It is important that this is discussed so that you can follow a similar routine to the home one.

Potties

Potties must be used in a separate area well away from food preparation and eating areas. The contents of potties should be flushed down the toilet. Potties must be cleaned with hot soapy water and disinfectant and dried thoroughly. There should be a separate sink that is used for this (not a basin that is used for hand-washing). Always use protective clothing when you are doing this.

Toilet training Tom

Amanda is a nanny and cares for Tom, who is just 2 years old, while his parents are working. Tom is a happy little boy who is still wearing disposable nappies all the time. Tom's mother is very keen that he should become toilet trained and has asked Amanda for her advice and help.

K2D140

➤ *How will Amanda know if Tom is ready to be trained?*

➤ *How should she suggest that she and Tom's mother go about this?*

Dressing babies and children

When choosing baby clothes, there are some important points to remember:

- Choose clothes that are easy to wash and dry.
- Natural fibres such as cotton are the most comfortable as they are more absorbent than synthetic fabrics.
- Clothing should be comfortable, and not too tight. This will allow for easy movement. Tight clothing, especially around the feet, can cause bones to become deformed.

Choose clothes that are comfortable and allow for free movement

- Clothes made of stretch fabric and with wide sleeves make dressing and undressing much easier.
- Avoid suits with feet, as it is tempting to continue using them after they have been outgrown. A footless suit with a pair of correctly sized socks is a better alternative.
- Clothes should have a flame-retardant finish.
- Avoid ribbons and ties. They may cause strangulation.

Children's clothes are usually made of material that can be easily washed. It is important to check before you buy that the clothes can be washed in a machine. Hand-washing sounds fine, but if you are busy it takes time, so restrict this to one or two special items.

Sleeping

Daytime sleeping

Babies and younger children may need a daytime sleep. It is very important to discuss this with the child's parents so that you are following their home routine and their wishes. If children are sleeping at nursery, it is important to provide a safe place for them to sleep. Cots, mats or beanbags may be provided. If children do not have their own cot to sleep in, then any sheets and covers should be changed for each child. The room should be properly ventilated and the temperature controlled so that the children do not become over-heated. Dimming the lights will also help to provide a restful environment. Children should always be supervised when they are sleeping so a member of staff should be with them all the time.

To prevent cot deaths, current research recommends that all babies should sleep:

- on their backs
- without a pillow
- feet against the bottom of the cot
- using sheets and blankets *not* a duvet
- in a room temperature of 18°C (68°F).

Checking on sleeping babies regularly or using a baby monitor can also be helpful in ensuring safety.

There is more information about rest and sleep in Unit CCLD 205.

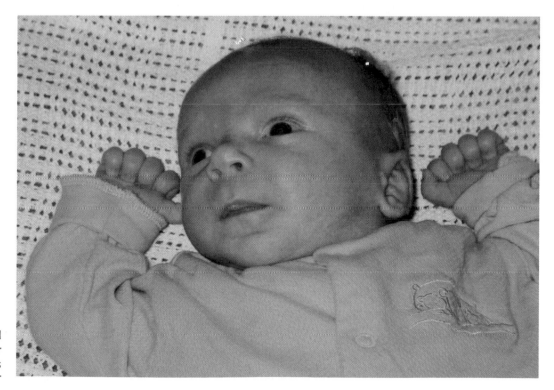

All babies should sleep on their backs

Practical Example

K2S141

Sleeping safely

Jasmine is a young mother who has a new baby, India, who is just a few weeks old. Jasmine and her partner have had lots of advice about how to look after India from relatives and friends. Some say she should sleep on her tummy, others say the side or back is best. They are most anxious about the baby when they put her down to sleep and they are not in the room.

➤ *What advice would you give Jasmine about caring for India when she is sleeping?*

➤ *How could they reassure themselves that India is safe when they are not in the room?*

➤ *What is the policy of your setting when babies are put down to sleep?*

Providing a safe clean environment for babies

Keeping the environment hygienic

K2S123

It is very important that strict hygiene procedures are followed in childcare settings, especially where babies are being cared for. Cross-contamination and cross-infection can be avoided.

Checklist for a hygienic environment

The environment:

- Keep kitchen work surfaces and implements clean.
- Use disinfectant to clean work surfaces regularly.
- Wash surfaces and implements with hot soapy water after they have come into contact with raw food, particularly meat, fish, and poultry.
- Wash tea towels, dish cloths and other cleaning cloths regularly on the hottest cycle of the washing machine, or use very hot water if washing by hand.
- Clean babies' toys at least each day or after each session with hot soapy water or disinfectant.
- Keep toilet areas clean. Disinfect the seats, handles, door handles and sink taps at least after each session. Keep rubbish bins securely closed and out of the reach of the children.
- Nappies and other waste involving bodily fluids must be securely wrapped and disposed of in the designated bins following the policy of the setting. Childcare workers must ensure that they wear latex gloves when handling any waste contaminated with bodily fluids. Wash your hands after doing this even if gloves have been worn.
- Any spills or accidents involving bodily waste must be mopped up using a 1% bleach solution and gloves and aprons must be worn.

- Any spills should be mopped up immediately. Separate mops should be assigned to the different areas of the setting, for example kitchen and bathroom.
- The bathroom area where babies are changed must be checked and cleaned regularly.
- Changing mats should be disinfected after each nappy change.
- Children should have their own potty.
- Children should have their own cot. If this is not possible, then the cot should be cleaned and the bedding changed before another child uses it.
- Babies should not share dummies or teething rings/rattles and these items should be sterilised regularly.

Personal hygiene (both practitioners and children):

Hands must be washed before:

- preparing food
- preparing babies' bottles or weaning food
- eating or drinking
- attending to skin or nappy rash
- giving a child's medicine.

Hands must be washed after:

- going to the toilet
- handling raw food
- changing nappies
- wiping noses
- coughing or sneezing
- touching pets or their equipment.

Animals:

- Keep pets free from infection.
- Keep pets out of food preparation areas.
- Wash and store pets' equipment separately.
- Keep pet food and litter trays out of children's reach.

Food preparation:

- Ensure that food is handled and stored correctly.
- Prepare food following the instructions on packaging and in recipes.

Nursery equipment

K2S123

All equipment must comply with safety regulations and must be used following the manufacturer's instructions. Look for the British Standards Institute and other marks of safety (see Unit CCLD 202).

Cleaning equipment

All equipment should be cared for correctly. This will include cleaning and checking equipment regularly. Cleaning should be carried out following the manufacturer's instructions.

Washable items can be cleaned using hot soapy water then rinsed and allowed to dry. Anti-bacterial sprays are useful but be careful that they don't replace thorough washing.

Soft toys can often be washed in the washing machine. Some soft toys can only have a surface wash. Follow the manufacturer's instructions.

Cleaning should be regular; how often will depend on the number of children using toys and equipment, but at least at the end of each play session or more often if there is a lot of use by a large number of children. It is useful to check on the cleaning methods when buying toys. Choose those that can be washed and cared for easily. Anything that needs dry cleaning will not be a practical buy.

Change and separation

Attachments

K2T130
K2D48

The quality of children's early close relationships is very important. Children need to develop close, affectionate, two-way relationships with those who care for them. These relationships are called attachments. Good attachments help children to feel secure, happy and confident.

Babies and young children will try to stay close to the adults they are attached to. They want to be cared for by them. By the end of their first year, they show that they prefer to be with these adults. These adults may include people such as their grandparents, aunts and uncles, as well as their parents. Babies and young children usually become unhappy if they are separated from them. They may show anxiety and cry if they are left with strangers. Babies and young children need good preparation, understanding of their needs and good substitute care if they are to be cared for successfully by others.

How attachments are formed

Attachments build up over a period of time. Their quality depends on how a parent and baby relate to each other both before and after birth. Attachments develop best:

- if pregnancy and birth are a good experience
- if the child is wanted
- in a happy and secure family environment.
- if there is good quality, close contact between infant and mother and other carers in the first three years of the child's life.

Attachments
develop best if
there is good
quality, close
contact between
infant and carers

Children need to
be cared for
in a happy
environment
that does not
change from day
to day

Providing good quality care

Attachments develop if practitioners meet children's needs and give them good quality care. Good quality care includes a practitioner:

- playing with the child
- cuddling them
- giving them individual attention
- having 'conversations' with them
- enjoying their company
- meeting their physical and emotional needs.

A baby or young child forms a stronger attachment with a person who plays and talks to them, than with someone who simply meets their physical needs.

You should always talk to and play with the young children in your care. In this way, you will be able to relate closely to them. A **key person** system is one where a worker is responsible for a particular child. This can help practitioners to form a special relationship with children in their care. Key persons can also form a positive and helpful relationship with a child's parents.

When a baby or young child starts nursery, it usually involves:

- separation from their main, familiar carer
- a change of physical environment
- feelings of loss.

This loss can affect a child's feelings of stability, security and trust. In general, children react most strongly to separation between the ages of 6 months and 3 years.

Why support is needed

Children have to adapt to a new setting when they start at a day nursery, a playgroup or school or go to a childminder. They will need help to cope with separation from the people to whom they are attached. They may have feelings of loss, anxiety and stress caused by the changes. Adults need to help them to adjust to their new setting.

Preparing for change

Children are immature and vulnerable. Preparation before any change can help children to adjust. Preparation has become part of the policy of most nurseries, childminders, pre- schools and hospitals. Practitioners can advise parents to prepare their children by:

- being sensitive to their needs and stage of development
- talking and listening to them
- explaining things to them and reassuring them honestly
- reading books and watching certain videos with them

- providing imaginative and expressive play to help them to express their feelings
- going on introductory visits
- providing personal details about their child and their cultural background.

Ways to help children to adjust to new settings

K2T130
K2D48
K2T1112

Childcare workers should take the child's age into account when providing care for any child in a new setting. Generally, separation is more difficult between 6 months to 3 years of age. The younger the child, the more they will benefit from a one-to-one relationship with a particular person. Some settings have a named key person for each child. This is the person who makes a relationship with a particular child. When possible they greet the child on arrival, settle them in and attend to their needs. The key person will also be responsible for observing the child, making records and sharing observations with parents. Practitioners should find out the particular needs and background of each child. They will then be able to respond better to their individual needs.

Settling-in

Most settings will have a settling-in policy. This is designed to help babies and young children adjust to a new environment. This will vary, but usually starts with a short initial visit. This gives the baby and parent chance to meet the key person and see the nursery. At the next visit, the parent stays with the baby and the key person plays alongside. The next time, the key person will take a more active role. Depending on the time available, more visits can be made until the parent leaves the child for a short period. The next step is to leave the child for a longer time while the key person builds up an attachment.

Starting at a new setting

When a young child starts a new setting, it is good practice for childcare workers to:

- welcome new babies, children and their parents warmly when they arrive and call them by the name they prefer
- make sure that a baby's or child's comfort objects are readily available to them if they are needed. This may mean keeping a blanket or a favourite toy in a particular place and knowing the policy of the setting. They should agree this with the parent
- show older children around so that the physical layout is less strange and becomes more familiar. Give them a special coat peg with a picture or label of their own. Provide a drawer to keep personal objects and work in. These will all help to make them feel they belong
- prepare other workers by passing on information about the child's needs
- introduce them to other workers in a relaxed way without rushing them
- reassure them and comfort them if they appear anxious or upset. It is important to observe children closely to be aware of any early signs of distress and respond to these

- be sympathetic. Help them to deal with routines and other things that are unfamiliar. Remember that even adults can find unfamiliar surrounding difficult

- provide new children with appropriate activities. These should include play and play that encourages the expression of feelings

- develop ways or strategies to encourage children to join in with activities. This may mean allowing them to play alongside an adult or other children for a while. It could mean letting them watch and gently encouraging them to join in with you or another child when they are ready

- allow them to adjust to the setting and the routines in their own way and in their own time. Children will vary in the time it will take them. This may depend on their previous experiences of change and on their age and their personality.

Encourage a new child to join in with other children when they are ready

Parents

Parents may well be distressed when leaving a baby or young child in your care. They may be feeling guilty about leaving their baby and anxious about how the baby will settle. To help parents, you must reassure them that they remain the most important people in their child's life. It is also very important that the policy of the setting includes sharing information with parents about their child's day. Settings often do this by keeping a diary of information that parents can read when they come to collect their child. Key persons should also be there to talk to parents.

Sharing information with parents

Babies make very rapid progress in their development during their first year. Most parents will be very anxious to know about their baby's progress. They will also wish to know about their baby's day, for example what they have done, how well they have fed and what they have eaten.

Many nurseries and childminders keep a daily written record for the parents to see at the end of each day. Feed charts will also provide information, for the nursery and the parents and can be used to record any changes.

Written records should also be used to give parents an opportunity to provide information for the nursery. Sharing information is a two-way process. This is very important when caring for babies, as changes in the care are frequently needed. A good example of this is feeding requirements. This will also help to ensure that parent's wishes and suggestions are put into practice.

Element 208.2 — Are you ready for assessment?

Provide safe physical care for babies and children under 3 years

You need to show that you can competently provide safe physical care for babies and young children under 3 years. To do this, you will need to be directly observed by your assessor and present other types of evidence. The amount and type of evidence you need to present will vary. You should plan this with your assessor.

Direct observation by your assessor

Observation and/or Expert Witness Testimony is the required assessment method to be used to evidence some part of each element in this unit. If your assessor is unable to observe you s/he will identify an expert in your workplace who will provide testimony of your work-based performance. Usually your assessor or expert witness will observe you in real work activities and this should provide most of the evidence for the performance criteria for the elements in this unit.

Preparing to be observed

You will need to show that, as you care for the babies and children, you can talk with them and build up a relationship with them. Babies and young children will often need comforting. You should know about individual children's comfort objects. Be alert to children's distress and provide comfort.

You will need to arrange to clean bottles and other equipment and to prepare a formula feed for your assessment. Try to ensure that you include bottles, teats, plastic cups, dishes and spoons in the articles you clean and sterilise. Prepare a bottle-feed following a baby's feed chart and the instructions on the tin. ▶

Arrange to feed a baby. Check the feed charts and make all the necessary preparations. Ensure that you and the baby are comfortable during the feed and that you talk to the baby. Smile as you talk to the baby and make eye contact. Make sure that you keep the teat covered when the bottle is put down. Clean and settle the baby after the feed and fill in the relevant records.

You will need to arrange to prepare and give a baby weaning food from a spoon and if possible provide some finger food. Try to make sure that this is relaxed and that you communicate and interact with the baby. Protect the baby's clothing and wash their hands before and after feeding. Consult the baby's feed chart before feeding and make your own entry afterwards.

Help children when eating and drinking at a mealtime or snack time. Ensure that you prepare the area where children will eat and drink by making sure that all the tables and utensils are clean and that there are enough suitable aprons and bibs if needed. Provide enough chairs of a suitable size and height for the children to be seated comfortably. Make sure that suitable cups, plates, bowls are provided so that the children can feed and help themselves. Create a relaxed atmosphere so that this is an enjoyable time.

You will need to arrange for your assessor to see you wash and dress a baby or young child and change a nappy. This is a tricky procedure so make sure you have done it a few times and feel confident. Make sure that you have everything ready before you fetch the child you are going to wash and change. Carry out the washing, changing and dressing in a careful and unhurried manner and follow the guidelines above. Pay particular attention to hygiene and safety. Don't forget to talk to the child and make sure that time is taken to let the child be free from the nappy. This should be a relaxed time where you have one-to-one contact with the babies and children. When you have finished changing, make sure that the changing area is thoroughly cleaned and left ready for the next user. Make any records needed.

Read the performance criteria carefully before your assessment.

Other types of evidence

You may need to provide other types of evidence in order to:

- cover criteria not observed by your assessor
- show that you have the required knowledge and understanding.

Element 208.3

Provide play and activities to encourage learning and development

Babies and young children are completely dependent on their main careers to meet all their needs. They need constant care and attention. They also need to play and learn if they are to grow and develop successfully.

Children progress at their own rate, but practitioners need to be aware of the stages of development so that they can provide what is needed to interest and encourage a child's development. Babies and young children learn using all their senses: touch, taste, smell, sight and hearing

There is more information about development in Unit CCLD 203.

The practitioner role

K2S126
K2D48

Babies and young children use all of the time, when they are not sleeping, for playing and learning. Practitioners, and especially a child's key person, are the most important play resource in any childcare setting.

Babies and young children are curious. They enjoy exploring their environment. They like repeating activities; they do this to perfect their skills. It is important to allow them time to do this and not to rush them when they are concentrating on their play. Daily routines, like feeding and changing, provide very good opportunities for practitioners to play and talk with babies and young children. It is very important that you support babies and children in their play and learning. This includes praising their efforts as they meet the challenges in their everyday experiences. Remember that, for a baby or young child, attempting to do something is very important. So do praise the children when they have a go even if they don't succeed. This is really important as some children will need to try something a number of times before they are successful. Praising the effort as well as the achievement will encourage them to do this.

Play activities to support different areas of learning and development

Physical development

Physical development is often described as having two aspects:

K2D121
K2D125
K2D48

- gross motor skills, which include big movements like walking, running and climbing
- fine motor skills, which include smaller movements, like using the forefinger and thumb to pick up small objects and turning a page in a book. These skills develop alongside hand–eye co-ordination.

Physical development is very closely linked to all the other areas of development. As babies and young children progress in their physical skills, their experiences change. For example, a baby that can sit up has her hands free to hold and explore objects more closely. As babies become more mobile, they can move to explore objects and places that they could not reach before. Although there are activities and equipment that can support the development of physical skills, the practitioner is still the key to progress in the first year.

Safety

K2S123
K2S124
K2D48

Babies walk at different ages, usually between 12 and 18 months. They will be very keen to use their new skill to explore the environment, so ensuring their safety is very important. There is more information about safety and safe supervision and risk assessment earlier in this unit and in Unit CCLD 202.

Once children can walk, they will enjoy a range of activities and equipment that will help them to develop their gross motor skills further.

How to encourage the gross motor skills needed for walking, 0–1 year

Babies make great progress in their physical skills in their first year. At birth they have little control of their bodies but by the time they are 1 year old, they will be well on the way to walking. To encourage the development of walking it is important to know about the stages of physical development:

- At 6 weeks to 3 months, babies will enjoy kicking vigorously. Time should be allowed in the baby's routine for her to kick with the nappy off and to lie on her back and her tummy. Talk to her and touch her hands and feet.

- At around 5–6 months, the baby will begin to sit and take her weight on her legs. Provide safe opportunities for sitting. Hold in a standing position so that she can bounce and practise taking her weight. Babies love this and find it fun to do.

- At 6–9 months, he may well be rolling and crawling to get from one place to another. You will need to provide a safe environment for the baby to practise these skills. You could use a simple tunnel or boxes for the baby to go through and climb into, or a ball or rolling toy to chase after.

- At 9–18 months, she may be pulling herself up to stand or walking with help. Provide safe walking opportunities by having stable furniture for the baby to use to pull herself up. Getting from one piece of furniture to another is a favourite game. Make sure that the pieces of furniture are steady and not too far apart. Hold the baby up in a standing position and support walking. Babies love this and will progress from having two hands held to one hand held. Encourage babies to walk from one person to another. Make the distances short to begin with and hold your arms out to her to give confidence. Praise her efforts even if she doesn't quite make it. This will encourage her to have another go. Walkers and push along toys can also be helpful. However, they need careful supervision as they can tip over or move too quickly.

- Babies who take longer to walk or who have a difficulty may need additional help. This could just be extra encouragement from you. Other children may need to use a walking aid or to get extra help from another professional.

Activities to develop gross motor skills, 1–3 years

Activity	Play and learning
Moving around	Opportunities to run and move around in safety will help children to develop their gross motor skills. This could include outdoor and indoor running games or dancing and moving to music.
Climbing frames	There is a range of climbing frames and it is important to provide one suitable for the children's level of skill. Children will develop balance co-ordination while strengthening their muscles. The chosen frame needs to provide a challenge, while not being too difficult. Support from you will help them have a go at something more challenging. (*continued on page 274*)

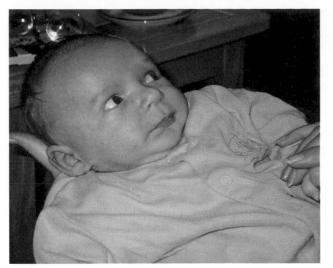

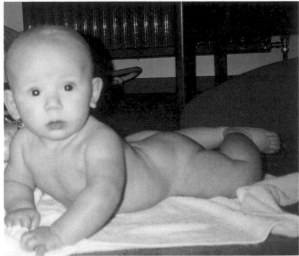

Stages in the development of walking

Activities to develop gross motor skills, 1–3 years (*continued*)

Activity	Play and learning
Slides	A small slide helps children learn to climb the steps. They will get a sense of achievement when they successfully slide down. You will be there to guide, praise and approve their efforts.
Play tunnels	Children enjoy hiding and crawling through these.
Rockers	A small rocker or see-saw will help to develop balance and co-ordination.
Soft play toys equipment	This will let quite young children can move around in safety and develop their gross motor skills.

K2D121
K2D122
K2D125
K2D48

Activities to develop fine motor skills and hand–eye co-ordination, 0–1 year

Age	Development	Role of the practitioner	Equipment/toys
0–6 weeks	Smiles Watches faces and near objects intently	Talking to the baby especially when feeding or changing	Mobiles Musical cot toys Pram toys
6 weeks–3 months	Watches and plays with fingers Holds a rattle briefly Vocalises especially when spoken to Beginning to control their head Watches hanging toys and will try to hit them	Talk to the baby and allow the baby to 'reply' Play finger and hand games like 'Round and round the garden'	Activity blankets Baby gym Pram toys encourage reaching and investigation Different rattles to hold
3–6 months	Sits with support Grasps objects using the whole hand Puts everything in the mouth	Provide safe opportunities for babies to sit. Put cushions around them in case they topple over. Provide safe object of a suitable size for the baby to grasp and put in their mouths Make time for the baby to experience the outside environment Very curious likes to look at everything	Soft hand -sized washable toys Small plastic bricks Small soft balls especially those with a rattle inside Pop-up toys Books with thick pages and bright pictures Outings in the pram or buggy to look at the outside world. Point out the birds, ducks, cars, etc.

9–12 months	Points at object Uses a pincer grasp to hold smaller object Claps hands	Play 'peep-bo' games and clapping games Point and name objects Allow the baby to feed herself Read books and encourage the baby to handle books Take the baby outside in a pram or buggy. Sitting outside on a rug to view the environment	Safe everyday objects, e.g. wooden spoons, saucepans, boxes, plastic jugs Stacking beakers Shape sorters Bath toys, jugs, sponges Bricks Books Supervised water play Outings in the pram or buggy

Activities to develop fine motor skills and hand–eye co-ordination, 1–3 years

- Cups and shapes that fit inside one another
- posting boxes
- building blocks
- interlocking bricks
- construction equipment, such as Duplo, Stickle Brix
- mark-making equipment, such as large crayons and pencils
- sand with equipment like spoons, spades and a variety of containers
- water with jugs and other pouring equipment
- suitable jigsaws
- finger painting
- using a cup, spoon or other feeding utensils
- fastening clothes.

K2D121
K2D122
K2D125
K2D48

You need to choose activities and equipment that are right for the children's stage of development. Remember that for manipulative play, the smaller the hands the bigger the pieces need to be.

Don't forget that everyday activities like using a spoon and trying to do up buttons and zips also help to develop hand–eye co-ordination and fine motor skills. You will need to be on hand to help with this. Show the children how it is done.

Babies and children with visual difficulties may need extra help when developing their fine motor skills. This is because, normally, the eyes would work closely with the hands to co-ordinate these movements.

Developing fine motor skills and hand-eye co-ordination

Listening and responding

K2D48
K2D121
K2D125

Babies are good listeners. Even before they are born they listen and respond to the sounds around them. Babies as young as 3 or 4 weeks old will show they are listening by moving their eyes towards someone speaking to them. As they move through their first year of life, babies show that they can listen and understand. By the time they are 1 year old, they will respond to what is said to them and begin to use words. They love sounds and will coo, babble and repeat sounds. They will listen to music and rhymes, especially if you do the actions.

Young children will respond to simple requests. They learn new words quickly and begin to use them in their speech. They continue to enjoy sounds and music.

Actively encouraging listening and responding

K2D48
K2D121
K2D122
K2D125

You need to spend time with babies and a good way to do this is to use everyday activities. You will be feeding and changing babies and young children and this is an ideal time to talk with the child and allow time for her responses. You can talk with babies as you dress them; count their fingers and toes and sing and play. Make this a fun time. Don't do all the talking –wait for her responses. Leave time for the baby to 'reply'.

Taped rhymes and stories are good to share with babies and young children. Make sure that some are for listening and some are for joining in. Don't forget that babies and young children like to hear familiar things. You should get to know their favourites and use them often. Babies will often link what they hear to what happens. For example, they get to know the sounds that their food is being prepared or the water running before being washed. Talk to them about these everyday sounds so that they can make the links.

Be ready to talk to the children about things that interest them. Listen to their questions and answer carefully. Introduce objects that you think might interest the children. These can be things you come across, for example flowers, birds or insects that you might see outdoors.

Action songs and games will encourage children to listen. Stories will encourage children to listen and respond. Use puppets, pictures or other props to encourage children to listen and join in.

All children under 3 will be using non-verbal as well as verbal ways to communicate. Children with communication difficulties should be encouraged to use non-verbal ways to join in.

Emotional and social competence

K2D48
K2D121
K2D122
K2D125

During their first three years, babies and young children become aware of themselves as separate from others. They need to be accepted and valued by their close carers and to become self-assured. They will gradually develop self-confidence and self-esteem. They need to feel that they belong and have a place within the group. Babies and young children make healthy emotional attachments. To do this they must make trusting and secure relationships with the important adults around them. As they acquire other skills, they will gradually be able to feed and dress themselves and become more independent.

Action rhymes like 'Round and round the garden' encourage listening and responding

Babies who are being looked after away from their parents or main carer will need to separate from their parents and make a secure relationship with one person in the setting. Most day care settings do this by having a key person who will be linked to a particular child. This will help a good relationship to be formed and will be a contact for the child's parents. Ideally the key person should:

- settle children when they arrive
- play with the children and give them individual attention
- enjoy the children's company
- have conversations with them
- cuddle them and encourage snuggling in
- change and wash them during the day
- feed and be with them at meals and snack time
- be with children as they rest or sleep
- be on hand when babies and small children wake after sleeping
- be available to talk to parents as they bring and collect their children.

When a key person is absent another familiar adult should help the child.

To help babies and young children feel that they belong, they will need their own place to keep their things. These could be their comfort objects or another link with home like a photo. A key person will be able to provide a consistent and comforting presence and form a special relationship with the child. Opportunities for children to become involved in domestic routines will help to provide links between the setting and home.

Help the children to build secure relationships with you. Make time to play and have fun. Always get down to the child's level so that they can see you properly. Provide some role-play opportunities so that the child can dress up and try out being someone else. Give all the children a chance to contribute to the group and always show that you value their efforts.

Allow babies to play by themselves for short periods of time. Choose a favourite toy and remain close by. Gradually increase the time that they play independently. Encourage the children to help with getting out resources and in tidying up and putting away. Let babies and young children feed themselves. Babies can help by patting or holding the cup or bottle. Older children can begin to use a spoon or other feeding tool. It may be messy, but it will enable them to develop important self-help skills. They will also improve their physical skills.

Usually, children under 3 will play by themselves (solitary play) or side by side with another child (parallel play). Children will begin to share and co-operate in their play as they become more experienced. It is important that you remember this when you are providing activities for babies and young children under 3 in group situations. The younger children are unlikely to share and co-operate with each other, so you must make sure that there are enough toys and materials for everyone. Most interactive games that children under 3 play are with their key

Play interactive
games like
peep-bo

person. These include peep-bo, tickling games, finger rhymes, clapping games, hiding games and chase.

Thinking and learning

K2D48
K2D121
K2D122
K2D125

Babies and young children are naturally very curious and are eager to explore the world around them. They do this by using their whole body and their senses of sight, touch, smell, taste and hearing. Their developing physical skills also help them to do this. For example, a baby of about 6 months will look at an object, grasp it and feel it, then smell and taste it by putting it in his mouth. As babies become more mobile, more of the world is opened up for them to explore.

Babies also remember past actions and use this to predict what will happen. For example, if the baby smells and hears the sound of food being prepared, he will expect that food is coming soon. Routines help babies and young children to learn about the pattern of the day. They will be able to remember the sequence of events providing you keep things the same. Involve them in the day-to-day things that happen in the setting, like tidying up and laying the table.

Babies and young children want to find out as much as possible. They can do this with support from their trusted key person.

Play activities to support development and learning could include opportunities to:

- explore materials and make marks, for example use cornflour and water in trays so babies can enjoy making marks in it. Use tools that will make marks in clay dough or wet sand. Offer a range of markers like crayons and felt pens
- examine materials that ensure that all the children see familiar symbols and marks, for example food packets, supermarket logos

Let children come to activities in their own time

- explore sounds, for example voices, musical instruments, tapes
- explore objects. Provide a collection of everyday objects to explore (be aware of safety). These could include cones, corks, boxes, material, vegetables, and fruit
- sort objects, for example children can help sort the washing, lay the table, sort out pots and pans in the imaginative play area, investigate different sized boxes
- explore sand (both damp and dry, water and dough play)
- use paint, with the fingers or selection of brushes
- investigate the outdoor environment. Look at the leaves, trees, flowers. Even small babies can touch the flowers. Older children can look at the puddles, stamp on the water with their wellies on
- explore their body movements. Babies need space to stretch and roll. Older children need to make a noise, run around and play games.

Children will have their individual preferences. For example, some children may not like the water or sand. Don't insist; allow them to come to these activities in their own time.

K2D48
K2D121
K2D122
K2D125

Imagination

Babies love imitating others. A baby will watch your face very carefully and will copy your movements. Try sticking out your tongue and making exaggerated mouth movements and sees what happens! As they become older, young children

Children love to use items in pretend play

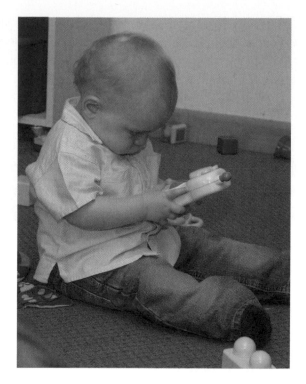

will recreate familiar scenes. This imaginative or pretend play lets the children try out ideas, feelings and relationships. They will do this using props like large empty boxes, cooking equipment and dressing-up clothes. Pretend play will often develop into quite complicated long games where children take on different roles.

Play activities to support imaginative play will include:

- playing with babies and young children in a way that will encourage them to imitate

- providing opportunities for pretend play like cooking, shopping, cleaning. You might set up these activities in the imaginative play area. Young children may not stop in this area; they will probably go off with items to play in other parts of the nursery.

- providing real objects for the children, like a camera, telephone, brushes and dustpans, hats, scarves, boxes. Let the children create their own pretend games with these

- small world playthings, which will enable children to recreate scenes and use them in pretend play. Small world play things include, people, animals, houses, cars, roads, tracks, engines, farm animals. Children will talk about what they create and may make up stories using their experiences.

You should encourage and support children's imaginative play. Sometimes you will be a part of this. For example, children love to give you a cup of tea or food as they play with the pots and pans. At other times, you may need to stand back. A child engaged in creating her own story with the small world playthings will need space to do this. You will need to be on hand to talk with them about this when they are ready. The materials, toys and equipment you choose should value diversity and encourage positive feelings. They should meet the needs of all the children. For example, small world playthings, cooking utensils, puppets, and books should reflect children and families from different cultures.

Element 208.3 — Are you ready for assessment?

Provide play activities to encourage learning and development

You need to show that you can competently provide play activities to encourage learning and development. To do this, you will need to be directly observed by your assessor and present other types of evidence. The amount and type of evidence you need to present will vary. You should plan this with you assessor.

Direct observation by your assessor

Observation and/or Expert Witness Testimony is the required assessment method to be used to evidence some part of each element in this unit. If your assessor is unable to observe you s/he will identify an expert in your workplace who will provide testimony of your work-based performance. Usually your assessor or expert witness will observe you in real work activities and this should provide most of the evidence for the performance criteria for the elements in this unit.

Preparing to be observed

Your assessor will need to see you interacting and playing with babies and young children in different situations. You must show that you know about and follow the safety policy of your setting. You need to be guided in your choice of activities by the plans of your setting. Try to include caring routines like feeding and changing as well as planned activities to stimulate development. Choose the play equipment carefully to suit the developmental stage of the children. Don't forget the importance of eye contact and talking with babies. Look back at the information above to help you with this. Show your assessor how your setting shares information with parents, including records of activities and development. If possible include indoor and outdoor activities.

Other types of evidence

You will need to present different types of evidence in order to:

- cover criteria not observed by your assessor
- show that you have the required knowledge and understanding.

Communicate with and respond to and interpret the needs of babies or children under 3 years

Element **208.4**

You will need to refer to Units CCLD 201, 203 and 206 as you work through this element.

How babies and young children communicate

K2G127
K2C128
K2D48

At birth babies communicate through crying. In this way, they make their needs known to their main carer. This crying is just a distress call at first. By the time the baby is 6 weeks old, the crying will be more purposeful and will indicate a particular need like hunger. From this time, the baby will develop a variety of ways of communicating using gurgling, babbling and squealing. These playful sounds are in response to the human voice and will be accompanied by kicking and arm waving.

From about 6 months, babies enjoy using sound and single simple words to communicate. Babies will understand what is said to them well before they can use words themselves. Young children will use single words and two words to convey meaning. By the time they are 3, children are using language as a means of sharing thoughts and feelings. There is more about the development of language and communication in Units CCLD 201and 203. You need to read these while you are studying this element.

Babies and young children often find separating from their parent or main carer stressful. Parents will also find this difficult and may be distressed themselves. It is important that practitioners are sensitive to parents' worries. This can be done by making sure that babies and young children are settled in to settings gradually and that parents can talk to the child's key person about their worries. This is described in more detail earlier in this unit and in Unit CCLD 205. Babies and young children will need to build a trusting relationship with their key person. When they are distressed, you will need to soothe and comfort them. You may need to gently distract them from whatever it is that has upset them.

How babies learn through everyday interactions with their primary carers

K2G127
K2C128
K2D48

Babies and young children are naturally social and seek out contact with those around them. They are likely to receive this contact from adults and older children, not from other babies. They need carers who recognise and are responsive to these early attempts at communication. If there is no response, babies will give up and opportunities to learn will be lost.

The following points are suggestions for ways to support early learning and communication:

- Provide a calm atmosphere that allows the baby to pick out familiar sounds and voices. This does not mean silence but acknowledges that baby cannot make sense of a very noisy environment;

- Use care routines as opportunities for communication with babies. Physical care may take up much of the baby's wakeful time. Changing and washing are good opportunities for close contact and chatting with a baby. Babies respond to the splash of the water and the feel of the cream on their skin. Time should be taken over these activities and a conveyor belt approach, where babies are whisked through the procedure as quickly as possible, should never be used.

- Ensure that feeding is relaxed and pleasurable. Bottle-feeding should be a one-to-one experience and there should always be time for a cuddle. When babies are being weaned, the spoon should be offered at a pace that suits the baby, not the practitioner. It will not be a pleasurable experience for anyone concerned if the childcare worker is spoon-feeding more than one baby at a time.

- Practitioners need to give babies their full attention. Babies thrive on this and will lose interest if the practitioner's attention is elsewhere.

- Take advantage of any opportunity to stimulate babies' curiosity about the world. Talk to them about the birds perching on the fence, the rain gushing out of the drainpipe. Point out and show them these things.

- When planning activities for babies, have realistic expectations about how they will respond and what they will get out of them. For example, hand printing on paper will be meaningless task to an 8-month-old. He will be far more interested in touching and tasting the paint.

Tips for talking with babies

Babies love to communicate. But for those who have had no previous experience of working with babies, talking with babies can be daunting. You don't have to be the parent to be 'tuned in' to the baby!

Think about the following:

- Get close to the baby. Babies love faces and respond to smiles.
- Use short phrases and ordinary words, not baby talk.
- Consider the tone and modulation of your voice. Babies respond to a slightly higher pitch than usual and to expressive speech.
- Remember that you are talking with, not at the baby.
- Pause and listen so the baby can reply. This rhythm should reflect the pattern of normal conversation.
- Repetition of the same or similar phrases is helpful, but don't overdo this.
- Follow the baby's lead and allow him to initiate the conversation. See what he's looking at or pointing to and respond.

Talking with babies

Communicating with young children

K2C127
K2C128
K2D48

- Make time for talk. Young children will be learning new words so it is important that you talk to them about what they are doing and what is happening. Work with the children in one-to-one situations, or in very small groups of two or three children.

- Young children will be interested in books and will love to look at books and hear stories. Listening to stories will help children to respond to sound and the rhythm of spoken language. Listening to stories will also help a child to learn new words. Contact with books will help a child to understand that the squiggles on the page mean something. This is an important skill in the development of reading and writing.

- Use story aids to tell a story. This will help the children to listen and follow the story.

- Use music. Include actions with rhymes and songs. This will help the children to join in and learn them.

- Pretend play, role play and dressing up will provide good opportunities for children to express their feelings and thoughts. Join in pretend play and discuss what the children are doing.

- Provide objects for the children to explore, investigate and talk about.

- Provide children whose home language is not English with the opportunity to ask questions and express their thoughts and feelings in their first language.

- Remember that children will understand what is said to them before they use language to express themselves.

Solving language and communication difficulties may need outside support. People who work with young children need to be aware of the early signs of speech and language difficulties. You should refer any concerns to your line manager for discussion with parents and, if necessary, advice and help can be sought.

Recognised language formats

K2S129

Children who are deaf or whose parents are deaf may have British Sign Language (BSL) as their first or preferred language. This is a distinct visual and gestural language, which has a grammar and structure that is different from spoken English. BSL should not be confused with Makaton. BSL is a sophisticated language that allows discussion of complex issues. Makaton is a system of simple signs that can be used for communication.

Using signs (gestures) and symbols (photographs, diagrams or drawings) can be helpful for all children including those with communication difficulties.

Element 208.4

Are you ready for assessment?

Communicate with and respond to and interpret the needs of babies or children under 3 years

You need to show that you can competently communicate with babies and children under 3 years, interpret their needs and respond to them. To do this, you will need to be directly observed by your assessor and present other types of evidence. The amount and type of evidence you need to present will vary. You should plan this with you assessor.

Direct observation by your assessor

Observation and/or Expert Witness Testimony is the required assessment method to be used to evidence some part of each element in this unit. If your assessor is unable to observe you s/he will identify an expert in your workplace who will provide testimony of your work-based performance. Usually your assessor or expert witness will observe you in real work activities and this should provide most of the evidence for the performance criteria for the elements in this unit.

Preparing to be observed

Your assessor will need to see you communicating with babies and young children. You should become familiar with talking to babies and responding to them. Make sure you get down to their level so that they can see you. Use smiles and gestures. Don't take over; wait for the baby

to reply. Do use the time that you spend changing and feeding the baby to communicate with her. Show you are pleased and enjoying talking with the baby, give verbal and non-verbal encouragement. Provide suitable activities to communicate with young children. Make time for talk and discussion in the day. Read stories and sing songs as part of daily activities in one-to-one situations or very small groups.

Read the performance criteria carefully before your assessment. Try to cover as much as you can

---

Other types of evidence

You will need to present different types of evidence in order to:

- cover criteria not observed by your assessor
- show that you have the required knowledge and understanding.

Reflecting on your practice

- Describe how observing babies has helped you to learn about their development. **K2D115**
- How are observations of babies and young children used in your setting? **K2M120**
- What important points do you record in your setting about a baby's feeding? What differences have you noticed about the way individual babies take their solid foods? **K2S134, K2S135**
- Describe some examples of activities that you have provided to encourage young children's imagination. **K2D121**
- Describe an occasion when you have responded to a baby's pre-verbal speech. **K2C127**

Support a child with disabilities or special educational needs

*T*his unit is about supporting a child with disabilities or special educational needs. The unit includes: how you care for and encourage the child; how you work to support the child to participate in activities and experiences; how you observe and record information about the child; and how you work in partnership with the child's family.

Disabilities and special educational needs may affect children in different ways. It is important that practitioners are aware of the needs of the child and their role in supporting the child.

This unit contains three elements:

⌣ *CCLD 209.1 Support a child with disabilities or special educational needs by providing care and encouragement*

⌣ *CCLD 209.2 Provide support to help the child to participate in activities and experiences*

⌣ *CCLD 209.3 Support the child and family according to the procedures of the setting.*

The national standards for this unit include a list of key words and explanations that you need to understand. You should read this carefully as you plan the activities for your assessment. Your assessor can help you to make sure that you are interpreting the standards correctly.

⌣ Introduction

It is very important to remember that as a practitioner in a supporting role, you should be working under the close supervision of qualified colleagues, including the Special Educational Needs Co-ordinator (SENCO). These colleagues will be advised and supported by professionals from other organisations such as the Local Education Authority (LEA). In your setting, you should have clear policies and procedures to guide you in your work with any child who has a disability or special educational needs. These policies and procedures are shaped by legislation such as the Special Educational Needs Code of Practice 2001.

You will need to observe and record information about the child and how they are getting on. Any interactions with the child, their parents and other professionals should be conducted in a professional manner.

Particular disabilities or special educational needs

K2D147

There are a large number of disabilities and special educational needs. It is not possible to give details of all of them. It is very important that, as a practitioner, you are aware of the needs of any child that you are working with. You will be able to find information locally, both in your setting and beyond the setting through local authority support, training and research with national organisations.

The diagram below gives examples of some of the more common disabilities and special educational needs that you may encounter.

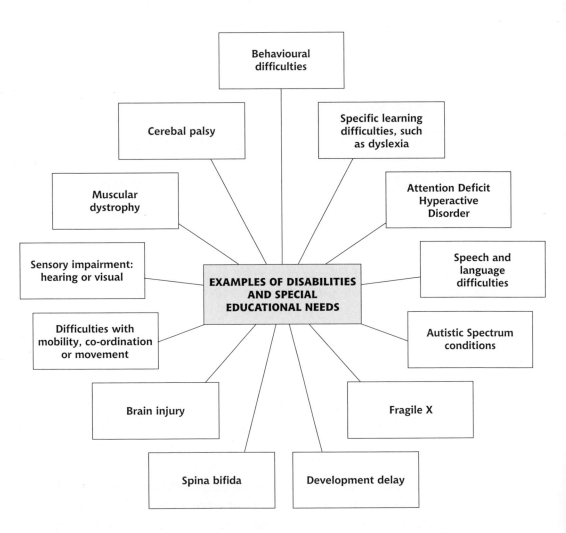

It is important to note that if you are working with very young children, they may be going through an assessment process. If you are working with older children, your setting may have a copy of any Statement of Special Educational Needs to inform your practice and the provision that is in place for the child.

Creating an inclusive environment

K2D146

An inclusive environment is one in which children and their families are included and none are excluded. This is achieved through having sound policies and through the attitudes and behaviour of all members of the establishment. It can be enhanced by the provision of equipment and activities that promote inclusion, avoid bias and present positive images. Such provision should permeate both the care and the curriculum that children receive.

Provision should include:

- sound policies that promote inclusion
- books, displays and pictorial resources that promote and represent a multi-cultural, multi-ability society
- resources for activities that enable all children to participate fully and represent themselves
- an environment which enables all children to participate to their full ability.

As a practitioner, it is important that you work within the policies, procedures and guidelines at your setting. In order to support and encourage a child with disabilities or special educational needs, you need to fully understand the important role that you play.

You also need to understand how your role fits in with roles of others:

- in your setting
- with the family of the child
- with the other professionals that you might come into contact with.

Working with a child with disabilities or special educational needs is a big responsibility. You are probably already aware of the challenges that such a role presents. Your role may be physically draining but also, we hope, stimulating and satisfying.

Regardless of the role that you play in supporting a child with a disability or special educational needs, you need to be aware that there are a number of laws and codes of practice to guide and govern what happens in your setting. At a local level, in your area and setting you should be aware of the policies and procedures in place for supporting children with disabilities and/or special educational needs.

Laws on disability and special educational needs

K2P142

- The **Education Act 1944** placed a general duty on local education authorities (LEAs) to provide education for all children, including children with special needs.
- The **Education Act 1981** was the main piece of legislation about special education. It laid down specific procedures for the assessment and support of children with special educational needs.

Appropriate resources enable all children to participate fully and represent themselves

- The **Education Reform Act 1988** requires LEAs to provide access to the National Curriculum for all children, including those with special needs.

- The **Education Act 1996** has now replaced, and included, the provision of the previous Education Acts.

- The **Children Act 1989** defines the services that should be provided for 'children in need' including those who are disabled.

- The **Disability Discrimination Act 1995** requires any services offered to the public to be accessible to people with disabilities. This is backed up by the Disability Rights Commission, which will support legal action in cases of discrimination against disabled people.

- The **Special Needs and Disability Act 2001** requires LEAs to provide parents of children with special needs (SEN) with advice and information. It strengthens the rights of children with SEN to be educated in mainstream schools.

- The **Special Educational Needs Code of Practice 2001** is the most recent code which applies to settings that receive government funding. It is divided into chapters that are intended to support and advise practitioners. You should be able to locate a copy of the SEN code of practice within your setting.

Other professionals involved in children's care, learning and development

These might include:

- play therapists
- physiotherapists
- child psychologists

Other
professionals
might be
involved in
supporting
the child

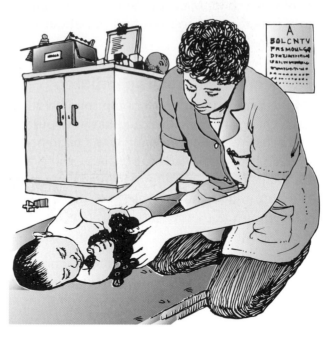

- doctors
- educational psychologists
- advisors
- social workers
- speech and language therapists
- health visitors.

Specialist local and national support

K2M143

You can access an enormous amount of additional information to help you to support children. Locally and nationally, there are organisations and individuals that your setting can contact. These include:

- National Deaf Children's Society
- Association for Spina Bifida and Hydrocephalus
- The Fragile X Society
- British Dyspraxia Foundation
- British Dyslexia Association
- Down's Syndrome Association
- Cystic Fibrosis Trust
- National Autistic Society.

These organisations have websites where you can find information. You should also be able to find details of training courses to help you to support the particular needs of a child. Many of these organisations have affiliated branches that operate in different areas. You can find out about these through your local authority and local directories.

Respecting and valuing children

K2D145

It is very important that all of the children at your setting are valued as individuals. Each child is an individual and has a unique range of qualities to be nurtured and respected. If you are working with children with disabilities or special educational needs on a regular basis, you may come across children with similar needs or disabilities. It is possible for practitioners to have preconceived ideas about children. You might be tempted to make stereotypical assumptions about children that you do not know very well. It is unacceptable to behave in this way when working with children.

As a practitioner, you should always work in a professional manner. You have a responsibility to the child and their family to do the very best that you can.

Language and terminology

It is important that practitioners use acceptable language and terminology. Practitioners must ensure that they do not use derogatory terms or language in relation to any child. Using inappropriate language can cause offence and upset. Such behaviour will be in breach of policy and practice guidelines. This is particularly important when working with children who have disabilities or special educational needs. In order to do this effectively, you will need to refer to documentation, seek advice from colleagues and respond to the preferences expressed by the child and their parents. Some basic guidelines are given in the table below.

Some guidelines on terminology

Terminology to avoid	Terminology to use
SEN child	Child with special educational needs
Wheelchair-bound	Wheelchair user
Disabled child, autistic child, etc.	Child with a disability, autism, etc.
Handicap	
Invalid	
Cripple	Disabled or disability
Normal (this implies that a disability is abnormal)	Non- or not disabled

It is also important that children in the setting do not learn to label other children. This can happen if practitioners express negative opinions about a child, their behaviour or needs. Other children might not understand the way that a child behaves or the levels of support that they need. This may cause children to be cautious or fearful of the child. Practitioners have a responsibility to all of the children. They can help children to understand each other through explanations where appropriate or by encouraging play and learning experiences which encourage positive interactions between all children.

Support a child with disabilities or special educational needs by providing care and encouragement

Element
209.1

Planning for a child's individual needs

K2D149

Planning enables practitioners to meet the needs of all children. Children are unique and planning for their needs should reflect this. The format may vary from setting to setting. For example, if you are working in an early years setting, a child with a disability or special educational needs will have an Individual Education Plan (IEP). An IEP is a plan that is designed to focus on the development, needs or behaviour of a child. Targets are set to enable the child to progress. If you are working in a less formal setting, such as a holiday club, there will be plans in place to support and meet the needs of the child. Behaviour support plans, care plans and programmes might also be used in other settings.

The planning system that you use will contain specific information about the child and targets for the child. Target-setting is a very important issue. Many people will be involved in the process, including:

- the child
- parents/carers
- SENCO
- specialist support staff
- professionals involved in meeting the child's needs
- practitioners.

Planning for any child is a very important process. You will have a role to play in the process too. You might be asked to observe the child, give feedback on progress and activities and to report any concerns. The level of your involvement in the planning process will vary depending on where you work.

Alternative and augmentative communication systems

K2C148
K2C4
K2C6

Some children use alternative or augmentative communication methods (AAC). This means that a child might use a device, a system or special communication method to enable them to communicate more effectively.

AAC can take many forms, including:

- communication boards
- voice output communication aids
- signing
- facial expression, including eye pointing and lip reading
- gesture
- symbols, pictures, photographs.

It is important that you and your colleagues learn how to use any communication system that a child is using. You might be able to get training in your setting or through your local authority. The parents of the child may be able to support the setting and give advice about where to get training.

Learning how to use a system will enable you, your colleagues and other children to interact and communicate with the child. However, if you are using a system that involves gesture or signing, consider the following points:

- Do you normally use your hands when you speak?
- Do you speak very quickly?
- Do you make eye contact with the person you are speaking to?

For example, if you are aware that you talk with your hands, you will need to address this behaviour. A child who is expecting to be signed to may become very confused if the adults around them are moving their hands as they talk to each other.

Children might use a communication device or system

Praise and recognition

As already mentioned, working with a child with disabilities or special educational needs can be challenging and rewarding. Children progress and develop at different rates. Progress in some areas might be rapid, but in other areas, a child might need repetitive experiences and activities broken down into small steps. It is incredibly important that practitioners strive to recognise and praise the efforts and achievements of the child. You might need to use praise and reward systems that have been agreed in the planning.

Element 209.1

Are you ready for assessment?

Support a child with disabilities or special educational needs by providing care and encouragement

You need to show that you can competently support a child with disabilities or special educational needs by providing care and encouragement. To do this, you need to be directly observed by your assessor and provide other types of evidence. The amount and type of evidence you will need to present will vary. You will need to plan this with your assessor.

Direct observation by your assessor

Your assessor will need to see you carry out these performance criteria (PCs):

CCLD 209.1 PCs 1, 2, 3, 4, 5, 6.

Preparing to be observed

You will need to plan your assessment carefully, so that you are observed during your normal work with a child with disabilities or special educational needs. Your assessor will need to see you providing care and encouragement, communicating with and sensitively supporting the child.

Read the performance criteria carefully before your assessment. Try to cover as much as you can.

Other types of evidence

You will need to present other types of evidence in order to:

- cover criteria not observed by your assessor
- show that you have the required knowledge, understanding and skills.

Provide support to help the child to participate in activities and experiences

Barriers preventing participation

K2D150

Barriers may exist which prevent the inclusion and participation of individuals. Legislation and policies already mentioned are in place to limit such barriers and to make people aware of what is expected. It is very important that settings are able to meet the individual needs of all children.

Barriers may include:

- *attitudes* – practitioners making assumptions about children's abilities, for example limiting participation because they feel that the child will not benefit
- *environment* – the layout of the setting, the location of activities, access points
- *staff and expertise* – additional staffing may be required. This might be all of the time or for specific activities like outdoor play or mealtimes. Expert support might be needed and additional training made available for existing staff
- *financial resources* – to enable the setting to make/purchase equipment, aids, adaptations or adjustments to activities or the setting.

Practitioners are expected to work to limit or remove barriers that prevent the participation or involvement of individuals.

Choice, participation and involvement are encouraged

Providing activities and experience

K2D151

It is essential that practitioners are aware of the needs of the child. Being aware of the suitability of the activities that you provide will help you to do the best that you can.

It is good practice to observe experienced colleagues. Doing this will help you to support the child and work to meet their individual needs.

You will need to use the planning that is in place as this has been developed with the age, needs and abilities of the child in mind.

It might be necessary to adapt or alter activities and experiences so that all of the children can participate. This does not mean making things easier or less of a challenge. Being imaginative and creative are key to providing suitable activities. If you are unsure of how to approach activities, you should ask for help and support. Some ideas are given in the table below.

Adapting activities for specific needs

Activity	Specific needs of child	Adaptation
Table-top lotto game	Difficulty with hand–eye co-ordination and fine motor skills	Add magnetic strips to game pieces for children to pick up using a large magnet *or* Use Velcro strips to help children keep the pieces in place
Ball games	Visual impairment	Use a ball which makes a sound, sit on the floor to play, children can sit with a partner feet to feet and roll the ball to each other.
Dressing-up clothes	Wheelchair user	Costumes with side tab or Velcro fastenings rather than seams
Story time	Hearing impairment	Use signs and actions Sound and sensory stories Role play Big books
Cooking	Dyslexia	Visual process cards using words and illustrations

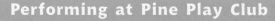

Practical Example

Performing at Pine Play Club

Vikki is working at a play club. She is supporting 10-year-old Oliver. Oliver has mobility problems and he is a wheelchair user. The club will be putting on a circus show, Vikki will be supporting Oliver and another child called Daisy. They need to decide on an act that they can perform together.

Vikki and the children have a chat about what they could do. Oliver suggests a juggling act. Daisy is worried because she cannot juggle. Vikki suggests that they practise a variety of juggling techniques. They do this and decide that using silk scarves is the most effective. They all agree that this is a great idea. They work hard on their act and make costumes to wear. Oliver is also keen to decorate his wheelchair for the show. Vikki suggests they look in some catalogues. They find some hoola hoops that light up and Olive thinks they would be great to put on the wheels of the chair.

The children really enjoy performing in the show. They are also able to share their skills with the other staff and children at the club.

➤ *Do you think this activity was suitable to the age, needs and ability of the children?* **K2D151**

➤ *How was Oliver involved in the planning for the event?*

Specialist aids and equipment

K2D152

The equipment that you need to use will depend on the needs of the child. Whatever equipment you are required to use, it is essential that you learn how to use it safely and appropriately. This is particularly important if you are using safety or lifting equipment. Such equipment may include:

- wheelchairs
- hoists
- feeding aids
- communication aids
- standing or walking frames
- splints and mobility aids
- medical equipment
- grab rails
- changing and toilet facilities.

If you are not sure how to use equipment or aids, you must ask. You might need specific training and you should not be using any specialist equipment until you have been trained to do so. You can research the range of equipment and aids through your setting, local support services and national organisations.

It is important that you are properly trained before attempting to use specialist equipment

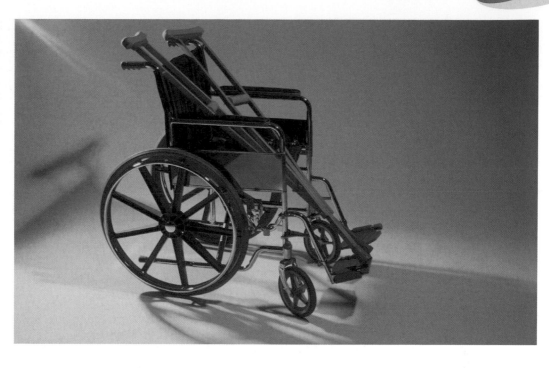

Are you ready for assessment?

Provide support to help the child to participate in activities and experiences

You need to show that you can competently support the child to participate in activities and experiences. To do this, you need to be directly observed by your assessor and provide other types of evidence. The amount and type of evidence that you will need to present will vary. You will need to plan this with your assessor.

Direct observation by your assessor

Observation and/or Expert Witness Testimony is the required assessment method to be used to evidence some part of each element in this unit. If your assessor is unable to observe you s/he will identify an expert in your workplace who will provide testimony of your work-based performance. Usually your assessor or expert witness will observe you in real work activities and this should provide most of the evidence for the performance criteria for the elements in this unit.

Preparing to be observed

You will need to plan your assessment carefully, so that you are observed at a time when you are working with the child. Your assessor will need to see you supporting the child participating in activities and experiences. This might include the use of adaptations and specialist equipment. You will need to show your assessor any adaptations to the environment you have made.

Read the performance criteria carefully before your assessment. Try to cover as much as you can.   ▶

> **Other types of evidence**
>
> You will need to present other types of evidence in order to:
>
> - cover criteria not observed by your assessor
> - show that you have the required knowledge, understanding and skills.

Element 209.3

Support the child and family according to the procedures of the setting

For this element, it will help to refer to Unit CCLD 201 in this book.

Building relationships with parents

K2D144
K2D153

It is the responsibility of practitioners to do everything they can to make parents feel welcome and valued. The needs and feelings of the parents must be considered, including parents who have had negative experiences.

Practitioners need to be aware that the parents of a child with disabilities or special educational needs will probably have many professionals involved in supporting their child. This may also have an effect on the parent's ability to build relationships. Being involved with so many people and organisations can be exhausting. It can also mean that the child and family experience many changes of personnel. You need to remember this as you work to build relationships with parents and families.

Parents and families of children with disabilities or special educational needs may experience a number of challenges. Such challenges may affect the relationships within the family and with the setting. Practitioners need to be aware of this, but should avoid making judgements or assumptions about any family.

There may be a number of children in a family. A child with a disability may be very demanding. For example, a child with autism may require one-to-one support and supervision. Parents may need to spend large amounts of time with the child, which may include attending to physical needs, waking nights or medical needs. Meeting the needs of the child may cause strain within the family. Families where children have physical disabilities may need to adapt their home and lifestyle; there may be financial constraints and limits to time available for individual attention for other children.

It is particularly important that parents and carers have confidence in the practitioner. Parents need to feel that they:

- are valued
- can trust you

- are able to share information about their child with you
- can ask questions
- can share concerns and worries
- are welcome within the setting.

Sharing information

Parents have the most knowledge and understanding of their child. If they are encouraged to share this, all will benefit. Legislation contained within the Education Reform Act 1988, the Children Act 1989 and the Special Education Needs Code of Practice 2001 places a legal responsibility on professionals to work in partnership with parents. Services provided for children in the public, private and voluntary sector must consider this.

Practitioners who work to support a child with disabilities or special educational needs will need to work closely with the child's parents, carers and family. It will help them to meet the care, learning and developmental needs of the child if they encourage parents to share information. For example, when the child arrives at the setting, it will be helpful to know about:

- sleep patterns
- feeding routines
- toileting routines
- general health
- incidents or changes of behaviour
- home events.

Communicating with parents

Receiving information in advance will help practitioners to provide for the needs of the child during the day. A bad night's sleep will affect most of us; practitioners may be able to meet the needs of a tired child by adjusting routines or allowing time for a rest.

Similarly, the setting can give regular feedback to parents that will enable them to support the needs of their child when they are away from the setting. For example, feedback about progress towards a target will give parents the opportunity to reinforce progress at home. As a practitioner, you will need to be clear about your role in providing feedback to others. It is possible that a senior colleague will do this.

Sharing information is going to be of huge benefit to the child. It will help practitioners to provide for the child's care, learning and development. Encouraging the parents and family to take a role in how you work in your setting will be helpful too. There are many ways that the setting can do this, including:

- involving parents and the child in planning and decision-making
- inviting parents to support the staff, for example advising staff about care routines
- meeting other parents at events
- participating in group sessions where possible.

Singing and signing

Jodie is 4 years old. She has communication difficulties and she uses basic signs to communicate with the adults at the crèche. The staff observe Jodie and notice that some of the other children are beginning to use gestures as they play. They give this feedback to her mother. She is delighted that the children are learning to communicate with each other. She suggests that she come in to the setting to teach the children and staff some songs and rhymes using singing and signing. The staff agree that this is a great idea. Jodie's mother teaches them a few songs over a period of three weeks. Soon the staff are able to lead the sessions and all of the children are keen to participate.

➤ *How did Jodie and her mother benefit from this activity?* **K2P144**

Jodie and her
mother sing and
sign

Are you ready for assessment?

Support the child and family according to the procedures of the setting

You need to show that you can competently support a child and family according to the procedures of the setting. To do this, you will need to be directly observed by your assessor and provide other types of evidence. The amount and type of evidence you need to present will vary. You should plan this with your assessor.

Direct observation by your assessor

Observation is the required assessment method to be used to evidence some part of each element in this unit. Expert witnesses could supply additional evidence. Your assessor will observe you in real work activities and this should provide most of the evidence for the performance criteria for the elements in this unit.

Preparing to be observed

You will need to plan your assessment carefully, so that you are observed at a time when you are working with a child and family. Your assessor will need to see you seeking help and supporting family members, giving feedback on progress to the child and recording the child's progress.

Read the performance criteria carefully before your assessment. Try to cover as much as you can.

Other types of evidence

You will need to present other types of evidence in order to:

- cover criteria not observed by your assessor
- show that you have the required knowledge, understanding and skills.

Reflecting on your practice

- Look at the communication systems listed on page 296. Research the use of any that you have not experienced. **K2C148**

- Think about the layout of your setting. Are there any barriers preventing children's participation. How could these barriers be removed? **K2D150**

- Why is it important to use specialist aids and equipment safely and according to manufacturer's instructions? **K2D152**

- How is partnership with parents encouraged at your setting? Why is this important? **K2P144**

Support children's and young people's play

Children and young people have a right to a variety of play environments that stimulate them and provide opportunities for risk, challenge and personal growth. This unit is about preparing and providing such opportunities. It is taken from the National Occupational Standards for Playwork PW2 and it is an optional unit for NVQ Level 2 in Children's Care, Learning and Development.

This unit contains four elements:

⌣ *CCLD 210.1 Create a range of environments for children and young people's play*

⌣ *CCLD 210.2 Offer a range of play opportunities to children and young people*

⌣ *CCLD 210.3 Support children and young people's rights and choices in play*

⌣ *CCLD 210.4 End play sessions.*

The national standards for this unit include a list of key words and explanations that you need to understand. You should read this carefully as you plan the activities for your assessment. Your assessor can help you to make sure that you are interpreting the standards correctly.

⌣ Introduction

If you are considering this unit as an option towards your NVQ Level 2 in Children's Care, Learning and Development, it is likely that you are working in a play setting. You will probably be working with children and young people aged between 5 and 15 years old. You might be working in:

- an out-of-school club
- a holiday club
- a play centre
- a play scheme

or any other play-based facility.

There are many similarities in supporting children and young people's play and in providing play opportunities for younger children. However, the differences are important. You must be sure that you understand how children's needs change as they get older. You must also understand how to adapt the environment, your style and practices to meet these changing needs.

Playwork assumptions and values

You must pay attention to the principles and values that underpin the National Occupational Standards for Children's Care, Learning and Development and make sure that your everyday work reflects them. You will find these listed in the Introduction section of this book.

Within the Playwork sector, there are some additional assumptions and values that you need to know about.

Assumptions

- Children's play is freely chosen, personally-directed behaviour motivated from within; through play the child explores the world and her or his relationship with it, elaborating all the while a flexible range of responses to the challenges she or he encounters; by playing the child learns and develops as an individual.

- Whereas children may play without encouragement or help, adults can, through the provision of an appropriate human and physical environment, significantly enhance opportunities for the child to play creatively and thus develop through play. In this way, the competent playworker always aims to provide opportunities for the individual child to achieve her or his full potential while being careful not to control the child's direction or choice.

Values

- The child must be at the centre of the process; the opportunities provided and the organisation which supports, co-ordinates and manages these should always start with the child's needs and offer sufficient flexibility to meet them.

- Play should empower children, affirm and support their right to make choices, discover their own solutions, to play and develop at their own pace and in their own way.

- Whereas play may sometimes be enriched by the playworker's participation, adults should always be sensitive to children's needs and never try to control a child's play so long as it remains within safe and acceptable boundaries.

- Every child has a right to a play environment which stimulates and provides opportunities for risk, challenge and growth of self-esteem.

- The contemporary environment in which many children grow up does not lend itself to safe and creative play; all children have the right to a play environment which is free from hazard, one which ensures physical and personal safety, a setting within which the child ultimately feels physically and personally safe.

- Every child is an individual and has the right to be respected as such; each child should feel confident that individuality and diversity are valued by the adults who work and play with them.

- A considerate and caring attitude to individual children and their families is essential to competent playwork and should be displayed at all times.

- Prejudice against people with disabilities or who suffer social and economic disadvantage, racism and sexism have no place in an environment which seeks to enhance development through play; adults involved in play should always promote equality of opportunity and access for all children, and seek to develop anti-discriminatory practice and positive attitudes to those who are disadvantaged.

- Play should offer the child opportunities to extend her or his exploration and understanding of the wider world and therefore physical, social and cultural settings beyond their immediate experience.

- Play is essentially a co-operative activity for children, both individually and in groups. Playworkers should always encourage children to be sensitive to the needs of others. In providing play opportunities, they should always seek to work together with children, their parents, colleagues and other professionals and, where possible, make their own expertise available to the wider community.

- Play opportunities should always be provided within the current legislative framework relevant to children's rights, health, safety and well-being.

- Every child has a right to an environment for play, and such environments must be accessible to children.

These assumptions and values underpin your learning and practice. They form the basis for good practice. You must therefore make sure that you think about them when planning for children's and young people's play.

Play and development

210K01
210K02

You may already have read Unit CCLD 206. There, we looked at the importance of play in children's learning and development. If you have not yet read it, you will find it useful to read through the unit before going on. In Unit CCLD 206, you will have learned about the importance of play. Children's needs will change as they get older, but the need for play remains. It is through play that children:

- practise new skills
- learn to relate to each other
- become independent and self-reliant
- interact with their environments.

As they develop, the need to explore and challenge themselves increases. This area can be seen as one of the main differences between providing play opportunities for young children, and planning for older children and young people.

Within a play setting, the focus should be on stimulating and challenging play. However, play and development cannot be separated. When children play, they develop.

Planning in a play setting does not have to link to a particular curriculum framework such as the National Curriculum or *Birth to Three Matters*. Instead, you need to have a good understanding of children's development to make sure that the activities and challenges you are providing are suitable for the age group with which you are working. Practitioners find it helpful to think about SPICE when they are planning:

Social play

S *Social interaction* Through play, children and young people will interact with each other, developing the practices and behaviours that are acceptable to the culture in which they live. They will learn tolerance and respect for others. They will take turns, negotiate and work together.

Physical play

P *Physical activity* Through play, children and young people will develop their large and small muscles. They will learn to assess risk, stretch their skills, develop a healthy and active lifestyle, develop control and co-ordination and strengthen bones and muscles.

Intellectual play

I *Intellectual stimulation* Through play, children will investigate, experiment, question, solve problems, create, imagine, develop memory and concentration, and learn about the people environment close to them and further afield.

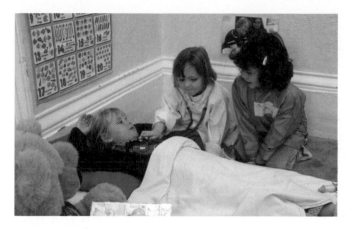

Creative play

C *Creative achievement* Through play, children and young people will develop their practical skills through imagining, designing and creating. They will work together and alone, using colour, texture, music and symbols (making one thing stand for another).

Emotional play

E *Emotional stability* Through play, children and young people will develop emotional attachments with the people around them. They will experience and act out a range of feelings. Their self-esteem and self-confidence will develop alongside other skills as they challenge themselves within their play.

The play environment must support the development of children and young people through play. The job of the playworker is therefore to plan and provide experiences, environments and activities in which children and young people can:

- challenge themselves physically, trying new skills, taking risks, learning about what they can do safely
- make decisions and choices for themselves, work and play co-operatively with others, become independent and self-confident, develop positive feelings about themselves and their abilities
- develop positive relationships with those around them, negotiating, compromising, expressing themselves and empathising (that is, understanding the feelings of others)
- investigate, explore, question, interact with the indoor and outdoor environment, solve problems for themselves and work with others to do the same
- respect, accept and understand the beliefs, practices and cultures of those around them, those in the local communities and those from further afield.

Being inclusive

K2D49.2
K2D50.2
K2D51.2

When you work with any group of children and young people, you will quickly become aware that a group is made up of individuals. Each individual will have his or her own ideas, thoughts, feelings, needs, interests and customs. Some may have additional needs that you must consider so that they can participate fully in the play experiences you provide. Some may have customs or practices associated with their faith or culture. This may mean that you will need to adapt some activities to enable them to join in. Some will have different social backgrounds – different family groupings, for example – that you need to know about in order to best support the child or young person.

The only way to be sure about the individuals' needs is to ask them and their families. They will not be insulted. It does not mean that you are ignorant about different religions, cultures or needs. It means that you respect them and want to do your best for them. It is through respect and understanding that we can develop a peaceful and accepting environment for children, young people and their families.

Element 210.1

Create a range of environments for children and young people's play

Let's start by asking some questions:

- Does your setting make all children feel that they belong?
- Do they feel safe and secure enough to be able to push the boundaries of their abilities?
- Are they able to make choices in their play, to 'direct' their own play and to be part of the decision-making process in the setting?

Putting children and young people at the centre of all the decisions you make will help them to grow in confidence and ability. They will learn to take responsibility for themselves, each other and their environment. They will learn to judge when to take risks without causing themselves or others serious harm. They will learn to make the right choices.

Where to start?

210K03
210K04
210K05
210K10
K2D49.1
K2D50.1
K2D51.1

No matter what age group you work with, you should always start with the child or young person. You need to identify their particular needs and interests. This is because you must recognise that children and young people have the right to have a say in their own lives. They are individuals and deserve to be listened to. When you take the time to find out about each and every child and young person in your setting, you will be sending them a clear message that says, *'You are an important person. What you want is important to me.'*

The result will be that the child's or young person's self-esteem will be enhanced. They will come to believe that they are cared about and that they are allowed to express their opinions. Their self-confidence will develop and this will have a direct effect on all other aspects of their lives.

There are other reasons why you should make your setting child-centred. If the children do not enjoy being at your setting, they will not come. If, however, they feel that they belong there and that their ideas are implemented, they will feel some responsibility and 'ownership' for the environment.

You can find out about the needs and interests of children and young people in several ways. You can observe them, noting down who they socialise with, what they enjoy doing, what their abilities are. You can talk to their families to find out about their lives and interests outside your setting. You can use your knowledge of how children and young people generally play and develop. And most importantly, you can ask the children and young people themselves. Spend time with them, showing interest in what they have to say. Hand out questionnaires, have a suggestions box, hold meetings with the children. Share your findings with your colleagues so that, together, you can make sure that the environment you provide reflects the needs and interests of all the children and young people.

Children and young people should always be involved in making decisions about their care, play and learning. They will have a wide range of interests. Some will have special needs that you need to take account of. All will have their own particular interests and you must consider them in order to provide appropriate play opportunities.

Practical Example

Finding out what people think

Deepesh works with children aged 5 to 11 in an after-school and holiday club. Every term, before the planning meeting, he gives out questionnaires to the children, their families and the playworkers. In the questionnaire, everyone is asked to look back at what went well last term and to look forward to what they would like to happen next term. However, Deepesh has noticed that some children do not return their questionnaires. He also realises that the younger children do not find it easy to write down what they think.

➤ *Why is it important for Deepesh to find out the opinions of the children, the parents and the playworkers?* **210K03, 210K04, 210K05**

➤ *What can Deepesh do to include those who do not return their questionnaires?* **210K05**

➤ *How can Deepesh include the younger, less able children?* **210K05**

➤ *What do you do in your setting to find out about the children and young people's interests and ideas?* **210K05**

Creating the right environment

210K06
210K08
K2D50.7
K2D51.7

There are many different locations for playwork settings – you might be working in a classroom or school hall where you have to set up and clear away for each session. You might be lucky enough to have sole use of the premises you use. Wherever you are based, you will need to think about creating a stimulating environment where the children and young people can make choices from the variety of experiences and activities you are offering.

This table will give you some ideas about what your setting should aim to offer. It will also help you to identify your own role in the children's and young people's experiences. Use the table below to think about ways you could improve your own practice to benefit the children in your care.

Improving your practice

Physical play Play where children use their large and small muscles, where they are physically active	• Is it fun? • Do you offer opportunities for indoor and outdoor activity? • Do you provide enough equipment or tools to go round? • Do you adapt what you offer to make sure that those with additional needs can join in? • Do you allow the children and young people to use what you have provided in their own ways, even if it is not what you planned? • Do you allow the children and young people to assess the risks of particular activities for themselves? • Have you made sure that what you are offering is suitable for the range of children's abilities and interests?
Environmental play Play which involves and/or raises awareness of natural elements and/or wildlife and their survival	• Is it fun? • Do you encourage the children to explore the natural and man-made environment? • Do you use natural materials wherever possible – sand, water, clay, earth, wood? • Do you make best use of the weather – allowing children and young people to use the wind, snow and rain in their play? • Do you support children and young people's interest in wildlife, insects, life cycles and habitats? • Are you a good role model, treating the environment with respect, getting muddy, wet or dirty in order to experience something interesting or new?
Creative play Play that is inventive and/or productive, for example writing, construction, artwork, music	• Is it fun? • Do you remember that creativity comes from within the individual and not from copying a model created by an adult? • Do you provide enough resources and equipment so that the child or young person can express themselves?

	• Do the children and young people have access to paint, paper, card, collage materials, dough, clay, and other open-ended items that can be changed? • Are the children and young people able to represent themselves with the materials you provide – for example, have you thought about different skin tones? • Are the tools accessible to all – have you thought about left- and right-handed scissors, the individual abilities of those in the setting, the importance of independence in play? • Do you show that it is the process that is important, not just the end product? • Do you demonstrate that you value the efforts and achievements of all those participating, by displaying a range of artwork and not just the 'perfect' creations? • Is there access to a range of creative experiences – music, movement and dance, drama, role play, writing, small world play?
Cultural play Play that celebrates and/or raises awareness of different cultures and their values and practices	• Is it fun? • Have you considered the backgrounds of the children and young people within your environment? • Do you offer the children and young people the opportunity to find out about people and practices from their own communities and from the wider world? • Do the materials and equipment reflect a wide range of cultures and backgrounds? • Do you celebrate a range of festivals from different cultures – not just the Christian festivals of Christmas and Easter? • Do you make an effort to find out about the customs and practices of all the children in your setting? • Do you make assumptions? Not everyone with the same beliefs have the same practices.
Imaginative play Play that involves 'pretend' roles or acting out fantasy situations	• Is it fun? • Are you responsive to the needs of the children regarding their imaginative play? Do you fetch extra resources when needed? • Do you allow imaginative play to flow freely, without adult intervention? • Are your resources varied and plentiful? Do they allow for symbolic play (when children make one thing stand for another)?

You will notice that the first question for each category is the same – Is it fun? It is sometimes easy to forget this point. You have to consider health and safety, learning opportunities, anti-bias and anti-discriminatory practice, but perhaps most important is that it should be fun. As long as you remain focused on the children or young people when planning the play opportunities, you won't go far wrong.

Think about zones

210K08
210K09
210K10

It is important when you think about your environment that you make sure it offers areas or zones to suit the needs of all the children and young people. These needs will not always be the same. Just as our moods can change daily, so can those of the children. They may feel tired, grumpy, energetic, chatty, sociable, cheeky, irritable or any other mood. As they progress towards puberty, these moods can become more extreme.

Your setting should provide areas or zones, inside and out, where they can:

- chill out
- chat
- work through strong feelings
- be alone
- be with others
- use up extra energy.

Think about how you can separate the zones. Large pieces of furniture, such as shelving units, book cases and seating can be used to separate sections of the room, without isolating the children or young people within. Carpets and rugs can create distinct areas. Screens and display boards are also useful. Creating these zones will allow the children and young people to choose where they spend their time and who they spend it with.

Flexibility with the environment is also very important. In order to encourage the children and young people in your setting to make their own decisions, you must accept that they may choose to adapt an area to suit their own interests or mood. This may include creating a den or moving resources. In this way, the children and young people will be creating their own zones. They will be taking ownership of the setting, being responsible for their own play, and this is to be encouraged.

Taking risks and being safe

210K07
210K18
K2D49.1
K2D49.6
K2D50.1
K2D50.6
K2D51.1
K2D51.5

Everyone working with children and young people has a responsibility for their health and safety. This can make practitioners feel nervous about providing challenging activities. However, as children get older, they have to learn to make their own decisions and be responsible for themselves. This involves learning to assess situations and decide for themselves what they can do safely. They will not learn how to do this if the people who work with them always make these decisions for them. Often, the children who are most nervous of trying new skills are those who have not had the opportunity to take risks for themselves.

Of course, you have to balance this growing need for independence with making sure they are safe from serious injury. You have to make sure that the challenges you provide are achievable, but also that they stretch the children's abilities. We all know how good it feels to achieve something we thought we would not be able to do. It makes us feel good about ourselves. We feel more self-confident and less worried about trying something new next time. Similarly, if we are unable to achieve our goals, despite our very best efforts, we feel deflated and less positive about ourselves. The same is true for the children and young people in your setting.

It is very important that you learn about the individual abilities of each child, and that you understand the norms of children's development – you can find more about this in Unit CCLD 203. With this knowledge and understanding, you will be able to provide appropriate challenges and opportunities for the children to make their own decisions, stretch their own abilities and stay safe.

In August 2002, the Play Safety Forum published an important statement that explores the issues relating to acceptable and unacceptable risk in play provision. It said:

> 'Children need and want to take risks when they play. Play provision aims to respond to these needs and wishes by offering children stimulating, challenging environments for exploring and developing their abilities. In doing this, play provision aims to manage the level of risk so that children are not exposed to unacceptable risks of death or serious injury.'

The full document can be obtained from the Children's Play Council or downloaded from their website. It is an important statement and it should be available in your setting.

It is important to offer challenging activities

St Luke's School Holiday Club

The playworkers from St Luke's School Holiday Club often walk the children to the local adventure playground. There is a variety of equipment on offer, including large climbing frames, swings, balance beams and ropes. The playground is suitable for the age group from the setting – 8–11-year-olds.

Some children are less confident on the equipment, sticking to the low apparatus within their comfort zones. Andrew notices that Harley, aged 9, is on the assault course climbing net. She has gradually climbed higher each visit, and has now pulled herself up to the top and is about to climb over the top and back down the other side.

➤ *What are the risks of allowing Harley to try?* **210K07**
➤ *What would the benefits to Harley be if she is allowed to continue?* **210K07**
➤ *Should Andrew intervene? Explain your reasons.* **210K07**
➤ *What opportunities for challenge and risk do you provide in your setting?*
➤ *How do you manage the risk?*

Policies and procedures

**210K11
210K12**

There will be many policies and procedures to follow in your setting. These will be based on the legal requirements of the Care Standards Act 2000 (National Standards), the Children Act 1989 and various pieces of Health and Safety legislation such as COSHH (Control of Substances Hazardous to Health, 2003) and RIDDOR (Reporting of Injuries, Diseases and Dangerous Occurrences Regulations, 1995).

You should make sure that your policies and procedures are working documents. You must be familiar with them in order to work to them, because Ofsted (Office for Standards in Education) will be checking that you know and understand them. For this unit, you will need to know about:

- your setting's health and safety policy
- your own job description
- policies and procedures for setting up activities, checking equipment and supervising play
- policies and procedures for the arrival and departure of children
- record-keeping and sharing information.

There are other considerations too, such as the policies of the owners of your building and the requirements of your insurance company. These should already have been taken into account within your setting's policies and procedures. If you are unsure about this, ask your manager or supervisor for advice. The purpose of the policies and procedures is to keep the users of your setting – the children and young people – safe and secure. They also give you clear guidance to follow when carrying out your duties and you should therefore regard them as a good thing. It may seem that they are too fussy or detailed but, if you are following them, you will know that you are fulfilling your duties and doing a good job.

Element 210.1

Are you ready for assessment?

Create a range of environments for children and young people's play

You need to show that you can create a range of environments for children and young people's play. Use the range categories to plan with your assessor. This will help you to gather as much evidence as possible on her visits. The amount and type of evidence you need to present will vary. You should plan this with your assessor.

Direct observation by your assessor

Observation and/or Expert Witness Testimony is the required assessment method to be used to evidence some part of each element in this unit. If your assessor is unable to observe you s/he will identify an expert in your workplace who will provide testimony of your work-based performance. Usually your assessor or expert witness will observe you in real work activities and this should provide most of the evidence for the performance criteria for the elements in this unit.

Preparing to be observed

You will need to arrange the indoor and outdoor environments for children and young people's play. To do this, you will need to find out about what they want in their play environments and gather feedback from them about what you have previously offered. You will also need to identify their play needs.

Make sure that the environments you set up are stimulating and challenging. Check that you have provided different zones and opportunities for different types of play. Check that all the opportunities are available to all the children. Make sure that you provide sufficient materials and resources. If possible, try to consult with the children and young people about aspects of the play environment while your assessor is observing you.

Read the performance criteria and range carefully before your assessment. Try to cover as much as you can.

▶

> **Other types of evidence**
>
> You will need to present different types of evidence in order to:
>
> - cover criteria not observed by your assessor
> - show that you have the required knowledge, understanding and skills
> - cover parts of the range.

Element 210.2

Offer a range of play opportunities to children and young people

Now that we have looked at the environments you provide, we need to take a closer look at the play opportunities you offer within them.

When thinking about the activities and experiences, there are many things to consider:

- the age and abilities of the children and young people
- the particular needs and interests of the children and young people
- the different environments your setting offers (indoor, outdoor, off-site)
- the need for variety and choice
- the resources you have available to you
- the zones you create for different types of play
- creating a balance between activities
- your own role in the play activities.

Choice and flexibility

210K08
210K09
210K13
210K15
K2D50.8,
K2D50.10
K2D51.9,
K2D51.11

It is important that the environment is organised. Routines will make the children and young people feel secure. It is likely that you will have plans in your setting, detailing the focus of play opportunities and the areas of development (SPICE, see page 310) to be covered. It is also good practice for these plans to consider health and safety aspects, the adults' roles and the resources needed.

However detailed your plans are, there is an important point to remember. The children and young people will not necessarily agree with them! You may have planned a wonderful session, full of imaginative activities and creative ideas. You may have spent a long time preparing the resources. But there is no guarantee that the children and young people will use the materials and equipment as you expected.

Is this allowed? Of course it is, as long as respect is shown for the environment, equipment and people around them.

Allowing children and young people to make choices gives them responsibility for their own activities. This, in turn, encourages their self-esteem and self-confidence.

It ensures that they learn from their own mistakes, solve their own problems, use their own imagination and creativity and negotiate with each other. It empowers them, enabling them to believe in themselves and helping them to express their thoughts and ideas now and in the future.

It is for these reasons that you should aim to provide flexible opportunities for play, both indoors and outdoors. Of course, you cannot have every single resource out for every single session. There are, however, practical things you can do. You can make sure that:

- extra resources are within reach for the children and young people to access them
- you are available to get what is requested
- what is planned can be developed or adapted by them, according to their own ideas or interests
- there is enough choice so that there is something for everyone attending your setting.

The materials and equipment you offer are therefore an important aspect of the setting. They should, wherever possible, be open-ended – that is, they should be flexible and adaptable. What you are able to provide will depend on different factors – your budget, storage options, availability of indoor and outdoor space. It will generally include:

Materials and equipment for activities

Type of activities	Examples of materials and equipment
Creative activities	Paper, card, scissors, glue, collage materials, brushes, pens, pencils, clay and tools, paint, word processing software packages Table-top games Bingo, battleships, chess, cards, quiz games
Role play and drama	Dressing-up clothes and costumes, mirrors, hats, accessories, face paints and make-up, tents, large coverings for making dens
Indoor activities	Snooker/pool table, computer, games consoles, dance mats, cooking
Quiet activities	Comfortable seating with books and magazines, sewing activity, TV and video/DVD
Construction activities	Building bricks, Lego, Meccano, work bench, woodwork tools
Activities using natural materials	Sand, water, clay, wood
Outdoor activities	Bikes, balls, football nets, basketball hoops, skipping ropes, parachute, cricket sets, rounders bat

Children and young people should make their own decisions about their play

The Den After-School Club

At the Den After-School Club, the staff are careful to plan a good variety of different activities for the children. They make sure that they balance the play opportunities, having quieter areas and making full use of indoor and outdoor space.

Sam has planned a bulb-planting activity outside. She hopes that the children will learn about their environment and about how plants grow. She expects that they will develop respect for the environment by caring for the plants as they grow.

She notices that several children have abandoned the bulbs and are playing 'cups' with the plastic plant pots, seeing how quickly they can stack and unstack the pots.

➤ *Should Sam intervene to get the play back on track? Explain the reasons for your answer.* **210K09, 210K13**

➤ *What skills are the children using in the adapted activity?*

➤ *Having observed this interest, what can Sam do now to support and encourage it?* **210K05, 210K06**

Balancing rules with choice

210K14

A lot of emphasis has been placed on the rights that children and young people have to make choices in their play. However, with rights there are always responsibilities. Children and young people need to understand that they must behave within a set of rules in order for everyone to be safe and to feel secure. These ground rules might cover topics such as behaviour and respecting the environment and equipment. They might be based on the setting's policies, but should be written in a way that all children and young people can understand.

It is important to involve the children and young people in setting the ground rules. You spend a lot of time trying to make them feel that they belong, that the setting is theirs. This hard work can be easily undone by adults setting rules that the children and young people have not been involved in.

You should talk to the children and young people about the rules for their club. It would be a good idea to give them time to prepare – you could plan a meeting for a week's time, suggesting that they think about what they would like to be included in the rules. During the meeting, a group discussion could be held so that all the children have their say. This way, they will understand why rules are important, they will have a better understanding of what the rules are and they will all feel a responsibility towards making sure the rules are followed. You should also discuss with them what will happen if the rules are not followed. What sanctions will be used? When there are clear guidelines and well known sanctions, there is less chance that they will be broken.

Once the general ground rules are set, you will need to remind the children and young people of them at appropriate intervals. There will be some play opportunities you provide where safety rules are important and need to be stressed every time. Rather than using a dominant approach – 'Don't do this ... don't do that' – you could ask the children and young people if they can remember the ground rules. This way, the rules come from them and they will be more inclined to remember them and remind each other about them.

Involve children and young people in making the rules

Of course, we all make mistakes. Things can go wrong and how you react to these difficulties may affect how quickly the situation can be resolved. A quick and quiet reminder of the rules is usually all it takes to keep things on track. Consistency is also important – everyone should follow the rules – including the adults in the setting. If your rules state 'No shouting', then make sure you don't shout either!

Element 210.2

Are you ready for assessment?

Offer a range of play opportunities to children and young people

You need to show that you offer a range of play opportunities for children and young people. Use the range categories to plan with your assessor. This will help you to gather as much evidence as possible on her visits. The amount and type of evidence you need to present will vary. You should plan this with your assessor.

Direct observation by your assessor

Observation and/or Expert Witness Testimony is the required assessment method to be used to evidence some part of each element in this unit. If your assessor is unable to observe you s/he will identify an expert in your workplace who will provide testimony of your work-based performance. Usually your assessor or expert witness will observe you in real work activities and this should provide most of the evidence for the performance criteria for the elements in this unit.

Preparing to be observed

You will need to be working in the setting with the children and young people. Make sure the setting offers choice and flexibility.

Make sure that you encourage the children and young people to choose for themselves. Be prepared to offer new ideas to the children about the way they can use and adapt the resources.

Read the performance criteria and range carefully before your assessment. Try to cover as much as you can.

Other types of evidence

You will need to present different types of evidence in order to:

- cover criteria not observed by your assessor
- show that you have the required knowledge, understanding and skills
- cover parts of the range.

Support children and young people's rights and choices in play

In this element, we move on to look at your role in children and young people's play. We have talked a lot so far about children and young people's rights – their rights to:

- play
- make decisions for themselves
- make choices
- develop responsibility for themselves
- become individual, self-confident people.

We have focused on how the playworker can set up environments and activities so that children and young people can exercise these rights. But your role goes further than this. There will be times when you will need to intervene in an activity or situation. There will be many other times when your intervention would be disruptive and unhelpful. You need to recognise these situations and act accordingly.

When and how to intervene

210K16
210K20
210K21
210K24

Health and safety issues

Sometimes, a child might over-estimate his ability and challenge himself to take a risk. If that risk might result in a serious injury or death, you *must* take immediate action. If the result might be an injury or damage to the equipment or environment, you might ask questions, such as 'What do you think will happen if that falls off? Is there another way to do it?' This allows the child or young person to retain control of the activity and to learn to consider the consequences more fully.

Effect on others

The right to adapt play opportunities is important, but this does not mean that the rights of others can be ignored. Sometimes, an activity can become so involved that it begins to take over other areas in the setting, affecting the play and rights of other children and young people. Other times, a loud and boisterous activity can lead to other children and young people feeling intimidated or frightened. If you do not intervene sensitively in these cases, conflict can arise. Usually, all that will be needed will be a comment from you to remind those involved of the ground rules – that they are not alone and that they need to respect the rights of those around them. You might also need to suggest a better location for their play – moving it outdoors might solve the problem.

Play runs out of steam

You might notice that the children at a particular activity appear bored or confused. This might be a cue for you to join them, make some suggestions or provide extra materials. Or it may be that this activity doesn't work, and you need to clear it away and ask the children what they would like to do instead. Whichever approach you take, you should be aware that your help may only be needed for a short while. Once the children begin to direct the play again, you can withdraw from the activity and observe from a distance.

Children or young people need help

Recognising when a child or young person needs your help is not necessarily straightforward. You may observe a child struggling to cut some stiff material or failing to set up a complicated game. He or she might even call you over to ask for help. However, sometimes frustration at being unable to do something turns into aggression towards the equipment or other people. On other occasions, a child might just flit from one activity to another without settling. You need to be alert to this and offer help before the situation develops. This help might be a quick fix, helping to cut through material and then leaving the child to his/her own creation, or it may be more sustained, setting up the complicated game and then playing with the child. You should take your cue from the child and be as involved as he or she wishes you to be.

Conflict

Conflict arises all the time and not all children will have learned the art of compromise and negotiation. You should always give those involved the opportunity to solve conflicts without your help. However, if this fails you will need to intervene. Your intervention should be used to help the children learn to deal with conflict situations themselves. You should ask them to talk to you about the situation, giving all parties the opportunity to be heard. You should ask questions to clarify what has happened and also to encourage all parties to see things from the other point of view. You should ask them what they think should happen next, getting them to talk to each other and negotiate a compromise. Finally, you should get them to think about how this situation can be avoided in the future.

When not to intervene

210K23
210K24

Becoming involved in children and young people's play may have positive benefits for them. But it may also have the opposite effect. The play belongs to the children or young people. They will have their own ideas, rules, team members and goals for their play. If you join in without an invitation, you may change the play. Their plans may not accommodate your presence. They may have to change their ideas and may not achieve their goals. You will have removed the responsibility for the play from them and all the benefits of self-directed play will be lost. Think about the following before intervening:

- Look at the body language and facial expressions. Are the children and young people focused and involved?
- Before you intervene in conflict, observe for a short time. Are they coping with disagreements through negotiation and compromise?

- Before you make decisions about risks, stop. What would be the possible outcome if the challenge goes wrong? What are the benefits of trying? Is the child or young person going carefully, judging the next step to take and analysing the risk for him or herself? Is it better in this event to let the child or young person judge the risk this time? Can you issue a verbal warning to think carefully instead of making the risk decision for him/her?

- Have you been invited to join in, either directly or through gestures or eye contact and facial expressions? What will your role be in the play? Do you know what the children/young people are working towards?

Overall, you need to make a judgement about whether to become involved or not, based on the above and on the individual circumstances. The more you work with the children and young people in your setting, the more tuned-in to their needs you will become. This will make it easier for you to make these decisions. As long as you remain focused on the child or young person as the centre of the play, you should not go too far wrong.

Supporting children's challenges

210K19
K2D49.3
K2D49.4
K2D49.6
K2D50.3
K2D50.4
K2D50.6
K2D51.3
K2D51.4
K2D51.5

The activities and experiences you plan for the children and young people in your setting will be based on their interests, ages and abilities. Because it is likely that you cater for different ages and abilities, this means that some activities might be too challenging for some of the children. When a child is unable to achieve their goals – completing a complicated jigsaw, climbing to the top of the assault course net – it can damage their self-confidence and self-esteem. If this happens on a regular basis, they will come to believe that they are not very good at activities. This can lead to the child being reluctant to try anything next time. They will have a 'can't do it' attitude which can continue throughout their lives. Meaningful praise and encouragement for effort as well as achievement will develop confidence. This means praising and encouraging specific actions – 'Well done' does not have the same impact as 'You did really well building that den, Shannon. How about finding a way of holding the shelter in place?'

It is therefore vital that the playworker is on hand to support the children to achieve their goals, without taking away the children's control or success.

You can do this by:

- observing carefully
- making helpful suggestions
- encouraging and praising
- asking questions to prompt the child in the right direction
- always allowing the child to complete the task. If you put the final piece of the jigsaw in, for example, the child will remember that he or she did not complete it.

Responding to play cues

210K23
210K24
K2D50.5
K2D51.6

Children and young people will not always tell you what they need or want. In fact, if you think about the way you get messages across to others, you will realise that facial expressions, gestures and body language are often more powerful than words!

It is estimated that two-thirds of communication takes place through non-verbal means. Practitioners therefore need to be tuned in to the non-verbal messages that children and young people are sending, and react accordingly. These play cues will tell you whether a child or young person is enjoying an activity, whether he or she is coping with it and whether or not he or she needs help. They can also help you to become aware of whether you should join in or whether it is better to observe from a distance. For example, a child flitting from one activity to another may be looking for someone to talk to. An activity that children avoid may need more variety of materials or extra resources.

If you feel that you do need to go and help, you should remember that the activity must remain child-directed. In other words, the children or young people have ultimate control over the activity, and this may mean that your offer of help or suggestion is rejected. If you are invited to join in, you should continue to take your cues from the children, following their ideas and not taking the play in your own direction.

Practical Example

Responding to play cues

Becky had been watching a clay modelling activity for a little while. She saw that the three 7-year-old children all appeared to have run out of ideas and were beginning to have 'sword fights' with the clay tools.

She joined the table and talked to the children about their models. They explained that they had been making dinosaurs. Becky asked them some open questions about where the dinosaurs might live and the children decided that they probably lived in a cave. Becky asked them if they would like to make a cave to display their dinosaurs. She then fetched some boxes, glue and paints and withdrew from the activity.

The children were motivated again and worked well together, cutting and sticking the boxes together to make a cave and then painting it. Over the next couple of days, they collected leaves and twigs and made an impressive dinosaur display, painting their models and then putting them into the cave.

➤ *What examples of good practice do you recognise from this example?*
   210K20, 210K21, 210K22

➤ *What effect did Becky's support have on the children's play?* **210K23**

> Becky could have told the children off for play fighting and insisted they sit and make some different shapes to keep them amused. What effect would this have had on the children's play? **210K24**

> Give some examples of when your involvement in children's play has had a positive effect. **210K24**

> When would you not get involved in an activity? **210K24**

It is important to judge if and when to intervene

Strategies for supporting children and young people's play

Having identified a play cue, you now have to decide how to respond. You should not make any assumptions about what is needed. You should listen carefully to those involved, make some suggestions if necessary, ask some questions to help those involved identify what they would like to do next and then take action to help. Below are some examples of what you might need to do:

- join the activity for a short time to remotivate the children and young people
- fetch extra resources, equipment or materials
- mediate in a conflict situation to help the children and young people resolve the situation
- make suggestions to help the child or young person to solve a problem
- take part in the game, if invited to do so
- remind them about ground rules so that play can continue safely
- encourage the children and young people to 'give it a go' and praise efforts

- be a good role model, demonstrating how to use tools and equipment safely
- carry out an on the spot risk assessment, taking into account the abilities of those involved and making suggestions if alternative methods are needed on the grounds of safety.

All of these strategies can be used without taking over the play. Judging when support is *not* needed is just as important as judging when it *is* needed. Learn to read the play cues children and young people give in order to decide if support would be helpful or unhelpful. And finally, do not forget that for play to be truly directed by the children, your involvement is not necessarily needed.

Element 210.3 Are you ready for assessment?

Support children and young people's rights and choices in play

You need to show that you can support children and young people's rights and choices in play. Use the range categories to plan with your assessor. This will help you to gather as much evidence as possible on her visits. The amount and type of evidence you need to present will vary. You should plan this with your assessor.

Direct observation by your assessor

Observation and/or Expert Witness Testimony is the required assessment method to be used to evidence some part of each element in this unit. If your assessor is unable to observe you s/he will identify an expert in your workplace who will provide testimony of your work-based performance. Usually your assessor or expert witness will observe you in real work activities and this should provide most of the evidence for the performance criteria for the elements in this unit.

Preparing to be observed

You will need to be working with children and young people as they play. Your assessor will want to see the way you encourage them to direct their own play, extend their own skills and explore their play environments. You will need to be alert to the play cues of the children and young people and act accordingly. Make sure that you do not take control of the play when you join in.

Read the performance criteria and range carefully before your assessment. Try to cover as much as you can.

Other types of evidence

- cover criteria not observed by your assessor
- show that you have the required knowledge, understanding and skills
- cover parts of the range.

End play sessions

All good things come to an end. Sometimes an activity will end naturally – goals achieved and resources used. Other times, it will be necessary to stop mid-activity. This may be because it is time to move on to another part of the session or time to clear up ready to go home. Either way, the ending of play sessions must be handled sensitively. Throughout this unit, we have discussed the importance of self-directed play, where the child or young person makes the decisions about the play. You will have thought carefully about the environment, equipment and materials and your own role. All this careful consideration can be ruined by you interrupting and stopping the play.

However, the reality is that you must adhere to your setting's routines. If you are in shared premises, it is likely that you will have a set time by which you must have cleared away and vacated. You must also ensure that the children and young people are ready to be collected at the correct time. And you must remember that routine is important to making younger children feel safe and secure – when they know what will happen at given times, they are able to predict the routine and this makes them feel more settled and less anxious. So, there are very good reasons why you must stick to the routine of the setting.

Balancing the requirements of the setting with the needs of the children and young people

210K25

In order to balance the two factors, you need to think about how you can give children and young people the opportunity to finish what they are doing before tidying away. There are several strategies that you can use:

- Make the children and young people aware of the routines of the session. If everything stops for snack time at 4:30 p.m., make sure they are all aware of this. You can display posters around the setting explaining the routine in words and pictures. You can use circle time to discuss the routine. And you can include the children and young people in reviewing the routine from time to time, asking for their opinions about the way the session is run.

- Give out timely warnings. Let everyone know when there are 10 minutes to go, and then 5 minutes. This will help the children and young people to pace themselves, complete their activity if possible or prepare themselves for a pause in the activity.

- Wherever possible, enable the children and young people to return to incomplete play activities. This will involve you having somewhere to store incomplete 'creations', perhaps overnight. Or it may mean being flexible enough for an activity to continue on after snack time instead of putting a different one out. Focusing on the needs of the individual child or young person will help you to make the right decisions.

- Explain why the play must stop. When children understand the reasons behind your decisions, they will be more inclined to conform.

Inevitably, there will be times when you have followed all the above advice, and you still are unable to prevent the disruption of an important activity. Sometimes the child or young person is so engrossed in what he or she is doing that it is impossible for him or her to pay attention to the time. Sometimes parents will arrive unexpectedly. In these circumstances, you need to be sensitive to the child or young person. They will be feeling frustrated and upset. You will need to remain calm. Tell him or her that you understand how it feels. Explain why the activity cannot continue and try to find a compromise. Maybe the activity can be offered again in the next session, or even continued at home. Above all, be as flexible as you can and try to offer the child or young person the opportunity to continue as soon as possible. Preparing everyone in the setting for the ending of the play session is the best way to avoid upset.

Tidy up time!

210K26

Tidying up is a chore that should be shared between the whole team – staff and children/young people. It is likely that it is an on-going activity throughout the session, as well as part of the routine at the end of play sessions. It is also likely that there will be some members of the team – adults and children/young people – who may be reluctant to help. However, it is important that everyone takes part.

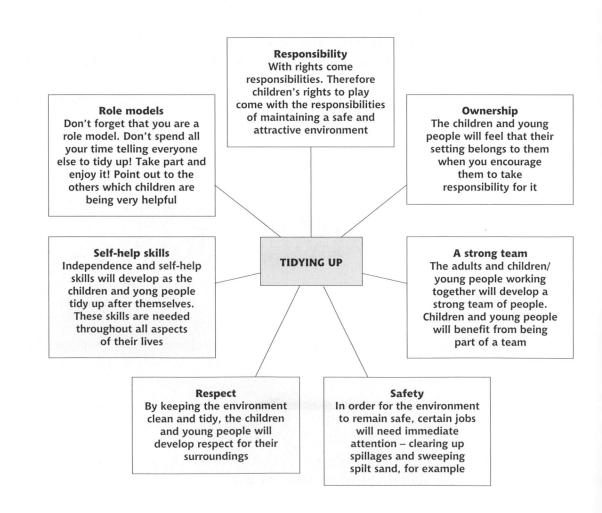

Responsibility
With rights come responsibilities. Therefore children's rights to play come with the responsibilities of maintaining a safe and attractive environment

Role models
Don't forget that you are a role model. Don't spend all your time telling everyone else to tidy up! Take part and enjoy it! Point out to the others which children are being very helpful

Ownership
The children and young people will feel that their setting belongs to them when you encourage them to take responsibility for it

Self-help skills
Independence and self-help skills will develop as the children and yong people tidy up after themselves. These skills are needed throughout all aspects of their lives

TIDYING UP

A strong team
The adults and children/young people working together will develop a strong team of people. Children and young people will benefit from being part of a team

Respect
By keeping the environment clean and tidy, the children and young people will develop respect for their surroundings

Safety
In order for the environment to remain safe, certain jobs will need immediate attention – clearing up spillages and sweeping spilt sand, for example

Reluctant children and young people can be encouraged to take part in several ways:

- Consider using rewards to entice everyone to participate. This can be verbal praise, choice of next activities, stickers and star charts or extra responsibility.
- Give specific jobs to them – for example, ask John to sweep the sand up and Ruby to take the paint pots to the kitchen.
- Use circle time to discuss why everyone needs to be involved.
- Make tidying up part of your ground rules, to be discussed and agreed by all those using your setting.
- Make sure the staff team are good role models. Make sure that they are consistent in their praise and encouragement.
- Agree strategies with the rest of the adult team to deal with persistent reluctance, and make sure everyone sticks to the plan.

Your setting will have its own tidy up procedures which you will need to follow. Make sure that you have a good understanding of them.

Home time

210K27

It is likely that the children will leave the setting at different times to go home. Your setting must have procedures in place for monitoring arrivals and departures. In the event of an emergency evacuation, you will need to know exactly who is on the premises at that time. Parents also need to have confidence in the safety and security of their children while they are in your care. Finally, Ofsted will check that these procedures are adequate during their inspection of your setting. Legislation laid down in the Care Standards Act 2000 states that your setting must have systems in place to record arrivals and departures.

Encourage everyone to take responsibility for the environment

It is your responsibility to find out about the procedures for your setting and make sure that you abide by them. Find out the answers to these questions:

- Who is responsible for updating the attendance register when children or young people arrive?
- How do you make sure that children only leave with the approved adult?
- How is the register updated to show the correct number of children on the premises?
- Where do you record the number of adults (including parents, visitors and volunteers) on the premises?
- How do you record the presence of unexpected visitors?
- Where is the register kept? Does it have a set place so that it can be easily collected in an emergency evacuation?
- What is your setting's procedure for dealing with an adult who comes to collect a child, when the parent has not notified you in advance?
- *For after-school clubs:* What would you do if you are expecting a child to arrive from school and they do not show up?
- *For Open Access settings (settings where children and young people are not required to be registered in advance):* How do you monitor arrivals and departures of children?

If you do not know the answer to any of these questions, you must go and find out.

Record-keeping

210K28

The register of attendance is not the only form of record-keeping you will need to carry out. Settings have a legal duty to keep various records of the children using their facilities. These include:

- personal details
- medical details, including allergies
- contact information for parents
- names of authorised people who can collect the child
- full details of any accident or illness occurring whilst the child is in your care
- records of dangerous occurrences (RIDDOR)
- financial record – fees, petty cash, invoices
- fire drills carried out
- incidents occurring which cause you concern
- health and well-being of the children or young people in your care.

These records must be up to date. In order for them to remain current, your setting will need to have systems in place for checking that there have been no changes. This might be by the staff speaking to each parent every term to make sure the records are up to date. If you need to get hold of a parent in an emergency, you do not want to be trying to track them down because they have changed their job and forgot to tell you.

Detail is also extremely important. Sometimes, what seems to be a minor accident in the setting can later develop into a more serious injury. The details in your records could be vital. Other times, your records might show up a pattern of behaviour or injuries which might indicate a child protection issue or a learning difficulty. Accident and incident records must be dated and timed, and include clear detail about:

- what happened
- who dealt with it
- whether it was witnessed
- what action was taken
- what advice was given to the parent.

They should also include the names and signatures of the staff, witness and parent.

Take a look at Unit CCLD 202 in this book for more information about keeping records of children's health and well-being.

All these records may be subject to the Data Protection Act 1998 and your setting may need to register with the Information Commissioner. If you or your setting is unsure about this, you should speak to Ofsted for guidance.

Confidentiality of this information is vital to maintain the trust that parents place in your setting. Records should be locked in a secure cabinet and access to them restricted.

Always complete your records as soon as possible

Element 210.4

Are you ready for assessment?

End play sessions

You need to show that you can end play sessions in a sensitive manner. Use the range category to plan with your assessor. This will help you to gather as much evidence as possible on her visits. The amount and type of evidence you need to present will vary. You should plan this with your assessor.

Direct observation by your assessor

Observation and/or Expert Witness Testimony is the required assessment method to be used to evidence some part of each element in this unit. If your assessor is unable to observe you s/he will identify an expert in your workplace who will provide testimony of your work-based performance. Usually your assessor or expert witness will observe you in real work activities and this should provide most of the evidence for the performance criteria for the elements in this unit.

Preparing to be observed

Your assessor will need to see the way you draw play sessions to a close. She will want to see you giving sensitive warnings that it will soon be time to tidy up. You will need to show her how you involve everyone in the tidying up activity, how you gather feedback from the children about their enjoyment of the activities and how you follow your setting's procedures for the safe departure of the children and young people. You will also need to complete any necessary records.

Read the performance criteria and range carefully before your assessment. Try to cover as much as you can.

Other types of evidence

You will need to present different types of evidence in order to:

- cover criteria not observed by your assessor
- show that you have the required knowledge, understanding and skills
- cover parts of the range.

Reflecting on your practice

- How do you ensure that children and young people are able to direct their own play within your setting and why is this important? **210K02**

- How do you encourage children and young people to assess risk and challenge for themselves? **210K07**

- How do you balance the rights and needs of all the children in your setting? **210K16**

- How do you decide whether or not to join in the play of children and young people? **210K21, 210K24**

- What are the procedures in your setting for:

  - ending play sessions **210K25**

  - tidying up and dealing with resources **210K26**

  - children and young people's departure? **210K2**

Index

Page numbers in *italics* indicate figures or tables